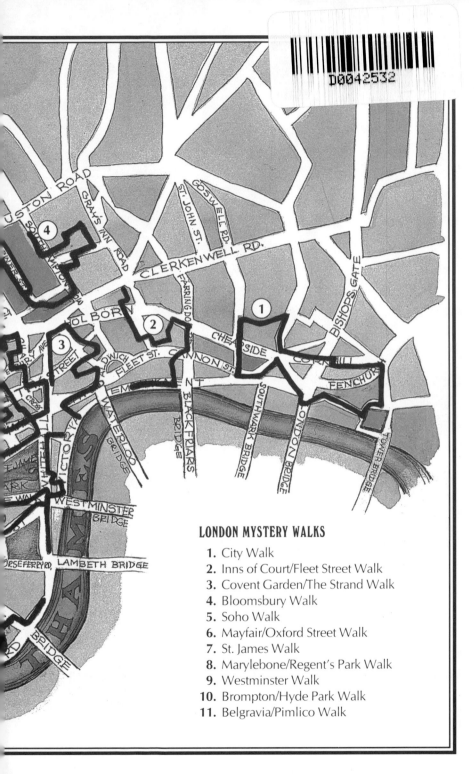

LONDON MYSTERY WALKS

1. City Walk
2. Inns of Court/Fleet Street Walk
3. Covent Garden/The Strand Walk
4. Bloomsbury Walk
5. Soho Walk
6. Mayfair/Oxford Street Walk
7. St. James Walk
8. Marylebone/Regent's Park Walk
9. Westminster Walk
10. Brompton/Hyde Park Walk
11. Belgravia/Pimlico Walk

MYSTERY READER'S WALKING GUIDE:
LONDON

MYSTERY READER'S WALKING GUIDE:
LONDON

ALZINA STONE DALE
BARBARA SLOAN HENDERSHOTT

MAPS BY JOHN BABCOCK

 **PASSPORT BOOKS**

Trade Imprint of National Textbook Company
Lincolnwood, Illinois U.S.A.

Published by Passport Books, Trade Imprint of National
Textbook Company, 4255 West Touhy Avenue, Lincolnwood, Illinois
60646-1975.
© 1987 by Alzina Stone Dale and Barbara Sloan Hendershott.
Maps by John Babcock, © Alzina Stone Dale and Barbara Sloan Hendershott.
Manufactured in the United States of America.
Library of Congress Catalog Card Number: 86-60564
6 7 8 9 0 IB 9 8 7 6 5 4 3 2 1

Dedication

To Ron and Chuck, who have cheerfully assisted us in any way they could, from reading mysteries and manuscripts to seeking out and marking maps to supplying quantities of much needed computer expertise. They also accepted gracefully our mental and physical absence while the book was being written.

CONTENTS

Special Helps

Bibliography   275

Index of Persons, Places, and Books   279

MAPS

Acknowledgments

Most authors say their book could not have been written without the aid and comfort of many people, but in our case it is the literal truth. Fortunately for us, devoted detective story readers lurk everywhere, eager to share their special knowledge with others of like mind. Out of many well-wishers, the following people deserve our special thanks. None of them are responsible for our slips and blunders; all of them may take credit for the book as it stands, for they are its mystery godparents.

We would like to thank:

Connie Fletcher and Barbara Metcalf for encouraging us to seek publication based on the initial idea. Les Zunkel, Ruth Howell, and Martha Mead for their book suggestions, and Mary McDermott Shideler for loaning us her copy of John Buchan's *The Three Hostages*. Julia and Paul Haynie, Carol and Jack White, and Joyce Hickey for encouragement and support; Martin Fornek for our photograph; Elizabeth Dale for the loan of her Catherine Aird mysteries, Kenneth Dale for dogsitting, and Phil Hendershott for doing whatever was asked.

Mary Sue Brown and the Adult Service Staff of the Elmhurst Public Library, Mary Goulding of the Suburban Library System, Betty Boyd and Donna Scullion of the York High School Library, Marilyn Roth of the Bridgman Public Library, the entire Staff of the Wade Collection, Wheaton College, and the salespeople at Fifty-Seventh Street Books, Chicago, for all their help in finding the facts and the books we needed.

Ann Rosenblum Karnovsky, Catherine Kenney, and Lenore Melzer for checking out special London restaurants and hotels for us. Damaris Hendry Day, Sarah Duncan, and Harriet Rylaarsdam for reading the walks in manuscript, and Mindy Ries for her help with indexing.

Two very special helpers were Peter ffrench-Hodges of the British Tourist Authority, who encouraged us and vetted the manuscript as well, and Dr. Margaret Nickson of the British Library, who gave us a special tour behind the scenes.

Among the societies important in the mystery world, the Midwest Chapter of Mystery Writers of America, to which we both belong, provided ongoing support and enthusiasm, as well as introductions to writers at home and abroad. The Chesterton Society provided assistance through the heroic efforts of its chairman Aidan Mackey and his wife Dorene, who checked and rechecked our manuscript, even calling up the Old Bailey. The Dorothy L. Sayers Historical and Literary Society, as always, provided splendid authoritative assistance on a wide variety of details. We owe particular thanks to Chairman Ralph Clarke, who wrote the Society's Sayers Walks which he allowed us to use. The many entertaining *Sidelights on Sayers* by Philip Scowcroft gave us essential clues, while Philip Scowcroft also vetted the entire manuscript for us over one weekend! The former Ruler of the Detection Club, Julian Symons, encouraged us and supplied information on his own mysteries, as did the present Ruler, H.R.F. Keating. Lady Antonia Fraser, then Chairman of the British Crime Writers Association, also provided us with useful information on the real locales of her mysteries, and cordial invitations to attend Crime Writers Association meetings of which we availed ourselves.

In London and by correspondence, we have had the fun of becoming acquainted with a number of our favorite writers and have hopes of meeting many more as we work on the succeeding guides. Among those who helped with this particular project were Catherine Aird, Marian Babson, Simon Brett, Amanda Cross, P.D. James, Jessica Mann, Anne Perry, Ellis Peters, and Ian Stuart. We also want to express our gratitude and affection to Robin Rue, our agent, who believed in the idea and sold it for us, and to the people at Passport Books, especially Michael Ross, our editor. Our cover artist and cartographer, John Babcock, also deserves a vote of thanks for the enthusiasm with which he did a great deal of time-consuming work, as does his wife who tracked the walks through the manuscript for him—and us.

We look forward to continuing to fill what seems to be a delightful void in the mystery-travel genre by creating more guides with the help of these devoted Dr. Watsons.

Alzina Stone Dale and Barbara Sloan Hendershott

INTRODUCTION: HOW TO USE THIS GUIDE

London, one of the world's greatest cities, is the center of the thriving English mystery world. Beginning with Charles Dickens and Wilkie Collins, who lived and worked in London, and including Edgar Allan Poe, who attended school there, nearly every mystery writer worth his salt has set at least one of his tales against a London backdrop. Even so American a writer as Robert Parker in his *The Judas Goat* took Spenser across the Atlantic to pursue his quarry in London. Because of the richness of its mystery associations, modern London is a mystery reader's mecca, filled with the real sights and sounds that give the stories their authentic atmosphere.

In the author's note to *Wobble to Death*, Peter Lovesey states that his "characters . . . are fictitious, but the setting is authentic"; this combination is repeated in the works of many other mystery writers. As a result, turn any London corner, and you will encounter the scene of a fictional crime or discover a haunt of a favorite detective or his creator.

London has always been a tourist's delight, a sprawling metropolis encompassing over 800 square miles; a key is needed to unlock its myriad streets and avenues, passageways and alleys. Many excellent guides have been written for just this purpose. Some focus on specialized areas, such as architecture, history, or literature, but if you want to hunt down the locale of a detective story, you will find these guides deficient. With the exception of the likes of Wilkie Collins, Sir Arthur Conan Doyle, and G.K. Chesterton, little is said about mystery writers, let alone their detectives. When the author of a detective story is mentioned, he is lumped with such writers as Geoffrey Chaucer, Samuel Johnson, and John Donne.

Faced with the knowledge that none of the existing guidebooks provided a mystery reader with a way of seeing London through the eyes of such characters as Philip Trent, Lady Molly, or Lord Peter Wimsey, we decided to write for ourselves, based on our favorite mystery writers and their works, the guide we would like to be using.

We determined that the guide must be a walking guide because everyone seems to agree that the only way to see London is on foot. Despite the excellence of public transportation and the availability of taxis, the London we sought was a London available only to those free to duck into a passageway, cut across a square, or poke into a cul-de-sac, while chasing an elusive sleuth.

The first thing we had to decide was which books to use for our guide. Our choice had to be personal because the number of mysteries that take place in London runs into the thousands. Our ambition was not to produce an encyclopedia of crime or even a handsome coffee table tome. We wanted something readable, a toteable book that could guide and entertain both our armchair readers and our London walkers. So, we each sat down and made a list of our favorite authors, being careful to mix types, periods, and sexes. Then we compared lists and kept the names that appeared on both. Next, we consulted such major classics on the detective story as Steinbrunner and Penzler's *The Encyclopedia of Mystery and Detection* and Julian Symons's *Mortal Consequences* to make sure that we had examples from all the tried-and-true mystery types. The resulting list included everything from apple-cheeked spinsters to superspies and ran the gamut from Patricia Wentworth's Miss Silver to Antonia Fraser's Jemima Shore and John Buchan's Richard Hannay. We covered a group of writers who would appeal to an audience of varied reading tastes and, at the same time, satisfy our own.

In planning the guide, we have not followed the established custom of dividing the book into sections on food, shopping, entertainment, museums, and sights. Rather, we divided London geographically into its historic neighborhoods, like Bloomsbury and Soho. Then we cross-indexed our authors (more than forty of them), detectives, and books (over one hundred of them), pulled out the geographic sites mentioned by or in each, and remixed them into these walking tours.

Each of the walks represents a neighborhood. There is a paragraph or two of introductory material about the area of the walk, followed by a list of the general points of interest, including all "must-see" spots listed by the British Tourist Authority. (We mention opening and closing times where appropriate.) Whenever possible, our restaurant suggestions are connected with one of the detective stories.

The walks are area-oriented rather than book- or author-oriented. If you want to follow a particular character or writer or want to know more about an unfamiliar one, look him or her up in the index. A map is included with each walk to make route following easier.

The starting and ending point for each walk is an underground, or "tube," station. We elected to use the tube because it is quick, efficient, and inexpensive. There are ten principal lines and 275 stations. In addition, many tube stations have lavatory facilities. In case a particular walk becomes too long or your time becomes too short, we have pointed out other tube stations conveniently located on the walk.

We have included many references to points of interest that do not fall into the natural range of a mystery walk but may, nevertheless, be of interest to the reader. The number of these spots you include in each walk will determine how long the walk will take. If, for example, you choose to go inside the National Portrait Gallery or Westminster Abbey, your walk will take that much longer. The walks are, on the average, about 3.5 miles long.

In preparing the guide, we made a number of discoveries about the authors and their stories. For instance, while each of the writers makes it plain that his story takes place in London, just where in London is not always clear. Dick Francis, for example, has his merchant banker Tim Ekaterin work in a new building with a view of St. Paul's "in the City." It might be on Gresham Street, Old Jewry, or Milk Street—anywhere north of the cathedral, where the bombs of World War II laid waste. Agatha Christie often gives a street address that sounds right but is totally fictitious and then has her characters—Tommy and Tuppence, for instance—eat at a Lyons Corner shop or have tea at the Ritz. On the other hand, she sometimes refers to the Ritz as the Blitz or combines two hotels into one, as is the case with the Ritz-Carlton and Bertram's. On such occasions, since we are walking a real city, we will take you to the Ritz. In still a different way, Margery Allingham, world famous for her evocative descriptions of London, invents squares and cul-de-sacs, locating them around the corner from real places. In *Black Plumes,* when David Field takes Frances Ivory from Sallet Square to the Café Royal for a sundae and walks her to Westminster Bridge by night, we are dealing with the imagined, as well as the real. The railway station in *Tiger in the Smoke* is probably Paddington, but a case can be made for its being Euston or Victoria or even Charing Cross!

We also discovered that many of the writers provided clues in their books to the sections of London in which they lived or had lived or of which they were particularly fond. Dame Ngaio Marsh, for example, had nearly all her characters live and several of her murders take place in Belgravia, near the Brompton Oratory. This is where she always stayed in London and where she and the "real" Charlot Lamprey ran gift shops before the war. Georgette Heyer's first flat after she married was in Earls Court, where her young, ex-convict social secretary, Beulah Birtley, lived in *Duplicate Death*. Dorothy L. Sayers lived and worked in Bloomsbury, as does Harriet Vane, while Jemima Shore lives near Holland Park, as does Lady Antonia Fraser.

We made a number of discoveries that delighted us. While pursuing Graham Greene's colonel in *The Human Factor,* we found Greene's own flat in tiny Pickering Place hidden behind a St. James's Street vitner. Chasing down P.D. James's well-educated Philippa Palfrey, we came upon the Courtauld Institute Galleries, with its magnificent Impressionist collection. Thanks to Agatha Christie, we had tea at the Ritz; we lunched in a pub in Shepherd Market, that maze of old lanes behind rich and modern Park Lane; and we stood on tiptoe to peek in the window of all that remains of bombed-out St. Anne's Soho to see where Dorothy Sayers's ashes are buried. Coming out of Carlton House Terrace, where Christie's Sir James Peel Edgerton lived, we were fascinated to discover the tiny gravestone marking the burial place of a dog that belonged to the German ambassador in 1934.

We hope you will use this guide to tour all of central London, beginning with the oldest part, the City, whose narrow streets still remind us of the medieval days of mysterious Richard III. Then move westward into legal London, reminiscent of Charles Dickens and today's Rumpole of the Bailey. Follow along into "intellectual" Bloomsbury and the foreign restaurants of Soho and into the spacious parks and squares of the true West End.

The time of day you elect to walk will be important. For instance, pub hours are 11:30 A.M. to 3:00 P.M. and 5:30 P.M. to 11:00 P.M. (except in the City, where morning hours do not begin until 11:30 A.M. and in Covent Garden, where they reflect the early hours of the market days). Your feelings about crowds, your shopping plans, and the number of museums that you wish to visit will all affect the time that you set out. (Before 8:30 A.M., London is uncrowded, and walking just about anywhere is a joy.)

If a complete tour is not your aim, use the index of persons, places, and books to chart your own tour.

The large map of central London shows you how the geographical sections of London lie in relation to each other, and the sectional maps show the route of each walk, as well as the neighborhood's principal streets and sights.

Our aim has been to give you a guide that is workable, whether you stay at home or sally forth armed with umbrella, camera, and guidebook to track down your favorites for yourselves. For, as G.K. Chesterton, one of the grand masters of detection, said in his "In Defence of Detective Stories," "Modern man has a great need for romance and adventure, which, paradoxically, he can find just around the corner in any ordinary London street." Or, as Sherlock Holmes observed and we echo, "It is a hobby of mine to have an exact knowledge of London."

MYSTERY READER'S WALKING GUIDE:
LONDON

1

CITY
WALK

BACKGROUND

The first walk begins in the oldest part of London, the square mile known as the City. The difference between London and the City of London can be confusing. They are actually two different administrative entities. The City of London, usually referred to only as the City, covers roughly one square mile; today it is the financial center of London. It is built on the site of the old Roman city of Londinium, as well as the walled medieval city. The street plan is that of the medieval city, and many of the old street names have been retained. One of the delights for visitors to this area is the curious street signs— Crutched Friars, Cheapside, Seething Lane, Bread Street, and so on. The approximate position of the Roman and medieval walls can be determined by such names as Moorgate, Aldersgate, and Newgate.

The Romans had arrived by 43 A.D., the first date in London's history. However, it is quite likely that there were Bronze and Stone Age settlements on the site before this. The first Roman town was sacked by Boadicea, but it was soon rebuilt and given walls and a bridge across the Thames. London quickly grew to be one of the largest towns in northern Europe. Today there is little left of the old Roman city: the

1

Temple of Mithras, which was discovered in 1954; a bit of mosaic floor uncovered by war damage to All-Hallows-by-the-Tower; a larger bit of mosaic under Bucklersbury; a number of smaller relics that can be seen in the London Museum; and, of course, bits and pieces of the wall, such as the part near the Tower of London. Remnants of medieval London can be found in a few churches and the narrow streets with odd names, but World War II bombs did such great damage to the City that much of what you see today has been restored or rebuilt.

More than half a million people work in the City during the day, but they evacuate at night, leaving the narrow streets and alleyways, the Wren churches, and the pubs to the resident population of 4,500 and the cats and dogs that are said to outnumber the humans.

LENGTH OF WALK: 3.8 miles

See map on page 5 for exact boundaries of this walk and page 228 for a list of detectives and books mentioned.

PLACES OF INTEREST

St. Paul's Cathedral, Ludgate Hill. Open daily, April–Oct., 7:30–6:00 P.M.; Nov.–March, 7:30–5:00 P.M. Free except for special areas, like the crypt.

Bank of England, Threadneedle Street. Tours by appointment only on alternate Saturdays. Free.

Mansion House, Mansion House Street. Tours by appointment only. Free.

Temple of Mithras, Queen Victoria Street. Second-century Roman ruin. Other remains from the site on display in the Museum of London. Free.

The Guildhall, Gresham Street. Open May–Sept., Mon.–Sat., 10:00–5:00; Sun., 2:00–5:00 P.M. Free.

Tower of London. Open March–Oct., Mon.–Sat., 9:30–5:00; Sun., 2:00–5:00 P.M.; Nov.–Feb., Mon.–Sat., 9:30–4:00. Admission charge.

The Changing of the Guard on Tower Green. Daily at 11:30 A.M. in summer; alternate days in winter. The Ceremony of the

Keys is by appointment only. It takes place every evening at
10:00 P.M. Free.

Barbican Arts Centre, Aldersgate. London's equivalent to New
York's Lincoln Center and Paris's Centre Pompidou. Part of a
postwar development, home of the Royal Shakespeare
Company. Free.

London Wall, Noble Street. Southwest section of a Roman fort
c. 100 A.D.

Museum of London, London Wall. Open Tues.–Sat., 10:00–6:00;
Sun., 2:00–6:00 P.M. Free. Remains of a Roman fort may be
seen by making arrangements at the reception desk. Free.

The Monument, Monument Street. Open May–Sept., Mon.–Sat.,
9:00–6:00; Sun., 2:00–6:00 P.M.; Oct.–April, Mon.–Sat.,
9:00–3:40. Admission charge.

All-Hallows-by-the-Tower, Byward Street. Open Mon.–Sat.,
10:30–6:00; Sun., 10:30–5:30 P.M. Services at 11:00 A.M.

St.-Mary-le-Bow, Bow Street.

PLACES TO EAT

Note: Eating places and pubs within the walk are open Mon-
day-Friday during lunch hours only. (Toilet facilities are also
limited.) Although Sunday is an ideal time to tour this area,
plan to eat elsewhere. A suggestion is Soho's Chinatown,
where you can find places open any day, any time.

Sweetings, 39 Queen Victoria Street. Mon.–Fri., 11:45–3:00 P.M.
London's first fish restaurant, established in 1830. The
atmosphere is Edwardian. 01-248-3062.

Bow Wine Vault, 10 Bow Churchyard. High-ceilinged bar popular
for salads, cheeses. Open Mon.–Fri., to 7:00 P.M. 01-248-
1121.

Ye Olde Watling, 29 Watling Street. The archetypal pub on the
ground floor features traditional pub food; upstairs is an
intimate restaurant that serves lunch from 12:00–2:15 P.M.,
Mon.–Fri. 01-248-6235.

Barbican Waterside Café, Level 5, Barbican Centre. Modern
cafeteria service, features open-air dining. Mon.–Fri., to
5:30 P.M. 01-638-4141

CITY WALK

Begin the walk at the St. Paul's Underground station. In *Inspector Ghote Hunts the Peacock,* H.R.F. Keating's visiting Inspector Ghote of Bombay, India, on his way to the Wood Street Police Station, arrived at St. Paul's station an hour and 27 minutes early, so he decided to walk to the Tower. (He reversed the route you will follow.)

Quite often in detective stories, it is said that someone went to the "City," usually on business. For example, Graham Bendix, whose wife was murdered in Anthony Berkeley's *The Poisoned Chocolates Case,* had an appointment in the City. The American millionaire, Rufus Van Aldin, in *The Mystery of the Blue Train* by Agatha Christie, also went to the City. In Christie's *The Golden Ball,* when George Dundas quit working for his uncle in the City, he was told that he was not grasping the Golden Ball of opportunity; however, while standing on the street, Dundas was picked up by a rich, eccentric young lady who was trying out suitors. Dundas proved to be properly adventurous and came in a winner. The unpleasant Arnold Vereker, who was found dead in the stocks in Georgette Heyer's mystery *Death in the Stocks,* was "a city man—mining interests," with irregular habits, which meant a series of girl friends at his riverside cottage.

Estonia Glassware Company was a front for the conspirators whom Tuppence and Tommy overheard in a Lyon's Corner shop. Tuppence, claiming to be Jane Finn, later showed up at the City offices and tricked the conspirators out of a 50-pound advance in Agatha Christie's *The Secret Adversary.*

The City was shaken by the disappearance of Ivor Harbeton of the Harbeton financial empire in Catherine Aird's *In Harm's Way.* Several people were suspected of doing away with him to prevent his taking over Tom Mellot's company—Mellot's Furnishings—Upholsterers to the Nation. There were similar financial upheavals when E.C. Bentley's Sigsbee Manderson, another rich American, was killed in *Trent's Last Case* and when Sir Reuben Levy was murdered in Dorothy L. Sayers's classic tale *Whose Body?*

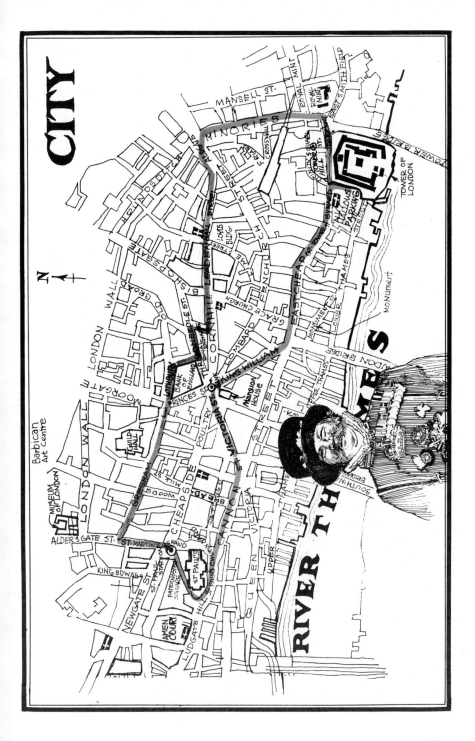

CITY

N

Barbican
Art Centre

MUSEUM
OF LONDON

Guild
Hall

Bank
of
England

Mansion
House

Monument

TOWER
OF
LONDON

RIVER THAMES

MINORIES

CORNHILL

LEADENHALL STREET

CHEAPSIDE

CANNON ST.

LONDON WALL

BISHOPSGATE

OLD BROAD

MOORGATE

THREADNEEDLE ST.

GRESHAM

KING EDWARD

ALDERSGATE ST.

ST. MARTINS

ST. PAULS

LUDGATE HILL

NEWGATE ST.

AMEN COURT

QUEEN VICTORIA ST.

LONDON BRIDGE

TOWER BRIDGE

ROYAL MINT

MANSELL ST.

EASTCHEAP

FENCHURCH

GRACE CHURCH

LOMBARD

POULTRY

PRINCES ST.

KINGS WILLIAM

SOUTHWARK BRIDGE

LOWER THAMES

UPPER THAMES

The City has its own City of London Police Force. The head-office is at 26 Jewry Street. Aird's Detective Inspector C.D. Sloan called the City Fraud Squad to find out about Ivor Harbeton's financial wheelings and dealings in *In Harm's Way*.

As you leave the station, walk southeast along Newgate Street, which becomes Cheapside. Turn right into St. Paul's Churchyard, a curving roadway that flanks the cathedral on the north. Take time to look at Paternoster Row, once the center of London's book publishing trade. In Ngaio Marsh's *A Wreath for Rivera*, 5 Materfamilias Lane (Paternoster Row), was the location of *Harmony*, a monthly magazine for which Edward Manx wrote highly intellectual theater reviews and the Marquis of Pastern and Baggott wrote a column of advice for the lovelorn. "One end of Materfamilias Lane had suffered a bomb and virtually disappeared, but the other stood intact, a narrow city street, with ancient buildings, a watery smell, dark entries and impenitent charm." In 1848, Charlotte and Anne Brontë came to London to see their publisher. They stayed in the Chapter Coffee House, which stood at the entrance to St. Paul's Alley, off St. Paul's Churchyard.

St. Paul's Cathedral, which was founded in 610, is located on Ludgate Hill, the second highest point in the City. The first cathedral building burned down in 1087. Its Norman replacement lasted until the Great Fire of 1666. Christopher Wren's masterpiece is the third building on the site. An example of English Renaissance architecture, St. Paul's has a Latin cross plan. Its appearance is Neoclassical, although there is much Baroque detailing. The dome is the second largest in the world, after St. Peter's in the Vatican. (Although the dome of St. Paul's appears to be a single structure, it actually comprises three separate parts: an inner dome, an outer dome, and a central dome.) The bell towers are the cathedral's most Baroque feature. The southwest clock tower houses three old bells. "Great Tom," the hour bell, was recast from Big Ben's predecessor at the Houses of Parliament. Down Ludgate Hill to the left is Ave Maria Lane, where you can find Amen Court. Until World War II, this was the home of Oxford University

Press, where Charles Williams worked as an editor. He described his office in the opening chapter of his first mystery, *War in Heaven*. Dorothy L. Sayers used to meet him there, and they often went to a nearby wine bar to argue theology.

Despite the incessant bombing of the City during World War II, St. Paul's survived, a tribute to the efforts of its fire-watching team; most of the surrounding buildings were destroyed. Today St. Paul's is an island of classic calm in a sea of skyscrapers. In Dick Francis's *Banker*, the new glass and stone office building of Ekaterin Merchant Bank on one side had a modern fountain where young Tim Ekaterin found his boss wading one morning. On the other side, the view was different. There was no fountain, but there was the sunlit dome of St. Paul's, which rose like a "Fabergé egg from the white stone lattice of the city."

The cross on top of the cathedral has been mentioned in several works of fiction. It figures in the title of G.K. Chesterton's *The Ball and the Cross* and in Charles Williams's *All Hallows Eve*. "The still-lifted cross of St. Paul's" gave the dead Lester hope as she scuttled along, sharing the ugly dwarf body with her dead friend Evelyn.

Historic associations with St. Paul's are legion. One that suits our purpose comes from A.A. Milne (author of *The Red House Mystery*), who wrote in his nursery rhyme, "King John's Christmas," that "King John was not a good man." It was here that the king submitted to the Papal Legate and promised to pay tribute to Rome just before he died from a surfeit of lampreys.

Frith and Henry (Lamprey) suggested that Roberta Grey look at the dome of St. Paul's; so, she obediently stared at it as they drove by in Ngaio Marsh's *A Surfeit of Lampreys*.

In Charles Williams's *All Hallows Eve,* artist Jonathan Drayton had a flat on the top floor of a building near St. Paul's. As one of the official war-artists of World War II, he did a painting of the City that showed the light of "co-inherence," or community, of the City, past and present. In a painting of Simon the Clerk's meeting, Drayton makes all the members of the audience look like insects.

If you have time, explore the cathedral, its crypt, and towers. St. Paul's is the church of the people of London, just as Westminster Abbey is the church of Royalty. It was a departure from tradition to have the 1981 wedding of the Prince of Wales and Lady Diana Spencer take place in St. Paul's.

The entire City is filled with reminders of Charles Dickens. Although the City in the Boz era was very different from the City today, many of the place names are the same, and some places Dickens knew can still be ferreted out. To find one such spot, turn right at St. Paul's and walk around its southern side to Godliman Street, turn right and walk the short distance to Knightrider Street. Here is the Horn Tavern, an unspoiled early nineteenth-century tavern that was called the Horn Coffee House in the time of jolly Mr. Pickwick, G.K. Chesterton's favorite Dickens character. Walk back north along Godliman Street to St. Paul's and go right, to Cannon Street. Head east along Cannon Street, where Edwards, the cigar-smoking private detective in Julian Symons's *The Blackheath Poisonings*, had a small office.

Continue to walk east toward the Tower along Cannon Street. Just past Friday Street, you will come to Bread Street, which runs north to Cheapside, crossing Watling Street. Cheapside was the High Street of the medieval City. With its many side streets, Cheapside was a huge open-air market. Although it originally was called after the Crown Inn, it was later named West Chepe from the Saxon word meaning "to barter" (East Chepe led to the Tower of London). The street was also used as the site for great guild pageants, royal tournaments, and other festivities.

John Milton was born in Bread Street, south of Cheapside, in 1608. The Mermaid Tavern, where Shakespeare and Ben Jonson met, was also in Bread Street. This is the street on which bakers used to gather to sell their wares. Milk Street, farther north, on the other side of Cheapside, housed the milk sellers in medieval times. Sir Thomas More, whom Josephine Tey's Inspector Grant considered the evil nemesis of Richard III in *The Daughter of Time*, was born in a house on Milk Street. Continue your walk along Cannon Street past the junction with Bow Lane, which was once the location of the City's shoemakers shops. It gets its name from the church of St.-Mary-le-Bow, which stands at the Cheapside end of the lane. The "bows" are the arches upon which the church stands. St.-Mary-le-Bow possesses London's most famous church bells. A "cockney" is someone born within the sound of Bow Bells. These are said to be the very bells that called Dick Whittington back to the City from Highgate in the fifteenth century. After he returned, he was made Lord Mayor four times before his death in 1422. The bells were shattered in World War II but have been recast. St.-Mary-le-Bow's steeple is judged to be the finest of Christopher Wren's steeples. You may wish to take a side excursion to look at St.-Mary-le-Bow, then come back to Cannon Street, and continue walking along it to Queen Victoria Street. Follow Queen Victoria Street to the left to the Mansion House, at the junction of Queen Victoria Street with Poultry, Threadneedle Street, Lombard Street, Cornhill, and King William Street.

The Mansion House is the official residence of the Lord Mayor of London, who must reside there during his one-year term of office. The building, which is Palladian in inspiration, was built from 1739 to 1753 and designed by George Dance the Elder. The Lord Mayor's private apartments are on the top floor. The state rooms, including the 90-foot-long Egyptian Hall, are elegant examples of eighteenth-century decor.

It was at Mansion House corner that Sir Julian Freke in Dorothy L. Sayers's *Whose Body?* set up the "accidental" meeting with Sir Reuben Levy.

To the left is Threadneedle Street, with its "old lady," the Bank of England. The Bank, founded in 1694, is girded by a massive, blank wall ornamented with mock-Corinthian columns. The wall, which is the work of Sir John Soane, who was appointed architect of the Bank in 1788, gives the Bank the appearance of an elegant penitentiary.

Elise Cubitt, in the Sherlock Holmes case of "The Dancing Men," tried to buy off Abe Slaney with 1,000 pounds in Bank of England notes. Plates for counterfeiting Bank of England notes were found by Sherlock Holmes, and a financial disaster was averted in "The Three Garridebs." Sax Rohmer's Fu Manchu tried to "buy" the newly appointed Governor of the Bank of England, Sir Bertram Morgan, by offering him his daughter and a chance to buy gold bullion in *The Trail of Fu Manchu*.

Between Threadneedle Street and Cornhill, across the street from the bank, is the Royal Exchange, with its classical portico. Founded by Sir Thomas Gresham in 1566, the first Royal Exchange was opened for commercial transactions by Elizabeth I, a first step in establishing London's future glory as financial capital of the world. In front of the imposing building stands a statue of the Duke of Wellington. The campanile of the Exchange is topped by an eleven-foot-long golden grasshopper, the crest of Thomas Gresham. The visitors gallery is open on weekdays.

South of the Royal Exchange is the street of bankers, Lombard Street. It was the site of the London office of the great Milligan railroad and shipping company run by Mr. John Milligan. In Dorothy L. Sayers's *Whose Body?* Lord Peter Wimsey visited Milligan here. Wimsey suspected Milligan of having kidnapped Sir Reuben Levy to stop a stock deal. Later, at a society luncheon, the Dowager Duchess discovered that Milligan thought he had been asked to open the Duke of Denver's bazaar. Mark Culledon, the murder victim in Baroness Orczy's *Lady Molly of Scotland Yard,* had his office in Lombard Street. Wilkie Collins's "Moonstone" was pledged to a banker in Lombard Street, as well.

In *Odds Against,* Dick Francis located the phony office run by Bolt, who was helping manipulate shares of race courses, on Charing and King, two fictitious streets presumably near Lombard Street. When ex-jockey, now private eye Sid Halley pretended to invest, he met Zanna Martin, Bolt's secretary, and took her to a pub across the road. It was "a warm, beckoning stop for City gents on their way home." When they left the pub, they walked through the empty City streets toward the Tower and found a quiet little restaurant in which Zanna Martin agreed to have dinner. Halley took her home on the underground.

Now turn and cross Lombard Street to the right and bear right again into King William Street. Walk down King William Street to the point where Cannon Street becomes Eastcheap Street. The next item of interest is the Monument, which is located on Monument Street, just beyond the point where Cannon Street becomes Eastcheap (so named because it was the eastern market in the medieval City). The Monument commemorates the Great Fire of 1666. The 202-foot stone column, designed by Sir Christopher Wren, is the tallest isolated stone column in the world. It is also 202 feet from the base of the Monument to the baker's residence in nearby Pudding Lane, where the fire started. By taking a side trek to your right on Fish Street Hill, you can enter the Monument and climb the 311 steps of the internal spiral staircase to the platform, which affords an unequaled view of London.

Continue east along Eastcheap, which becomes Great Tower Street and then Byward Street. Before you reach Tower Hill, you will arrive at the ancient church of All-Hallows-by-the-Tower.

All-Hallows was first built by the Saxons in the seventh century. World War II bombing, which gutted the church, revealed the remains of a wall of the original Saxon church. In the crypt, two Roman tessellated pavements are displayed, along with a detailed model of Roman London. The three Saxon crosses discovered after the Second World War are London's most important Saxon artifacts. The most valued possession of the church is its font cover, which undoubtedly was carved by Grinling Gibbons.

In Edgar Wallace's *The Crimson Circle,* St. Agnes on Powder Hill is probably All-Hallows-by-the-Tower. It is described as a church that escaped the ravages of the Great Fire of 1666, only to be smothered by the busy city that grew up around it. Entrance to the church was up an alley that led from a side passage. This was the first and only meeting place of all the members of the criminal Crimson Circle. Thalia Drummond came to the meeting disguised as a female crook.

You are now on Tower Hill, with the Tower Hill Scaffold

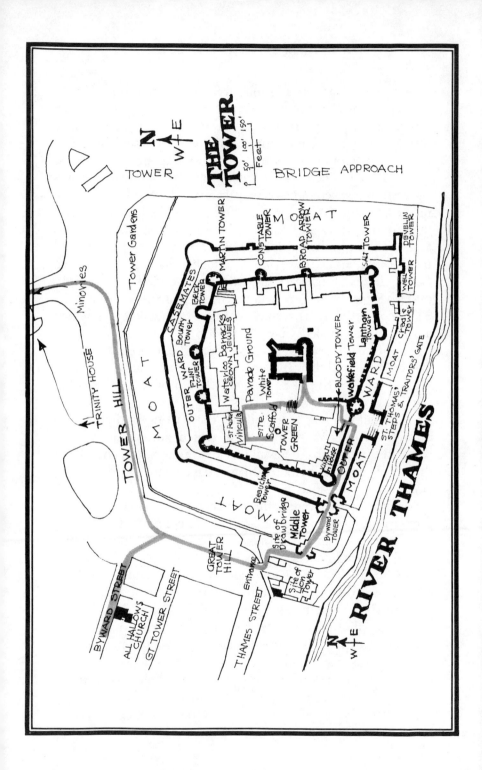

Memorial to your left. The chained area marks the location of the Tower Hill scaffold, where 125 well-known people were officially executed between 1347 and 1747. Among the victims were Sir Thomas More, Thomas Cromwell, and the Duke of Monmouth.

Following Tower Hill to the left around the north side of the Tower, you will come to the London Wall. The wall stands in a sunken garden that marks the ground level in Roman times. Because the Tower of London itself will take several hours to investigate, you might consider seeing it at another time. You should arrive at the Tower as early as possible, especially in summer, when the line-length is unbelievable. (Tour buses tend to begin disgorging their contents around 11:30.)

Characters in mystery stories often find their ways to the Tower. In *Inspector Ghote Hunts the Peacock,* H.R.F. Keating's Inspector Ghote came upon the Tower from a different direction than you did. But when he saw the Tower, the outline was unmistakable. "He had looked at it a thousand times in advertisements, in newspaper articles, on calendars. Beyond it was Tower Bridge, the one that could be raised to let ships pass. And there must be the mighty Thames itself. For a second he was surprised, shocked almost. The water of the great river was not, as it had been on a hundred brightly colored maps, a crisp and inviting blue. It was instead plainly a dirty brown. . . . The grim old building seemed that moment to hold for him in one graspable whole all the past centuries of this noble, sea-girt isle."

In Margaret Yorke's *Cast for Death,* the entreaties of the Greek policeman Manolakis to see the Tower made (don) Patrick Grant admit that he had never been there. "We'll go by boat . . ." Grant decided. As they approached the Tower, he launched into a fluent description of the young Elizabeth in the rain, a tale equal to any Greek legend. Grant found himself quite moved as they passed within the huge walls wherein so much tragedy had dwelt.

The Tower was originally built within the southeast angle of the City walls, but then it was extended east to cover 18 acres. The commander of the Tower is an army officer who is called the Constable of the Royal Palace and Fortress of London. His duties are performed by a Major and Resident Governor, like General Mason in John Dickson Carr's *The Mad Hatter Mystery.*

In Martha Grimes's *The Dirty Duck,* an American tourist, Harry Schoenberg, looked rapturously at Traitors' Gate, the 60-foot watergate from the Thames, through which accused traitors, such as Elizabeth I, were brought to the Tower.

The Tower has often served as a backdrop for real intrigue and even murder. The most famous case of murder associated with the Tower is that of the "Little Princes"—Edward V and the Duke of York—reputedly smothered in the Bloody Tower by order of their uncle, the Duke of Gloucester, later Richard III. In Josephine Tey's *The Daughter of Time,* the hospitalized Alan Grant of Scotland Yard investigated this case scientifically. He found many discrepancies in the records and concluded that Richard was not guilty as charged.

The Tower of London played a central role in John Dickson Carr's classic locked-room tale, *The Mad Hatter Mystery.* It is about a mysterious Edgar Allan Poe manuscript and a prankster who delighted in placing hats in unlikely places. You can explore the Tower by following the action of Carr's plot.

Enter the Tower near the site of the Lion Tower (where the Royal Zoo was kept) and go past the Middle Tower and under the gate of the Byward Tower. This is the way the commandant's secretary, Robert Dalrye, drove General Mason when they returned from Holborn. (General Mason had been attending a luncheon at the Antiquaries Society [see Mayfair Walk] with Sir Leonard Haldyne, Keeper of the Jewel House.) Walk along the south side of the Tower in the Outer Ward. To the right are the steps that lead below St. Thomas' Tower, built by Henry III, to Traitors' Gate. Here, in a dense fog, on the areaway steps, Phil Driscoll, with a crossbolt in his head, was found. Look down, as Dr. Gideon Fell did; no need to climb to the bottom.

Now walk to the left across the Outer Ward to the Wakefield Tower, where Henry VI was murdered in 1471 (by Richard III, according to Thomas More). The Crown Jewels used to be kept here, but are now in the Jewel House along the north wall. Across from Wakefield Tower is the Bloody Tower, where the Little Princes purportedly were smothered. It was here that Sir Walter Raleigh spent 13 years writing *The History of the World* before being executed on Tower Hill. (He was buried in St. Margaret's, Westminster. See Westminster Walk.) The police used the Little Princes' room in the Bloody Tower to examine Driscoll's body in Carr's mystery.

From Wakefield Tower, you can see the White Tower itself, with its four capped towers. Its 12–15-foot-thick walls are built of white Caen stone from Normandy. Begun by William the Conqueror, it was originally a formidable fortress. The White Tower contains several interesting collections, including one of medieval arms and armor, from which the Carr murder weapon supposedly came. The rounded-arch Chapel of St. John, the oldest church in London, was the place where Wat Tyler and his peasant mob grabbed old Archbishop Sudbury and murdered him. It was underneath a set of stairs on the south side of the White Tower that the bones thought to be those of the Little Princes were found during the reign of Charles II. They were reverently placed in Westminster Abbey. (See Westminster Walk.) In Tey's *The Daughter of Time,* Inspector Grant said sarcastically that every English schoolboy remembered the council scene in Shakespeare's *Richard III,* where Richard denounced his brother's lords as traitors and sent them straight from the White Tower to the block on Tower Green.

In *Watson's Choice,* Gladys Mitchell's redoubtable Dame Beatrice Bradley was amused when, at a Sherlock Holmesian house party given by Sir Bohun, his older nephew refused to wear a black velvet tunic and deep lace collar, declaring that he "wasn't one of the Princes in the Tower."

From the White Tower go left to Tower Green. It is located between the late Perpendicular Gothic Chapel of St. Peter ad Vincula at the north end and the inner facade of the King's House at the south. It is a serene bit of grass, of which the historian Macaulay, a favorite of G.K. Chesterton, said there "was no sadder spot on earth." The bodies of a number of Tower victims are buried under the peaceful green sod. In the middle of the Green, outlined with granite, is the site of the scaffold where the more illustrious of the Tower victims were granted the mercy of private execution. It was here that such as Anne Boleyn, Lady Jane Grey, Catherine Howard, and the Earl of Essex were beheaded. In Carr's mystery, Laura Bitten, Phil Driscoll's mistress, asked one nice old Beefeater if this was where Queen Elizabeth was executed. The guard, shocked by her historical ignorance, answered that "Queen Elizabeth had not the honor. . . . I mean, she died in her bed."

Beyond Tower Green, to the east of St. Peter's, is the former Waterloo Barracks. If the line is not terribly long, take the stairs to the cellar stronghold built in 1967 to house the Crown Jewels. (This is the building Sir Leonard Haldyne was in charge of in Carr's mystery.) Most of the jewels were sold or melted down during Cromwell's day, so the oldest now is St. Edward's Crown, made for the coronation of Charles II. Of much interest to mystery buffs is the Crown of Queen Elizabeth, made in 1911. In it was placed the fabulous "Koh-i-noor" diamond, which was given to Queen Victoria by the Punjabi Army. In Agatha Christie's *The Secret of Chimneys,* Anthony Cade was not impressed to hear that the prime minister of Herzoslovakia knew where the Koh-i-noor was. "We all know that, they keep it in the Tower don't they?"

Finish your tour of the Tower by returning to Byward Tower to exit to Tower Hill. Turn right on Tower Hill and follow it around the walls until you come to the Minories. (There is a pedestrian underpass that will take you to the Tower Hill Underground Station if you choose to end your walk here.)

Turn left on Minories and walk north. H.R.F. Keating in *Inspector Ghote Hunts the Peacock* mentioned that Ghote climbed a slight ascent going along the "oddly-named" Minories. The name came from the Minoresses, who were nuns of the order of St. Clare. In 1293, they founded a convent here; it stood outside the City wall.

Walk up Minories to Aldgate, passing Fenchurch Street Station on your left. Turn left across Aldgate to Leadenhall Street. In an office in Leadenhall Street, Hosmer Angel was supposedly a cashier in Sir Arthur Conan Doyle's Sherlock Holmes tale "A Case of Identity." The offices of the Dagger Line were on Leadenhall Street in A.E.W. Mason's *The House in Lordship Lane*. Walk west along Leadenhall Street, which is filled with big City banks, and past St. Andrew's Undershaft, whose shaft was a Maypole. Then turn left down Lime Street, the home of Lloyds of London, the great international insurance underwriters. The street also figured in Sherlock Holmes's case of "The Mazarin Stone" by Sir Arthur Conan Doyle as the street on which Van Seddar lived.

At the place where Leadenhall Street turns into Cornhill, Bishopsgate leads off to the right. Bishopsgate was the site, in the fifteenth century, of Crosby Hall. Richard III lived there, and later, before he moved to Chelsea, so did Sir Thomas More.

Walk down Cornhill and turn right on tiny Royal Exchange Buildings (an alley) to Threadneedle Street. Slightly to your left and across Threadneedle Street to the north is Old Broad Street, where Lord Peter Wimsey found the tobacconist's shop with the name Cummings, not Smith. It was the place Tallboys mailed his alphabet letter to his stockbroker each week using letters from Pym's Nutrax ad in Dorothy L. Sayers's *Murder Must Advertise*.

Turn right off Threadneedle Street into Bartholomew Lane. Follow it north to Lothbury and turn left. Follow Lothbury west; it will become Gresham Street. Cross Old Jewry and Ironmonger streets and keep walking along Gresham Street until you come to Guildhall Yard. The Guildhall is to your right.

The Guildhall, the City's most important secular building, has stood on or near its present site since the eleventh century. It was the meeting place of the important City Guilds, the banners and coats of arms of which are displayed on the gatehouse, together with replicas of the ancient wooden giants, Gog and Magog. The City is administered from here by the Court of Common Council, which developed from the ancient Court of Hustings. Huge ceremonial dinners are given in the restored fifteenth-century Great Hall.

The Guildhall is associated with Lord Mayors, such as Sir Richard Whittington (the one with the cat). In Catherine Aird's *In Harm's Way,* George and Tom Mellot agreed to divide their family's farm in Kent. George was to run the farm while Tom "went off to do a Dick Whittington." Aird's Detective Inspector Sloan thought to himself that it was funny that only one Lord Mayor got into the history book, but perhaps it was because he also got into a nursery rhyme.

Come out of Guildhall Yard and continue walking west (to your right) on Gresham Street to Wood Street. This is the site of the Wood Street Police Station, off Cheapside at the corner of Wood Street and Love Lane, where Inspector Ghote arrived early for the international conference on drugs in H.R.F. Keating's *Inspector Ghote Hunts the Peacock.*

If you wish to visit the London Museum, turn right and follow Wood Street to London Wall (the street Inspector Ghote took to the Tower), where you turn left. The Barbican, a postwar complex of apartments, shops, restaurants, and theaters, is just north of the London Museum. When you have finished at the Museum, take London Wall west to Aldersgate, where you turn left. Follow Aldersgate, which becomes St. Martin's le Grand, to St. Paul's Underground Station. If you decide to skip the Museum and are ready to complete your walk, follow Gresham Street to St. Martin's le Grand and turn left. This will bring you back to the St. Paul's Underground Station and the conclusion of the walk.

2

INNS OF COURT/ FLEET STREET WALK

BACKGROUND

This walk combines legal and newspaper London, or Fleet Street and the Inns of Court. They coexist in the ancient no-man's-land between the City of London, which ended in the west at Ludgate, and Temple Bar, where Westminster began. The Inns of Court are located on a north-south axis that runs along Gray's Inn Road and Chancery Lane, crosses Fleet Street, and ends at the Thames River Embankment. Fleet Street, a part of London's main east-west axis, is an extension of the Strand, which stretches from Temple Bar to Ludgate. Located on the Fleet River, which rises in Hampstead Heath and flows into the Thames at Blackfriars Bridge, Ludgate was the western gate of the medieval City. Both the law and the press consider themselves a class apart, standing between the government and the governed, and their geographic place-ment reflects this.

By the time of the first Elizabeth, legal London, with its four major Inns of Court, was known as the third English University. There, young barristers had to eat their dinners and pass their examinations in order to be called to the Bar. Many of the buildings are quite old, and they are set in handsome squares and tiny courtyards unsuspected by the passing tourist unless he catches a glimpse of a black robed and bewigged barrister rushing along.

Fleet Street is the name given to the whole area east of the Strand. Spreading into small winding alleyways and cul-de-sacs, it is where London's newspapers have been published since the time of Charles I. The local taverns (the City's name for pubs) have been inhabited by a mixture of lawyers and journalists since the time of Fleet Street's famous son, Dr. Samuel Johnson. G.K. Chesterton, a typical journalist in modern times, liked to work in a wine bar and then wander amiably down the center of Fleet Street or take a cab 200 feet to drop off his copy. Other detective story writers, such as Edgar Wallace and E.C. Bentley, were journalists by trade and worked in Fleet Street. Like Scotland Yard, the area is also the hangout of many fictional characters who appear in our detective stories.

LENGTH OF WALK: 5 miles

It can be covered in two parts, each about 2½ miles long. One covers the Inns of Court; the other, Fleet Street and the Old Bailey. The entire walk can be covered in a morning and an afternoon or on two separate days. But *both parts* should be done on a weekday, if possible, because the Courts and most restaurants and taverns are closed on weekends. Although the major legal holiday periods are August and September there, cases are tried at the Old Bailey and the Royal Courts all year round.

See map on page 23 for the boundaries of this walk and page 231 for a list of the detectives and stories covered.

PLACES OF INTEREST

Inns of Court (closed weekends):
  Gray's Inn
  Lincoln's Inn
  Inner Temple
  Middle Temple
Royal Courts of Justice, The Strand. Open Mon.–Fri., 10:30–4:30 P.M.

Temple Bar, Fleet Street/The Strand.

Staple Inn, High Holborn.

Public Record Office Museum, Chancery Lane. Open Mon.–Fri.,
1:00–4:00 P.M.

St. Clement Dane's Church, The Strand.

The Old Bailey (Central Criminal Court). Open 10:15 to rising of
the Courts.

Dr. Johnson's House, 17 Gough Square. Mon.–Sat., 11:00–5:30
P.M.; closed Sun. Admission charge.

Sir John Soane's Museum, Lincoln's Inn Fields. Tues.–Sat.,
10:00–5:00 P.M. (Closed in August.)

Somerset House, The Strand. Mon.–Fri., 8:30–4:30 P.M.

PLACES TO EAT

Taverns: Regular pub hours (except for a few open for Fleet Street,
but closed weekends). Reservations are a good idea.

El Vino, 47 Fleet Street. Wine bar. Ties required, women not
served at bar.

Ye Olde Cock Tavern, 22 Fleet Street. Elizabethan. 01-353-8570.

Ye Olde Cheshire Cheese, 145 Fleet Street. Dr. Johnson's haunt.
Reservations needed. 01-353-6170.

The Devereux Pub, Devereux Court. G.K. Chesterton's
Distributists met here. 01-583-4562.

Edgar Wallace Pub, 41 Essex Street.

Lunch or Tea: The Royal Courts of Justice Café, the Strand. The
Central Criminal Courts canteen, Old Bailey.

—— INNS OF COURT/FLEET STREET —— WALK

INNS OF COURT

Begin this walk by coming out of the Southampton Row exit of the Holborn Underground Station. Turn left to walk up Southampton Row. At Fisher Street, cross Southampton Row and follow Fisher Street to Red Lion Square. Walk through the square to Princeton Street and on to Bedford Row. In Dorothy L. Sayers's *Strong Poison,* Joan Murchison, who had been planted in the law office of Norman Urquhart to look for suspicious goings on, walked around Red Lion Square after the office closed to kill time before going back to burgle the office safe. She did that successfully, using the techniques she had learned in Limehouse from Bill, the ex-burglar, now a Salvationist.

Turn right into Bedford Row, which is a street of dark brick houses dating from the 1700s, most with a brass plate listing barristers' or solicitors' names. The difference between a solicitor and a barrister is that the solicitor does everyday legal work, such as writing wills or conveying property, and the barrister, whom solicitors "instruct" or "brief," goes into Court to plead cases. It is the glamorous barrister who wears the black gowns and wigs; John Mortimer's Rumpole of the Bailey is a barrister, while Dorothy L. Sayers's precise little Mr. Murbles is a family solicitor.

Norman Urquhart, the solicitor cousin of the poisoned Philip Boyes, had his office in Bedford Row in Dorothy L. Sayers's *Strong Poison.* Sayers must have associated this street with lawyers, for it was also the place in *Unnatural Death* where Inspector Charles Parker found Mr. Tripp, the lawyer whom Mary Whitaker consulted about the new inheritance law. Tripp told Parker a frightening story of being lured to a deserted house in Hampstead Heath to write a will for a dying woman who then tried to murder him. (In many detective stories, dangerous attacks occur in the wilds of Hampstead Heath or Epping Forest.)

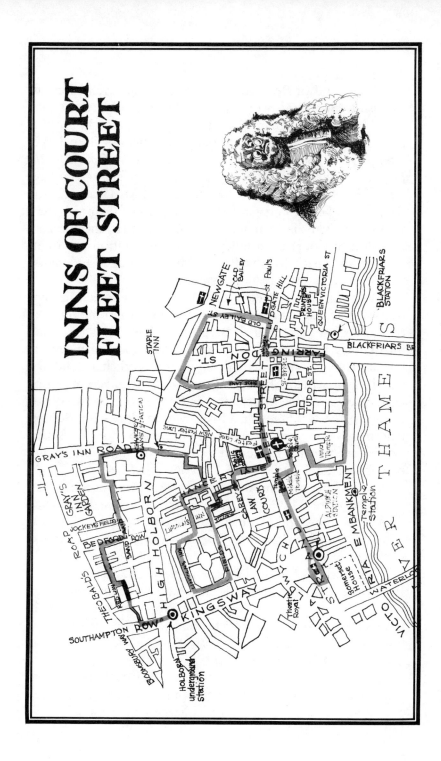

INNS OF COURT
FLEET STREET

At the end of Bedford Row, turn left and walk along its extension, Sandland Street, past Jockey's Fields. It was here that Margery Allingham placed the Queen Anne house that held the offices of the ancient publishing firm of Barnabas & Company "at the Sign of the Golden Quiver" in *Flowers for the Judge*. Go into the open gateway to Gray's Inn Gardens, where Pepys and Addison walked and which Charles Lamb declared to be the best gardens of the Inns of Court. A stern sign warns you that you are there only on sufferance because each Inn of Court is an independent organization run by its Benchers (Masters of the Bench who are judges and senior barristers) and an elected Treasurer.

Walk through the Field Court, where an ancient catalpa tree is associated with the memory of Gray's most famous son, the Lord Chancellor Francis Bacon, who was Gray's Treasurer, into Gray's Inn Square, where the heavy bomb damage has been repaired. You can see the rebuilt medieval chapel, library, and hall in which Shakespeare's *Comedy of Errors* was first performed in 1594. Matthew Bouff, the solicitor in Wilkie Collins's *The Moonstone,* had his offices in Gray's Inn Square. Another more recent luminary of Gray's Inn was F.E. Smith, Lord Birkenhead, who helped to prosecute G.K. Chesterton's brother for libel in the 1913 Marconi Trial.

It was in Gray's Inn that Sayers's Mr. Towkington, a barrister friend of Mr. Murbles, had his chambers. He invited Parker, Wimsey, and Murbles over to try his port and get the definitive word on the new inheritance statute in *Unnatural Death*.

Leave Gray's Inn by the ancient stone gateway into Gray's Inn Road; then turn to your right and walk south to High Holborn. The solicitor Reginald Colby had his offices in Gray's Inn Road. It was there he denied that he had ordered a hired car to meet Mrs. Benson at the airport in Patricia Moyes's *Who Is Simon Warwick?*

Standing at the northeast corner of High Holborn and Holborn, across the roadway you can see the marvelous black and white timber and plastered Elizabethan front of Staple Inn. This corner is another boundary of the ancient City, marked with two stone obelisks called the Holborn Bars. Originally, the Staple Inn was used by the Wool Trade's Merchants of the Staple. Its overhanging facade, although much restored, is a real survivor of the Elizabethan era. It was the place where Dr. Johnson wrote *Rasselas* in a week to pay for his mother's funeral.

Cross Holborn and walk through the gateway marked Staple Inn, and you will find yourself behind Staple Inn in the quiet eighteenth-century courtyard in which the Wimsey solicitor, Mr. Murbles, had his chambers. In Sayers's *Clouds of Witness,* Murbles had Wimsey, Sir Impey Biggs, and Lady Mary to lunch in a "delightful old set of rooms with windows looking out upon the formal garden with its odd little flower-beds and tinkling fountain. The chambers kept up the old-fashioned law atmosphere which hung about his own prim person. His dining room was furnished in mahogany, with a Turkey carpet and crimson curtains." On Murbles's sideboard stood some pieces of handsome Sheffield plate and a number of decanters with engraved silver labels round their necks. There was a bookcase full of large volumes bound in law calf and an oil-painting of a harsh-faced judge was over the mantelpiece.

Walk through the court past the little fountain on your left; then turn right past the Southampton Buildings and follow the passageway that leads to Chancery Lane. Cross Chancery Lane and take the Stone Buildings' gate into Lincoln's Inn, the second great Inn of Court, whose records begin in 1422.

Lincoln's Inn's most famous sons were Sir Thomas More (whom Josephine Tey thought had defamed Richard III) and Prime Minister William Pitt the Younger, whose politics, with the help of the Duke of Wellington, finally finished off Napoleon. Ann Dorland's insulting lawyer, Mr. Pritchard, has his office in Lincoln's Inn in Sayers's *The Unpleasantness at the Bellona Club;* and the very expensive and distinguished barrister hired to defend Isabel Mortimer in Julian Symons's *A Three Pipe Problem* has his chambers there, too. This Inn may also be where Ellis Peters's charming young oboist, Charlotte Rossignol, came to see the solicitor of her archeologist uncle, Alan

Morris, in *City of Gold and Shadows*. Mr. Stanford was described as "small and nimble, clever and froggish . . ." but he
was also definitely upset when her uncle had been missing for a
year. Finally, in John Creasey's *Leave It to the Toff*, the Honorable Richard Rollison, D.S.O., M.C., M.B.E., received word
of a strange and sinister legacy from Gammon & Hanbury,
solicitors with a Lincoln's Inn address.

As you come into Lincoln's Inn, on your left is the Old
Square, with an ancient chapel that was bombed in World War
II and the red-brick Old Hall, in which the High Court of
Chancery used to meet. This Hall was the scene of the famous
trial of *Jarndyce* v. *Jarndyce* in Charles Dickens's *Bleak House*, in
which the foggy proceedings took so long they used up the
estate.

Walk across the open area, turn left past the Victorian red-
brick New Hall, and go through the gateway into Lincoln's
Inn Fields, a large square with houses grouped about its edges.
A number of infamous executions took place there, and John
Gay wrote verse about the footpads and bad lighting. Turn
right and walk around Lincoln's Inn Fields to reach the home
of architect Sir John Soane on the north side at No. 13. It is
now a museum, inside of which is a hodgepodge of books,
busts, furniture, and the Picture Room, with its famous set of
Hogarth's *Rake's Progress*. No. 58 Lincoln's Inn Fields was the
home of Charles Dickens's good friend and biographer John
Forster. Dickens described it as the home of the sinister lawyer
Tulkinghorn in *Bleak House*. At the southeast corner, you can
see tiny Portsmouth Street, where the Old Curiosity Shop may
have been.

Complete your walk around Lincoln's Inn Fields and leave
again by the main gate to Lincoln's Inn. On your right is New
Square, where Michael Gilbert had his office and where the
firm of Horniman, Birley, and Craine had its offices in *Small-
bone Deceased*. Keep walking straight ahead to the northeast
corner of New Square. Turn to your right and walk a short
way until you can find the passageway on your left that will
take you into Star Yard; then turn right and go south through
Star Yard to an ancient archway.

Walk under the archway toward Carey Street. Set into this archway between two sets of stairs to lawyers' chambers (or offices) is two-storey Wiley's Legal Bookstore, with some satirical prints of legal beagles in the shop windows. Established in 1830, Wiley's has a wonderfully old-fashioned interior, jammed with books and prints and paperbacks of John Mortimer's Rumpole stories. After looking in vain for a cartoon of a *woman* barrister, we bought a lawyer daughter an inexpensive eighteenth-century print of Newgate Prison (on the site of the Old Bailey).

Coming out of Wiley's, turn left on Carey Street and walk to Chancery Lane. Across the street at Chancery Lane, you will see the large, gray Public Record Office, which stretches one block east to Fetter Lane. Only serious researchers are allowed to work here, where for thirty years Dorothy L. Sayers's Somerville College friend, Muriel St. Clare Byrne, read, collated, and edited her lifework, *The Lisle Letters*, which were published in 1982. (Lord Lisle, the illegitimate son of Edward IV and nephew of Henry VIII, ended up in the Tower charged with treason. The Crown kept his correspondence, which provided Byrne with a superb contemporary glimpse of Tudor England.) Byrne co-authored the play *Busman's Honeymoon* with Sayers.

The general public can go into the Public Record Office Museum, to the left of the main entrance in the slightly sunken site of a medieval chapel for converted Jews. In the museum, you can see a copy of Shakespeare's signature; the Domesday Book of William the Conqueror, which celebrated its 900th birthday anniversary in 1986; the signed confession of Guy Fawkes, whose effigy is "murdered" every November 5th with bonfires (although he was hanged); and the gaol (jail) book from "Hanging" Judge Jeffrey's Bloody Assizes after the rebellion of the Duke of Monmouth.

As you leave the Public Record Office, turn left (south) and walk down Chancery Lane to Fleet Street. (You will come out near the junction of the Strand and Fleet Street, which is marked by Temple Bar.)

At this point, you have walked about 2.4 miles. If you want

to continue, the next part of the walk is Fleet Street. You can stop for lunch or a snack at one of the many taverns clustered about Temple Bar or, having made a reservation ahead of time, continue the walk until you reach the Cheshire Cheese at 145 Fleet Street and have lunch there. (The Cheshire Cheese marks the 3-mile point.) Then you can finish the walk in the afternoon or end it by walking back up Chancery Lane to the Chancery Lane Underground Station by Staple Inn.

FLEET STREET

Take a good look at the ancient City boundary marker in Fleet Street called Temple Bar. The memorial marker, crowned by a bronze griffin, has small statues of Queen Victoria and Edward VII. It replaced a handsome Wren gateway, torn down because it restricted traffic. Officially, the reigning monarch must always stop at Temple Bar before entering the City. There, in a colorful ceremony that reflects the ancient freedom of the City, the Lord Mayor presents him or her with the Sword of London, which is then returned, and grants the king or queen the freedom to enter the City.

Near Temple Bar, the original Anodyne Necklace pub once stood. Its painted sign displayed a chain of beads, the anodyne necklace, that could produce cures for such ailments as teething, fits, and convulsions in children. American writer Martha Grimes called one mystery *The Anodyne Necklace,* but she arbitrarily moved the pub itself to London's seedy East End.

Turn left on Fleet Street, which, like the Fleet Prison, takes its name from the Fleet River. "There's Fleet Street," said Henry Lamprey to Roberta Grey in Ngaio Marsh's *A Surfeit of Lampreys.* "Do you remember 'up the Hill of Ludgate, down the Hill of Fleet'?" (When the Lampreys drove Grey from the East End, where she docked, they covered the same trip described by Marsh in her autobiography, *Black Beech and Honeydew.*)

Many mystery characters aspired to be members of Fleet Street's journalistic fraternity. In Julian Symons's *The Blackheath Poisonings,* Paul Mortimer wanted to become a Fleet

Street reporter, but his merchant family felt it was not a genteel profession. (They sounded very much like the family of G.K. Chesterton, who wanted him to be an artist instead of a journalist.) But numbers of detective story writers became journalists of one kind or another, among them, Edgar Wallace, G.K. Chesterton, Anthony Berkeley, H.R.F. Keating, Graham Greene, and E.C. Bentley. Others, such as Dick Francis, worked for the media for a time. He wrote a racing column for the *Sunday Express;* Dorothy L. Sayers wrote guest editorials and did book reviews of crime fiction for *The Sunday Times.*

Many real British newspapers are mentioned in mysteries, but many were made up to serve the writer's purpose. Among the fictitious ones is the nameless newspaper in which Edgar Wallace's Thalia Drummond, who was working undercover to capture the head of the Crimson Circle, ran an ad for a job. In Agatha Christie's "Jane in Search of a Job," Jane Cleveland religiously read the *Daily Leader*'s "Agony and Personal" column and answered an ad to impersonate a Grand Duchess. In *Forfeit,* Dick Francis's sports writer, James Tyrone, worked on the fictitious *Sunday Blaze.* On Saturdays, Tyrone went to the races. Then he had Tuesdays to Thursdays to think up some galvanizing subject to write about and Fridays to bring in his copy for the sports editor to vet. Dorothy L. Sayers's star reporter, the dark-haired, blue-eyed Salcombe Hardy, worked on the *Daily Yell.* Hardy was a large man who was usually drunk, but managed to report many Wimsey adventures, including the Wimsey's honeymoon in *Busman's Honeymoon.*

In *Whose Body?,* Sayers also mentions a number of other newspapers: the *Chronicle,* the *Banner,* and the *Daily Mail.* In *Murder Must Advertise,* her indefatigable young reporter, Hector Puncheon, worked for the *Morning Star,* where every Friday morning the Pym's Publicity Nutrax ad gave away which pub to use for drug distribution. Young Puncheon, wide awake after reporting on a warehouse fire and a heroic cat, ate a 3:00 A.M. breakfast of grilled sausages in a Fleet Street café, then strolled on a fine but chilly morning past the Griffin at Temple Bar, the Royal Law Courts, and St. Clement Dane's before turning north and going into a Covent Garden pub where he was mistakenly given a shipment of cocaine.

In *Trent's Last Case*, E.C. Bentley's artist, Philip Trent, had written several free-lance articles about murders that baffled the police. He did them for Sir James Molloy, a strong, clever Irishman, who was editor-in-chief of the *Record* in a building across Fleet Street from its sister evening paper, the *Sun*. In G.K. Chesterton's Father Brown story "The Purple Wig," a spineless editor who altered his own copy on orders of his publisher worked at the *Daily Reformer*. G.K.C. himself resigned from the Liberal *Daily News* rather than be edited by its owners, the Cadbury (chocolate) family.

Begin to walk east (to your left) along Fleet Street. Along your route, there are many places of interest to watch for. For instance, directly across from Temple Bar you can see 1 Fleet Street, where Child's Bank used to stand. Just beyond it at No. 22 is Ye Olde Cock Tavern, Fleet Street's oldest tavern, dating back to Elizabethan times. Its gilded cock sign was carved by Grinling Gibbons, and it was a favorite of Dr. Johnson, Charles Dickens, and other literary lights. At the Cock Tavern, Sayers's Hector Puncheon, tackling a well-deserved beefsteak after a long day's reporting suddenly realized that the packet of white powder he had been given that morning might not be soda and dashed out to a chemist's to have it analyzed.

No. 47, across the road on the south side of Fleet Street, is El Vino, a wine bar once patronized by G.K. Chesterton and suspiciously like Pommeroy's Wine Bar, inhabited after Court by that Old Bailey hack Rumpole, who liked to drink his claret (Chateau Fleet Street) in John Mortimer's *Rumpole of the Bailey*. El Vino is "infamous" today for its strict dress code—men must wear ties—and for not serving women at the bar.

As you walk along the north side of Fleet Street, you will pass St. Dunstan's in the West (the last church within the City), with a stone wind tower built like an earlier one at York. Although the Great Fire of 1666 stopped east of here, the church was rebuilt in Victorian Gothic. John Donne was once its vicar, and Isaak Walton was its vestryman. Inside are the figures of legendary King Lud and his sons, brought here when old Lud Gate was torn down. Across the street on the south side at No. 70 is The Falstaff, now only a basement room, where Sayers's Lord Peter Wimsey, Charles Parker, and reporter Salcombe Hardy lunched together in *The Unpleasantness at the Bellona Club*. A little farther on at Fetter Lane, on your left, you will pass the site of Clifford's Inn, the oldest inn in Chancery. The offices of the *Daily Mirror* are at the top of Fetter Lane.

Cross four more tiny cul-de-sacs going east on the north side of Fleet Street, and you will come to Hind Court. Turn left to follow Hind Court until it turns into Gough Square, where you will find Dr. Johnson's four-storey brick house. It is now a small museum in the attic of which the Great Lectioner wrote his dictionary. G.K. Chesterton, who liked to call himself a "Grub Street" scrivener, adored dressing up to play the role of Dr. Johnson and wrote a play about him.

Return from Gough Square to Fleet Street; go one short block to Wine Office Court, and turn left to walk into Wine Office Court. On your right, you will see the most famous Fleet Street tavern of them all: the Cheshire Cheese, beloved of both Dr. Johnson and G.K. Chesterton. It still reeks of authenticity, with sawdust on the floor, low-raftered and plastered ceilings, and such traditional old English pub food as roast beef, steak and kidney pie, and the Chesterton's favorite: Welsh rarebit. Cecil Chesterton and his journalist bride Ada (a.k.a. J.K. Prothero) held their wedding breakfast here in 1916.

When you leave the Cheshire Cheese, turn left and walk back to Fleet Street. You will be in front of the *Daily Telegraph,* where for many years E.C. Bentley was a leader (editorial) writer. Next door is the black tile and chromium, 1930s *Daily Express* of Lord Beaverbrook, the Canadian press magnate. Across Fleet Street to the south is Bouverie Street and then Whitefriars, the site of the world-famous magazine *Punch* and the former offices of the *Daily News,* where G.K. Chesterton, Hilaire Belloc, and E.C. Bentley all worked before the First World War. It is also the home of the *Daily Mail* and the gossip sheet *News of the World* that mentioned Rumpole of the Bailey so frequently. At one of these Fleet Street papers, Ian Stuart's bank inspector, David Grierson, met a reporter named Carlton, who let him use the newspaper's morgue in *A Growing Concern*.

Keep on walking along Fleet Street until you reach Shoe Lane. Here, across Fleet Street to the south, is Reuters, the international news agency. As you turn left to walk north along Shoe Lane, you see the very modern, concrete and glass International Press Centre. The Press Club is located here on the first floor.

The British Crime Writers' Association (C.W.A.), founded in 1953 by John Creasey and Nigel Morland, meets at the Press Club. Like that of the Mystery Writers of America (and the Detection Club), its membership is restricted to people who have published detection or crime fiction, but members are very cordial to visiting strangers from overseas who ask their help in sleuthing London. The C.W.A. holds a yearly awards dinner in May at which the Gold and Silver Dagger awards are presented. Many of the writers included in this guide have won the coveted daggers, including Julian Symons, John Le Carré, H.R.F. Keating, P.D. James, and Ruth Rendell; while others, such as Margaret Yorke, have also served as chairmen.

Continuing north on Shoe Lane, you will pass the *Evening Standard*. Follow Shoe Lane as it bends to the east, past St. Andrew's, one of Wren's largest churches, across from the City Temple, the "cathedral" of the Free Churches. Take Plumtree Court to your right, and you will come out on the iron Victorian bridge that connects Holborn with Holborn Viaduct.

In this vicinity, near the London Wall, Margery Allingham and her husband, Pip Youngman Carter, had a flat before and during World War II. You can sense that the atmosphere here is very like that portrayed in her fictional St. Peter's Square in *Tiger in the Smoke*, but the vague landmarks Allingham gives her reader all point to Paddington Station and Marylebone.

Turn right and walk along the viaduct over the top of Farringdon Street, past the Holborn Viaduct Railway Station. On your left, you will see the Crusaders' Church of St. Sepulchre without Newgate, with its restored fifteenth-century tower. Captain John Smith, who was rescued by the Indian princess Pocahontas, is buried here, but it also had criminal associations. It once had a watch house to prevent surgeons or students from St. Bartholomew's Hospital (to the north, up Giltspur Street) from body-snatching. The hospital, the oldest in London still on its original site, is just south of the oldest church in London, St. Bartholomew the Great.

"St. Bart's" was not only the place where Dr. Watson once worked, but also where he met Sherlock Holmes in the pathology lab in Conan Doyle's *A Study in Scarlet*. The Pathology Museum, with its plaque commemorating this "historic event," unfortunately is closed to the public now.

At St. Sepulchre, the great tower bell tolled as the condemned prisoners passed by on their way from Newgate Prison to Tyburn Hill (at Marble Arch). The prisoners were housed across the road in Newgate Prison on the site of the Central Criminal Courts, or the Old Bailey, the scene of so many famous and fictitious detective story trials. From St. Sepulchre's, you can clearly see the Old Bailey's famous copper dome, topped by the statue of Justice. Contrary to tradition, Justice *is not* blindfolded; she stands there sternly holding aloft the scales of justice and her sharp sword.

From St. Sepulchre's, cross to Old Bailey Street, which was widened here to allow room for the crowds who liked to watch a good hanging. You are near a well-known pub, the Magpie and the Stump, where the aristocracy used to rent rooms to watch executions and where John Dickson Carr's heroine Caroline Ross in *The Bride of Newgate* waited to be sure she was both a bride and a widow. John Mortimer said that Rex's Café used to be there, too, where Rumpole got the best scrambled eggs in London, but it has been replaced by an Indian restaurant, and "even Rumpole can't stomach tandoori chicken for breakfast." Rumpole then patronized the Public Canteen across the street in the Old Bailey itself, but its food was not as good as the prisoners' fare in the cells beyond that scarred, old oaken door from Newgate.

The original Old Bailey was built in Edwardian times. It

had only four courts built around a great hallway, with a marble staircase decorated with murals and memorials to the noted prison reformer, Elizabeth Fry. Young lawyers still hope a trial in the Court No. 1 or No. 2 will mean instant fame. To Rumpole's disgust, the modern wing of the Old Bailey has courts with carpeting, chairs, and air conditioning.

To gain admission to the drama of the courtrooms, you must line up at the Public Gallery entrance. Court sessions begin at 10:15 A.M. and 1:45 P.M. daily. A quick word of warning: Leave your camera at home for you may not take it into Court with you. A sign suggests that you leave it in one of the pubs across the street—a somewhat unnerving idea. Many of the crowd will be anxious friends and relatives of the accused; some will be retirees with time on their hands; others will be tourists and school groups who have come to see justice done. If you know a barrister or solicitor, an introduction from one can get you a seat in the court itself. On most days, the crowd is very like the amusing bunch of newcomers and old hands described in the opening chapter of Michael Gilbert's *Death Has Deep Roots*. In Cyril Hare's *Tragedy at Law*, Justice Barber was murdered just outside the Central Criminal Court.

In addition to scenes in which the incomparable Rumpole attempts to thwart the Bull's tendency to help the prosecution in *Rumpole of the Bailey*, many other detective story scenes were enacted here. Some defendants were innocent; some were guilty. Among them was Isabel Mortimer, whose trial and conviction for the poisoning of her lover, Roger, and her mother-in-law, Harriet, were described in detail in Julian Symons's *The Blackheath Poisonings*. In *The Man in the Queue*, Josephine Tey's Inspector Grant thought that suspect bookie Lamont would need bigger guns when he came up for trial at Old Bailey. Mike Wedgewood was also tried here in Margery Allingham's *Flowers for the Judge*.

In *Fog of Doubt*, Christianna Brand's Doctor "Tedward" was tried for murder in Court No. 1. In *Duplicate Death*, Georgette Heyer's Beulah Birtley was convicted of criminal fraud because her fiance, "Terrible Timothy" Harte, wasn't "an Old Bailey chaser" (a different name for the lawyers Rumpole called "Old Bailey hacks"). Most memorably, in Dorothy L. Sayers's *Strong Poison,* Lord Peter Wimsey first saw Harriet Vane in the dock on trial for poisoning her lover. "There were crimson roses on the bench; they looked like splashes of blood. The judge was an old man. . . . His scarlet robe clashed harshly with the crimson of the roses."

When you have had enough Court atmosphere, come out, turn left, and walk down Old Bailey Street. At Ludgate Hill, turn right and walk past Old Seacoal Lane, where the Fleet Prison once stood. In Charles Dickens's *The Pickwick Papers,* Mr. Pickwick, incarcerated after refusing to pay his fine, treated Mr. Jingle with charity and secured his release from poverty and squalor. (Pickwick was G.K. Chesterton's favorite Dickens character, and he called his beloved father "a bearded Mr. Pickwick.")

Keep walking along the north side of Ludgate Hill to Ludgate Circus and the bright red King Lud Pub, tucked under the arches of the Ludgate Viaduct. In Sherlock Holmes's time, this pub was renowned for its welsh rarebit, which was available from early morning to late evening on its free lunch counter.

In *Forfeit,* Dick Francis's reporter Tyrone walked a drunken sports writer named Bert down Fleet Street to Ludgate Circus. He then went to check on his typewriter at a repair shop. As Tyrone came back from Ludgate Circus, he heard a woman screaming and found Bert dead on the pavement below his newspaper office.

Cross Ludgate Circus to the northwest corner, where you will find a large memorial tablet to Edgar Wallace, who regarded himself as a journalist, not a detective story writer. Turn right, across Fleet Street, and walk south along New Bridge Street until you come to Bride's Lane. This was the site of the Bridewell Prison. Turn right and follow Bride's Lane; then go up the steps into St. Bride's Passage, which leads into Salisbury Square, where you will find St. Bride's Church. This is the so-called Cathedral of Fleet Street. Its many-tiered, "wedding cake" spire is Wren's tallest. The diarist Samuel Pepys was baptized in St. Bride's, and the poet Richard Lovelace, who died in Gunpowder Alley (Shoe Lane), is buried there. The church was gutted by bombs but was rebuilt with donations from the London newspaper. Its tiny area is similar to P.D. James's fictitious Pie Crust Court, off Pie Crust Passage, which was an alley so narrow one man could hardly get through. In *Unnatural Causes,* Adam Dalgleish, coming to interrogate Justin Bryce about the murder of mystery writer Maurice Seeton, found himself in an eighteenth-century courtyard so carefully preserved it looked artificial.

Now retrace your steps to New Bridge Street and turn right to walk towards Blackfriars Bridge. Across the wide roadway, you will pass the entrance to Printing House Square, just north of Queen Victoria Street, where the *Times,* queen of the London papers, was published until 1974. Printing has been done near Ludgate Circus since a pupil of William Caxton, Wynkyn de Worde (buried at St. Bride's), started a shop here. King Charles I authorized the first official London Gazette in 1627. The *Times* itself began publishing in 1785.

The *Times* is often mentioned in detective stories. In Sayers's *Whose Body?* Lord Peter put an ad in the *Times* about the pince-nez found on the body in the Thipps's bath in Battersea. Like many other Londoners, Lord Peter routinely "took" the *Times* and the *Times Literary Supplement,* which Bunter offered to Charles Parker when he came to breakfast.

East of Blackfriars Bridge and south of Queen Victoria Street, by the site of the old Blackfriars Theatre, was the warehouse flat of Jeremy Jones and Peregrine Jay. In Ngaio Marsh's *Killer Dolphin,* they got the chance to run the Dolphin Theatre, which they could see across the Thames on Bankside, near Shakespeare's Globe. In Dame Ngaio's last book, *Light Thickens,* which was her final paean of praise to Shakespeare's *Macbeth,* this flat had been converted into a family residence for Jay, his wife, Emily, and three sons. At the end of the mystery, the Jays entertained Superintendent Alleyn there. From their patio, they watched the river traffic and the tour boats going back and forth between Westminster and the Tower.

Not far downriver from Blackfriars and Puddle Dock is the

Queenhithe Dock, which was one of the four original City deep-water harbors. In *Unnatural Causes,* P.D. James's widowed Superintendent Adam Dalgleish lived there in a flat that looked out over the Thames. Suspiciously, in *The Skull Beneath the Skin,* Cordelia Gray had moved nearby into a City "warehouse" flat off Thames Street. Dickens's David Copperfield spent a miserable time in the vicinity of Blackfriars, washing and labeling bottles in Murdstone and Grimby's warehouse. (For the factory where Dickens himself worked as a boy, see Covent Garden/The Strand Walk.)

At the end of New Bridge Street, near the Blackfriars Bridge where it branches off to the right to the Victoria Embankment, is the entrance to the Blackfriars Underground Station. In Sayers's *Murder Must Advertise,* knowing he was being followed, Lord Peter Wimsey daydreamed about luring his assassins into some secluded spot, such as the Blackfriars subway or the steps beneath Cleopatra's Needle, then facing them and killing them with his bare hands.

Follow the Victoria Embankment to the right, crossing John Carpenter's Street, Carmelite Street, and Temple Avenue, which is an extension of Bouverie Street. Young E.C. Bentley, down from Oxford and reading for the Bar at the Temple, moonlighted at the *Daily News.* He walked up Bouverie Street by night to help put the paper to bed and then walked home. In this way, he kept up his adolescent habit of long night walks, like those he used to take with G.K. Chesterton, which G.K.C. mentions in his dedication to Bentley in *The Man Who Was Thursday.* Later, as a full-fledged editorial writer, Bentley walked to work from his home in Hampstead, composing *Trent's Last Case.*

On the right, you will pass the beautiful Inner Temple Garden (closed to visitors). The two Inns of Court, known as the Inner Temple and the Middle Temple, were formed from the property of the military order of the Knights Templar. Their task was to guard the pilgrims en route to the Holy Land during the Crusades. The order became so big and rich and powerful that in 1312 the King of France conspired with the Pope to destroy the order and seize its wealth. Their example was followed by the English kings, who first gave this choice spot to the other order of knights, the Knights Hospitalers of St. John of Jerusalem. When that order, too, was closed down, lawyers began to lease the land and organized themselves into two legal societies and were granted the freehold of the land by James I in 1608.

When you reach Middle Temple Lane, turn right and go up Middle Temple Lane. (This is the boundary between the Inner Temple—nearer the City—and the Middle Temple.) As you did in the courtyards of Gray's Inn and Lincoln's Inn, you will see doorways with staircases similar to those of an Oxford college, with a row of names. Among them is the name of John Mortimer, creator of Rumpole, himself a Q.C., or Queen's Counsel, one of the most august senior barristers.

To the left, go by the Middle Temple library and Middle Temple Hall, at the southern edge of Fountain Court. Middle Temple Hall was bombed in the Blitz but was restored to much of its former grandeur: paneled walls and a spectacular double hammerbeam roof, beneath which Shakespeare's own company is supposed to have put on *Twelfth Night* in 1602. Fountain Court, with its small fountain, seats, and shade trees, was described by law clerk Charles Dickens as an oasis in the dry and dusty channels of the law.

Turn right and walk across to Elm Court and into Crown Office Terrace, past the Temple Gardens, where Shakespeare began the Wars of the Roses. In "Rumpole and the Man of God," Mortimer's Rumpole walked through the Temple Gardens to his chambers one late-September morning and then set out for the Old Bailey.

You are now in the Inner Temple and going past the Inner Temple Hall, also rebuilt after the Blitz. Beyond Crown Office Terrace is the open space called King's Bench Walk. In King's Bench Walk at Staircase No. 9, there lived a young barrister named Montague Druitt, who drowned himself in the Thames. After his death, Druitt was suspected of having been Jack the Ripper. The other popular legend about that scourge of the East End prostitutes is that he was really Eddie (Prince Albert-Victor), Duke of Clarence and heir to the throne. The

Prince died young in 1892. Marie Belloc-Lowndes, sister of Chesterton's friend Hilaire Belloc, wrote *The Lodger,* which is the most famous fictional story about this mysterious person.

Austin Freeman's detective, Dr. Thorndyke, had his chambers at 5A King's Bench Walk. In Ngaio Marsh's *Black as He's Painted,* the African ruler known as the Boomer had eaten his dinners at the Temple as a law student. Both E.C. Bentley and G.K. Chesterton's brother-in-law, Lucian Oldershaw, who were friends and classmates since St. Paul's School and Oxford, read law at the Temple but followed careers in journalism. Just beyond King's Bench Walk are the Paper Buildings, where, in Georgette Heyer's *Duplicate Death,* young barrister "Terrible Timothy" Harte lived while wooing Beulah Birtley, the ex-con social secretary of the murdered Mrs. Haddington. Another Heyer lawyer, Giles Carrington, had his own flat in the Temple in which he entertained Superintendent Hanna-syde in his comfortable, book-lined sitting room in *Death in the Stocks.* In real life, Heyer's husband, Ronald Rougier, had his chambers there, too.

Turn left and go past Tanfield Court until you see the famous, round Temple Church, again badly bombed, but beautifully restored. It is one of five surviving circular churches in England, built like the church of the Holy Sepulchre in Jerusalem. Inside the church, you can see the battered stone effigies of the Templars. Just north of the church, where the porch has sunk into the hillside, the poet Oliver Goldsmith is said to be buried. Now go straight out Inner Temple Lane under the seventeenth-century arch into Fleet Street again.

Turn to your left and walk west again. Pass Devereux Court, where you will see the Devereux Pub, which can also be reached from Fountain Court. In *Forfeit,* the Devereux was the place where Dick Francis's newspaper men on the *Sunday Blaze* go for a lunch of cold meat and pickled onions, ending with cheese and another half pint. It was also the site of Distri-butist League meetings and "singalongs" when G.K. Chester-ton was chairman and editor of *G.K.'s Weekly,* published in Essex Street, which is the next lane leading south to the river. At 40 Essex Street is the Edgar Wallace Pub, dedicated to the memory of the prolific journalist-cum-detective story writer.

You are now across the Fleet from the Royal Courts of Justice, or Law Courts, where civil law is practiced. These courts once met at Westminster, but more space was needed; so, in 1882 this huge Gothic building was built, with its enormous central hall, mosaic floor, and 50 courts. As you enter under the porch, you can see signs for judges' changing rooms, and up and down the steps go bewigged and gowned lawyers and their clients, sometimes followed by the media.

You can sit in a courtroom and listen to a case, look at the small legal museum, or have a cup of tea in the Royal Courts of Justice cafeteria. Patricia Moyes's lawyer, Ambrose Quince, was in Court No. 5 when Scotland Yard's Henry Tibbett came to see him in *Who Is Simon Warwick?* Marian Babson's *The Lord Mayor of Death* also featured these courts.

Just past the Law Courts in the middle of the Strand stands St. Clement Dane's, a Wren church whose bells were immortalized in the nursery rhyme "Oranges and lemons say the bells of St. Clements." It was the parish church of Dr. Johnson, whose statue is in the yard.

It was from the now-gone Clements Inn to the north that Wilkie Collins's Walter Harkright began his long evening hike to his mother's cottage in Hampstead in *The Woman in White*. He hiked back a few days later to "meet his fate" (a woman in white) in the road near Regent's Park. Just beyond Aldwych is the London School of Economics, where Georgette Heyer's boorish peer, Lance, was an instructor in *Duplicate Death*.

If you continue west along the Strand, you will come first to St. Mary's le Strand, another handsome, war-damaged Wren church. Walk past King's College on the south side of the Strand, and you will come to the open courtyard of Somerset House on the site of the mansion built by Edward VI's uncle, the Lord Protector. Later on it became the headquarters of the Parliamentary Party, and there, after his death, Oliver Cromwell lay in state. Today Somerset House contains the national archives of wills, which you may consult for a fee, but births, marriages, and death certificates have been moved to another location.

In many detective stories, Somerset House has furnished our sleuths with some sinister facts. In *An Unsuitable Job for a Woman*, P.D. James's Cordelia Gray went there to trace Mark Callender's parentage and read his grandfather's will. Lord Peter Wimsey consulted the archives in *The Unpleasantness at the Bellona Club* and in "The Piscatorial Farce of the Stolen Stomach" and sent Miss Climpson to discover who the personae were in the Dawson murder in *Unnatural Death*. In the case of "The Speckled Band," Sherlock Holmes examined the will of the Stoner sisters' mother. From Somerset House, go to the Aldwych Underground Station, which ends the walk.

3

COVENT GARDEN/ THE STRAND WALK

BACKGROUND

This walk covers the heart of London's performing arts world. It contains a heady mix of hotels, restaurants, and theaters. Lying between the financial City and the government at Westminster, Covent (convent) Garden was built on the site of the Westminster Abbey gardens, which were seized by Henry VIII, then sold to the Russells, dukes of Bedford. They, in turn, used it to create the first planned urban development in London. Until 1974, Covent Garden was the old central produce market of London, excitingly alive in the wee hours, when everyone else slept.

Before Charing Cross Road was opened in 1887, rambling St. Martin's Lane was the route used to go from Covent Garden to the Strand. The Strand itself has been the major land route between London and Westminster since Roman times. It was as full of traffic centuries ago as you will find it today. When the Covent Garden area began to be developed, the Thames River's shoreline was lined with palaces of the Tudor aristocracy—Somerset House, Durham House, Savoy House,

42

and Northumberland House. The once-fabulous palaces now have given way to hotels, shops, and restaurants. It is this kind of neighborhood that has been well known in detective fiction since the time of Sherlock Holmes.

LENGTH OF WALK: 4 miles

This walk can be ended at 3 miles at Covent Garden Underground Station.

See map on page 45 for the boundaries of this walk and page 235 for a list of the detectives and stories covered.

PLACES OF INTEREST

St. Martin's-in-the-Fields, St. Martin's Place.
Covent Garden:
   St. Paul's Church. Closed Sun.
   London Transport Museum. Open daily, 10:00–6:00 P.M.
      Admission charge.
   The Royal Opera House
Bow Street Police Court, Bow Street.
Cleopatra's Needle, Victoria Embankment.
The Theatre Royal, Drury Lane.
Queen's Chapel of the Savoy, Savoy Hill. Open Tues.–Fri.,
   11:30–3:30 P.M.; Sun. service, 11:15 A.M.
St. Martin's Theatre, West Street. Ongoing production of Agatha
   Christie's *The Mousetrap.*

PLACES TO EAT

Lyons Corner House, the Strand. New version of gold and white,
   inexpensive restaurants that once dotted London. Garden
   Restaurant serves full meals; brunch and afternoon tea also
   served. Open daily to 8:00 P.M.
Tutton's, 11-12 Russell Street, Covent Garden. Inexpensive
   restaurant café built in old Potato Market. Tables on the
   sidewalk. Serves international dishes. Open daily 9:00 A.M. to
   11:30 P.M. 01-836-1167.

Rule's, 35 Maiden Lane. A "clubby" restaurant, very English in atmosphere, with Victorian decor and good English fare. Expensive. Cover charge and no credit cards. Reservations needed. 01-836-5314. Open to 11:30 P.M. Closed Sat., Sun., and month of August.

Simpson's-in-the-Strand, 100 Strand. An English institution famous for its roasts. Reservations needed. Open Mon.–Sat., to 10:00 P.M. 01-836-9112.

The Salisbury, 90 St. Martin's Lane. Theatrical pub opposite the Coliseum, with gorgeous etched glass, paneling, bronze nymphs, and red velvet alcove seating.

—— COVENT GARDEN/THE STRAND —— WALK

Begin this walk at the Charing Cross Underground Station. In Nicholas Blake's mystery about a publishing house in the Strand, *End of Chapter,* his sleuth, Nigel Strangeways, takes the Charing Cross Underground Station from his flat west of Kensington Gardens on Campden Hill Road. You should take the exit called St. Martin's-in-the-Fields. This exit will bring you up on the east side of Trafalgar Square, right in front of South Africa House, a favorite spot these days for picketing.

Turn left and walk north across the east side of the square to Duncannon Street. Cross Duncannon Street, and you will find yourself in front of the colonnaded classical church of St. Martin's-in-the-Fields, designed by James Gibbs. This is the parish church of both the Admiralty and Buckingham Palace. Charles I was baptized here, and George I was its first church warden. Today it is famous for its noontime concerts.

Pause on the wide steps of St. Martin's to look down Duncannon Street toward the Strand. Across the Strand, you will see the high sandstone facade of the Charing Cross Railway Station and Hotel. It is built over the site of Warren's Blacking Factory, where the young Charles Dickens was sent to work when his father was in Marshalsea Prison for debt. In "A Scandal in Bohemia," Sherlock Holmes's Irene Adler and

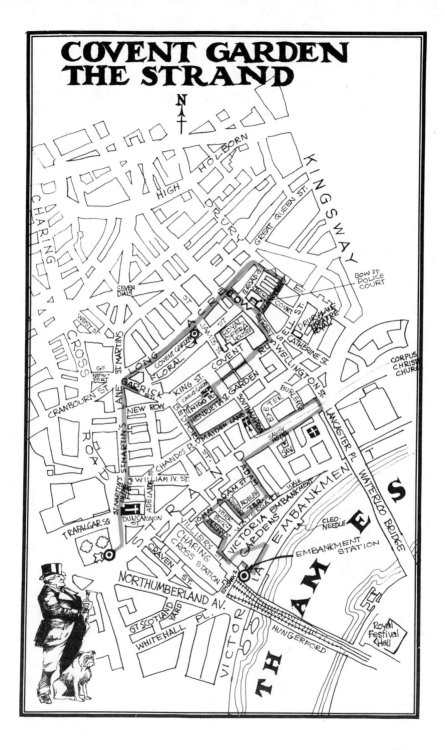

COVENT GARDEN
THE STRAND

N

SEVEN DIALS

BOW ST. POLICE COURT

HOLBORN

HIGH

DRURY

GREAT QUEEN ST.

KINGSWAY

DRURY LANE THEATRE ROYALE

ROYAL OPERA HOUSE

BROAD ST.

COVENT GARDEN

FLORAL ST.

LONG ACRE

WEST ST.

ST. MARTINS

CHARING CROSS ROAD

CRANBOURN ST.

GT. NEWPORT

GARRICK ST.

NEW ROW

KING ST.

COVENT GARDEN

INIGO PLACE

HENRIETTA ST. GARDEN

MAIDEN LANE

BEDFORD ST.

CHANDOS PL.

WILLIAM IV. ST.

ADELAIDE ST.

DUNCANNON ST.

ST. MARTIN'S LANE

ST. MARTINS

CATHERINE ST.

WELLINGTON ST.

SOUTHAMPTON ST.

BURLEIGH ST.

EXETER

SAVOY

CORPUS CHRISTI CHURCH

LANCASTER PL.

WATERLOO BRIDGE

VICTORIA EMBANKMENT GARDENS

ADAM ST.

YORK BKGS.

WATERGATE WALK

EMBANKMENT

CLEO. NEEDLE

EMBANKMENT STATION

JOHN ADAM ST.

VILLIERS ST.

CHARING CROSS STATION

CRAVEN ST.

TRAFALGAR SQ.

NORTHUMBERLAND AV.

GT. SCOTLAND YARD

WHITEHALL

PL.

VICTORIA

HUNGERFORD

THAMES

Royal Festival Hall

45

her future husband, Godfrey Norton, escaping from the King of Bohemia, left London from Charing Cross Station. In *The Secret Adversary*, Agatha Christie's Tuppence Cowley took the train there to chase after the villains who kidnapped the American, Jane Finn.

In the station yard, you can see the gray stone monument known as Charing Cross. The original cross was one of 13 "Eleanor crosses" Edward I put wherever the coffin of his queen rested on its final journey from Lincoln to Westminster Abbey. Until the civil wars in the seventeenth century, the cross was at the head of Whitehall, where the statue of King Charles I is today.

Charing Cross is a well-known London landmark. The Lampreys dutifully pointed it out to New Zealander Roberta Grey in Ngaio Marsh's *A Surfeit of Lampreys*. In Charing Cross Hotel, above the station, in "The Adventure of the Bruce-Partington Plans," Sherlock Holmes set up the capture of Hugo Oberstein and the recovery of the Bruce-Partington Plans.

Turn right and walk north on St. Martin's Place. As you cross William IV Street to St. Martin's Lane, glance toward your right. The street behind St. Martin's-in-the-Fields is Adelaide Street. In Julian Symons's *The Blackheath Poisonings*, after her lover's death, Isabel Mortimer walked out of Charing Cross Station, across the Strand to Adelaide Street, went among the narrow streets and alleys, and stopped at a tall, narrow house. It was one of an undistinguished pair of houses that had survived among butchers and greengrocers selling slightly spoiled goods. Here she went upstairs to her love nest to collect her belongings.

It was also on Adelaide Street that Margery Allingham placed the Grotto, the restaurant started after the First World War by the Dominques, close friends of Polly Tassie, who ran the museum at Tether's End. Allingham described the Grotto as a place beloved of two generations of Londoners for its food, served in a long narrow room "as warm and private as an old-fashioned family dining room."

Across William IV Street, you will be on St. Martin's

Lane, which was the original way north from Charing Cross, but was superseded as a major traffic route when Charing Cross Road to the west was carved out in 1887. Along its east side, St. Martin's Lane still has eighteenth- and nineteenth-century buildings. A number of theaters are located on or about St. Martin's Lane, which is almost exactly the dead center of the theater district.

Theaters are often used as the setting for detective stories because they are inhabited by people who act out their emotions dramatically and because theaters classically embody the kind of "locked room," or controlled environment, so beloved of mystery writers. Many detective story writers themselves have been passionately fond of the theater.

Perhaps the all-time stagestruck writer was Dame Ngaio Marsh. She wrote some of her very best stories about murder in the theater, including her last one, *Light Thickens,* a virtuoso description of Peregrine Jay putting on a perfect but unlucky *Macbeth* (in keeping with the theatrical tradition that performing *Macbeth* is unlucky). Ngaio Marsh became Dame Ngaio, not for writing mystery stories, but for acting, directing, producing, and generally encouraging the theater in New Zealand. In her autobiography, *Black Beech and Honeydew,* Marsh said that she never regretted the time she had spent producing Shakespeare instead of writing mysteries.

Marsh is closely followed in theatrical fame by Josephine Tey, who wrote successful plays under the name of Gordon Daviot (her real name was Elizabeth MacIntosh). Sir John Gielgud became a star when he played the lead in her *Richard of Bordeaux.* Tey also wrote several of her mysteries about the theater. She separated her careers by using the name of her maternal great-great-grandmother for mystery publication. Dorothy L. Sayers wrote a successful detective-story play, *Busman's Honeymoon,* in collaboration with her friend Muriel St. Clare Byrne and then went on to write religious drama. The creator of Jemima Shore, Lady Antonia Fraser, is married to playwright Harold Pinter, who she declares does not influence her work—except that she wrote no fiction before they met, and he *does* read her books. Simon Brett writes about an actor,

Charles Paris, who is more often "resting than working," and uses theatrical backgrounds in a number of his mysteries—for instance, *Murder in the Title* and *Not Dead, Only Resting*. At Oxford, Brett was president of the prestigious OUDS and worked in television for the BBC and LWT. Many others, like P.D. James in *The Skull Beneath the Skin,* have used the theater as their stage set.

For most of us, however, the most successful mystery writer in British theater will forever be Agatha Christie. She wrote several successful plays, including *Witness for the Prosecution,* but it is *The Mousetrap* that has made theatrical history with the length of its London run, which continues to the present day.

There are also a number of fictional theaters mentioned in our detective stories. Josephine Tey vividly described an entire group in *The Man in the Queue:* the Irving, where Greek tragedy proved not to be popular; the Playbox, next door, which was exclusive and ignored the existence of the pit; and the Arena, which had a three-week ballet season, 10 people for the gallery, and a queue for the pit. Then there was The Woffington, home of London's own musical comedy and to which a long line of patrons had come to see the actress Ray Marcable perform for the last time in *Didn't You Know?,* which had run for two years. Waiting in that queue, a man was stabbed.

Another fictional theater was the Imperial. In *The Skeleton in the Clock,* John Dickson Carr's "Old Man," Sir Henry Merrivale, once took the Dowager Countess of Bray there to see Lewis Waller play *Beauclaire.* In *Murder Unprompted,* Simon Brett's middle-aged actor, Charles Paris, actually got to the West End in a play called *The Hooded Owl,* but the Variety Theatre was too far off Shaftesbury Avenue to count. Another fictional theater was the Frivolity, where Lord Peter Wimsey was seen attending a performance of *Say When!* with a Royal Personage in Dorothy L. Sayers's *Murder Must Advertise.*

In many of her stories, however, Sayers uses real theaters. In *Whose Body?* she had Lord Peter airily suggest to Charles Parker that they quit work, go home and lunch, and go to the Coliseum, whose shows were not taxing to the mind. The Coliseum is the first theater you pass walking north, up the west side of St. Martin's Lane. Look up and you will see a tall, vertical black sign proclaiming the London Coliseum. Built in 1902 to rival Drury Lane, the Coliseum has a three-piece revolving stage, three tea-rooms, and a roof garden, as well as a giant globe lit up with spotlights. But in recent times it has been more culturally "highbrow": It was home to the Sadler's Wells Ballet until 1968 and is currently dedicated to opera.

Begin to walk north along the east side of St. Martin's Lane. You will pass the tiny alleyways of Brydges Place, Mays Court, and Goodwin's Court. Stop here to peek at its tiny row of narrow eighteenth-century houses with bow windows. The master furniture maker Chippendale had his workshops here, but later, in *Bleak House,* Charles Dickens called this part of London a slum.

Next, you will pass the Quaker Friends' Meeting House. Across the street is the Salisbury Pub, a charming tavern with etched glass, where actors congregate, and the Duke of York's Theatre. It is next to another tiny, gaslit street called Cecil Court, which runs west from St. Martin's Lane. Although its shops do not include a theatrical flea market, Cecil Court is the best candidate for Antonia Fraser's Memory Lane, an alleyway in the heart of London's theaterland, where Jemima Shore went with the elderly Prideaux brothers to Tony Jerrold's "Stage Whispers." Several Cecil Court shops sell secondhand books, maps, and prints.

The next street you cross is New Row, at the end of which is Moss Brothers, famous for renting formal attire, from hunting pinks to peers' robes. Continuing beyond New Row along St. Martin's Lane, across the street you will see the Albery Theatre; then you will come to a crossroads where Cranbourne Street and Great Newport Street, to the west, meet Garrick Street and Long Acre to the east.

The Arts Theatre Club, known for its avant garde productions, is to your left in Great Newport Street. In P.D. James's *An Unsuitable Job for a Woman,* a group of Mark Callender's Cambridge friends were attending a play there when he was murdered near Cambridge.

North and west of this corner on West Street are the twin

theaters, St. Martin's and the Ambassadors. Agatha Christie's all-time success, *The Mousetrap*, opened at the Ambassadors in 1952. It was transferred to the St. Martin's in 1974, and, as everyone knows, it is *still* playing there. *The Mousetrap* was originally a radio play written for the BBC as a birthday present for Queen Mary. On April 13, 1958, it became the longest running play of any kind in the history of British theater. Dame Agatha had made over the rights in the play to her small grandson, Mathew. By 1961, when Mathew was captain of the Eton cricket team, the family took the entire team to see the show. Tickets are still available, so pick your night and come back to see this classic case of theatrical homicide.

North of here, to your left on Charing Cross Road, is the Phoenix Theatre, where Josephine Tey's actress Marta Hallard was playing when Inspector Grant was laid up in the hospital in *The Daughter of Time*. When his landlady, "Tink" (Mrs. Tinker), visited him wearing her best "blacks," Grant asked her to go around by St. Martin's Lane to the Phoenix Theatre and give old Saxon at the stagedoor a note telling Hallard, "For the love of Mike find me a copy of Thomas More's History of Richard III." As *Murderess Ink* points out, once upon a time Charing Cross Road was the secondhand bookstore of the world, where you might hope to find a copy of any mysteries you lacked, perhaps even one by a favorite author that you had never read. But those days are gone forever, and you can often find more mystery books for sale in America.

At the corner of Garrick and Long Acre is the Garrick Wine Bar. Turn to your right and walk a short distance along Garrick Street, named, of course, for the famous eighteenth-century actor, David Garrick. No. 15, a tall, dirty, gray stone building with ironwork trim on the south side of the street, is the unmarked Garrick Club.

The Garrick Club is primarily an actors or theatrical club, an appropriate place for Ngaio Marsh's leading actor, Sir Dougal, to be feted after the opening night tour de force production of *Macbeth* in *Light Thickens*. Inside, it has a notable collection of theatrical paintings and a "long table" at which diners can sit informally. According to its new Ruler, H.R.F. Keating, the Detection Club now holds its twice-yearly meetings (but not the Initiation Dinner, which is still held at the Café Royal) at the Garrick Club.

The Garrick Club was also the club of Brigadier Sir James White, head of British Intelligence in Evelyn Anthony's series of thrillers starring superspy Davina Graham. The Brigadier worked in a Whitehall office off Birdcage Walk, but in *The Defector* he even had Graham bring the Russian defector, Sasanov, to lunch at the Garrick Club. Realizing there was no institution like a gentleman's club in Russia, Sasanov admired the bronze busts and marble inscriptions, the portraits and scenes from famous plays, and the glass cases of mementos of past celebrities. But he could not imagine any setting less appropriate to the head of British Intelligence than this flamboyant eighteenth-century club.

Turn right, away from the Garrick Club, and walk back to the intersection of St. Martin's Lane and Garrick Street. Then turn right again and walk along Long Acre, which is one of the older streets in Covent Garden and was once the home of Covent Garden's wholesalers. Edmund Crispin's private eye, Mr. Snerd, had his business office in Long Acre in *Frequent Hearses*. When Snerd sold a letter he had stolen from the Cranes to the news media, the CID came to Long Acre to look for him.

With its vintage lamp posts, Long Acre still has an old-fashioned charm. There are many different shops (selling art, apparel, and food) and bookstores to browse in. As you approach the modern-day "shopping mall," created out of old Covent Garden, you cross a succession of small alleys and courtyards: Rose Street, Conduit Court, Langley Court, and James Street, with the Covent Garden Underground Station. Beyond James Street is tiny Hanover Place (this is the time to thank London for posting white street signs on every corner). The crowds get thicker and thicker, for the whole Covent Garden area is a fabulous place for all kinds and conditions of tourists and shoppers to loiter and window shop. The next cross street is Bow Street, where you will be turning right. At the corner of Long Acre and Bow is the cream- and red-brick office of the *International Herald Tribune.*

Bow Street is rich in murder and mystery associations. Walk south to Floral Street, across which is the Royal Opera House, with a facade of gigantic columns and classical pediment, which occupies the northeast corner of Covent Garden.

It was inside the Opera House, in *Swan Song,* that Edmund Crispin's attractive writer, Elizabeth, watched tenor Adam Langley rehearsing *Der Rosenkavalier.* "She sat in the large, rococo splendour of the opera house, where tier upon gilded tier of boxes and galleries, radiating on either side from the royal box, towered into the upper darkness and callipygic cherubs and putti held the pillars in a passionate embrace."

E.C. Bentley's Philip Trent came back from Europe to haunt the opera in hopes of seeing Mabel Manderson. He finally met her at a performance of Wagner's *Tristan and Isolde* and fell in love all over again. (In 1929, Dorothy L. Sayers published a translation of an early Anglo-Norman version of the Tristan story as a kind of prelude to her later translation of Dante's *Divine Comedy.*) In the case of "The Red Circle," Sherlock Holmes and Dr. Watson also attended a performance of a Wagner opera.

Walk back from the Opera House to the corner of Long Acre and Bow Street. Cross Bow Street and continue down Long Acre to Drury Lane. The northern part of Drury Lane is old and narrow, with coffee bars and pubs; it is easy to imagine the spot as the lodging place of the actress Nell Gwynn, mistress of Charles II and mother of several of his ducal sons. In Drury Lane, at a fictional pub called the Stag at Bay, Dorothy L. Sayers's Lord Peter and Scotland Yard's Charles Parker's men caught the drug dealers they had been chasing in *Murder Must Advertise.*

Across Drury Lane, Long Acre takes a jog and becomes Great Queen Street. In *Murder Must Advertise,* reporter Hector Puncheon went into another pub, the White Swan, on Great Queen Street, where he accidentally gave the drug gang's code word and was passed cocaine by a man in evening dress. Puncheon also reported to the Connaught Rooms, at 61 Great Queen Street, to cover a luncheon with a distinguished airman

(Charles Lindbergh?). Further along Great Queen Street, named for the wife of Charles I, Henrietta Maria, is the Freemason's Hall.

To the left, at the corner of Great Queen Street and Kingsway, is the Methodists' West London Mission, which used to be Kingsway Hall, where Hector Puncheon reported on a political meeting. It might also be the sinister Simon's Hall in Holborn, where Charles Williams's Simon the Clerk hypnotized his followers in *All Hallows Eve.* Dorothy L. Sayers worked at 75 Kingsway as a copywriter at Bensons, an advertising firm that had a spiral iron staircase like the one in *Murder Must Advertise.* Bensons' staircase was later adorned with a plaque to Sayers, but the firm has since moved away. She also used Bensons in two Wimsey stories, "The Image in the Mirror" and "The Man with No Face."

Instead of walking all the way to Kingsway, turn right on Drury Lane and walk past Broad Court to Martlett Court. Turn right again and walk back to Bow Street. At Bow Street, turn right again and find the bureaucratic-looking front of the famous Bow Street Police Court, with an iron railing along the sidewalk.

The first court opened here in 1740. In 1748, the famous playwright and novelist Henry Fielding and his half-blind brother, Sir John, became the presiding magistrates. It was from this court that the pre-Scotland Yard detectives, called the Bow Street Runners (or Robin Redbreasts, after their red waistcoats), were sent out to improve on the work of the notoriously inefficient Watch. The Runners remained the chief detectives in London until Sir Robert Peel, the Home Secretary, formed the uniformed Metropolitan Police (Bobbies) in 1829. Both G.K. Chesterton, in his essay "In Defence of Detective Stories," and Dorothy L. Sayers, in her introduction to Gollancz's first collection of detective stories, praised Sir Robert Peel and his police for bringing law and order to modern society and for giving them a new romantic hero to write about—the detective. John Creasey wrote a history of the development of the London police beginning with its Bow Street days in his novel *The Masters of Bow Street.*

In *Murder Must Advertise,* Lord Peter Wimsey in his role as Death Bredon was seen entering the Bow Street Court dressed in a dark suit. In Georgette Heyer's Regency mystery, *Regency Buck,* Lord Worth's brother, Captain Audley, promised to escort Judith Tavener personally to Bow Street to put the Runners on the trail of her missing brother. It was also the court at which Kevin John Athlone, lover of Jemima Shore's murdered friend Chloe, was arraigned for Chloe's murder in Antonia Fraser's *A Splash of Red.* Sherlock Holmes appeared at the Bow Street Court with Dr. Watson in the case of "The Man with the Twisted Lip," while Gideon, the Scotland Yard detective of J.J. Marric (John Creasey), saw a brassy-haired woman brought up before the Bow Street magistrate in *Gideon's Wrath.* In real life, G.K. Chesterton's brother, Cecil, was arraigned here for libel in 1913.

Turn left at the Bow Street Police Court and walk back along Bow Street to the corner of Russell Street, where Bow Street becomes Wellington Street. One short block to your left, up Russell Street, you will see the Theatre Royal, Drury Lane, on Catherine Street. It is across from the pub at No. 29 called Nell of Old Drury, after Charles II's most famous theatrical mistress, who lived in Drury Lane. There are many pubs in this area, but this one, which used to be called the Lamb and then the Sir John Falstaff, is especially good. It serves real ale.

The Theatre Royal, Drury Lane, has some of the only Georgian features still surviving in a London theater. It was begun by royal charter under Charles II (after the Puritans were kicked out), but this is the fourth building on this site, which has its own ghost, the man in gray. In Regency times, John Dickson Carr's Dick Derwent in *The Bride of Newgate* knew the actors at Drury Lane well, for his mistress Dolly was one of them, while he had his fencing salon nearby. Drury Lane is currently the London home of such musicals as *42nd Street* and *Chorus Line.*

Adjoining the Theatre Royal on the corner of Russell Street was the Rose Tavern where, in 1712, a duel between Lord Mohun and the Duke of Hamilton ended with both men dead. Turn left on Russell Street, known in the seventeenth and eighteenth centuries for its many "literary" coffee houses. Boswell first met Samuel Johnson in 1763 at Tom's Coffee House, which was located over a bookshop at No. 8. Follow Russell Street into Covent Garden.

To the left as you come into Covent Garden is the London Transport Museum, whose real stagecoaches, buses, trains, and tubes are housed in the old flower market. To your right, facing the Central Market, is Tutton's, a modern combination café, pub, and restaurant, made out of an old potato market. With sidewalk tables and an international menu, Tutton's is open for food and drink from 9:00 A.M. to 11:30 P.M.

Originally, Covent Garden was the convent garden of Westminster Abbey. Seized by Henry VIII, it was then sold by the Crown to the first Earl of Bedford, who built himself a house facing the Strand in 1552. Then the fourth earl hired Inigo Jones to lay out a residential quarter to the north, stretching to the Bedford House Gardens on the south, of which only the northwest corner now remains. In 1661, the Duke of Bedford established a small market that grew into London's principal fruit, vegetable, and flower garden until it was relocated in 1974. Covent Garden was then converted into an attractive, high-ceilinged pedestrian mall, with shops and sidewalk cafés on two levels. It has become a favorite haunt of tourists from everywhere. A performance of some kind is often going on in the open space at the end of the covered arcades of the Central Market, near the colonnaded two-storey building with the Punch and Judy restaurant on the upper floor.

It was before its 1970s' transformation that Dorothy L. Sayers's reporter Hector Puncheon walked into Covent Garden after a night spent covering a warehouse fire. He saw the market filled with vans and lorries laden with fruit and flowers. Porters were unloading stout sacks, crates, and barrels filled with living color and scent, but they were sweating and grumbling as if their exquisite burdens were so much fish or pig iron. Puncheon had come to Covent Garden because its pubs had (and still have) early opening times for the benefit of the market men.

Walk through the Central Market with its blue arches and red stalls to the open area where you will see the red-brick back of St. Paul's Church, Covent Garden, known as the actors' church. When the Duke of Bedford asked for an inexpensive building, Inigo Jones designed for him what is called "the handsomest barn in Europe." St. Paul's still has Inigo Jones's eastern portico with Tuscan arches. It was the backdrop of Covent Garden in *My Fair Lady*, based on G.B. Shaw's *Pygmalion*. (Shaw was the public's favorite debating rival of G.K. Chesterton.) The church entrance is on the far side, at Inigo Place, which runs into Bedford Street. The churchyard between King Street and Henrietta Street, joined by Bedford Street, is still lit by gaslights decorated with a ducal coronet in honor of the dukes of Bedford.

Inside the church (which is closed on Sundays) are many memorials to actors. There are said to be more famous people buried here than in any London church except St. Paul's Cathedral and Westminster Abbey. In 1905, G.K. Chesterton preached a series of "lay" sermons here, and in 1978 the Dorothy L. Sayers Historical and Literary Society held a Thanksgiving Service here in her memory.

If you want to walk the shorter version of this walk, turn right at King Street at the northern edge of Covent Garden and then go right again to James Street and Long Acre for the Covent Garden Underground Station.

If you plan to continue on, you might like to stop for refreshments. For a cup of tea or coffee and a "monster" cookie, drop in at Mr. Rockwell's American Diner, which is decorated with huge replicas of *Saturday Evening Post* covers by Norman Rockwell. You can sit and listen to the music groups playing to the audience that gathers on the church steps and in front of the Central Market. Or you can walk back through the market to try Tutton's next door to the Old Chelsea Winestores (whose wine list it serves).

When you are ready to go on, turn left in front of the back of St. Paul's Church to find tiny Henrietta Street and follow it. At No. 14 Henrietta Street, you will see the bright blue display windows of Victor Gollancz, whose yellow-jacketed, hard-backed, crime thriller series featured the works of Dorothy L. Sayers, together with many other mystery writers and the Detection Club's own collaborations.

The writer Jane Austen, whose *Northanger Abbey* is one of the classic spoofs of the thriller genre, often visited her brother Henry in London and in 1813 stayed with him at No. 10. At the end of Henrietta Street, turn left and go one short block on Bedford Street to Maiden Lane. Turn left again and walk slowly up Maiden Lane toward Southampton Street. Near Bedford Street, you will pass the back—or stagedoor—of the Adelphi Theatre, whose front is on the Strand. A nineteenth-century actor was stabbed to death here by a fellow actor who wanted his part. When Ginger Joe was collecting alibis for Lord Peter in *Murder Must Advertise,* he discovered that Mr. Haagedorn of Pym's Publicity had a leave of absence to attend his aunt's funeral the day Victor Dean was killed on the agency staircase but was actually seen leaving a matinee at the Adelphi Theatre.

Halfway up Maiden Lane on the north side of the street at No. 35 is a creamy yellow building with a red awning and a large brass shield on a column by the double front door. This is Rule's, the famous theatrical restaurant. Its worn but polished brass plate still proclaims that it serves "luncheons and dinners and late suppers, the choicest vintage wines, liqueurs, spirits, and cigars of the finest quality." With its richly comfortable Victorian furnishings and excellent English food, Rule's was a favorite eating spot of Charles Dickens and the Prince of Wales who became Edward VII, both of whom had private alcoves in which to dine. One of Dickens's *Sketches by Boz* was called "Covent Garden." Rule's is still popular with royalty and VIPs, but its clientele, who are largely English, act as if they were in their private club. Rule's has a cover charge, does not accept credit cards, and is never open in August.

Rule's was popular with detective story authors and characters. Dorothy L. Sayers and her college friend, Muriel St. Clare Byrne, met there for lunch to plot their play, *Busman's Honeymoon.* Lord Peter Wimsey took various guests there. Among them was Cattery staffer Joan Murchison after she had successfully burgled Norman Urquhart's office safe in *Strong Poison*. In Patricia Moyes's *Who Is Simon Warwick?*, Sir Percy Crumble was seen eating at Rule's with lawyer Ambrose Quince and Bertie Hamstone. All of them were implicated in the murder of one claimant to the Charlton fortune.

On the south side of Maiden Lane is a blue historical plaque showing where the French writer Voltaire once lived, and toward the end of the block you will pass the tall, dark bulk of Corpus Christi Roman Catholic Church, where G.K. Chesterton's brother Cecil was married in 1916 before he went to the Front in World War I and where Cecil's requiem mass was said after he died of a war-related illness in France in 1918. (The church is not open.)

Walk to the corner of Maiden Lane and Southampton Street, where you should turn right. No. 25 Southampton Street is Boulestin's, a well-known restaurant. In *Murder Must Advertise,* Lord Peter met Pamela Dean there before they drove to the fancy dress ball to meet Dian de Momerie. At No. 34 Southampton Street, you will find the feminist Virago Bookstore. It is plentifully supplied with a selection of books by our mystery writers in both new and secondhand editions. In the basement, you will find the secondhand books, including copies of hard-to-find stories by Baroness Orczy, and you may happen upon a wine party for an author.

Keep walking south on Southampton Street until you reach the Strand, where you will turn left to walk along the north side of the street. In Anthony Berkeley's *The Poisoned Chocolates Case,* a forged letter was mailed by night from the Southampton Street Post Office, which was directly across from the Hotel Cecil, where Crimes Circle member (and suspect) Sir Charles Wildman had been attending a reunion dinner of his old school.

Called the noisiest street in all London, the Strand is jammed with traffic, as befits the oldest route by land from the city of London to Westminster. Once lined with noble palaces, it is now filled with hotels, restaurants, and shops. Either way, the Strand itself has a special atmosphere.

Robert B. Parker's American detective, Spenser, walked

up the Strand in *The Judas Goat* and passed a London cop walking along with his hands behind his back, walkie-talkie in his hip pocket, and his nightstick concealed in a deep pocket. Spenser felt an excited, tight feeling in his stomach knowing that he was "in the old country, the ancestral home for people who spoke English and could read it."

In *The Man in the Queue,* Josephine Tey's Inspector Grant walked up the Strand at dusk. It was "as brilliant as day and crowded, the ebb of the late home-goers meeting the current of the early pleasure seekers and causing a fret that filled both footpath and roadway." He walked up "the gaudy pavement . . . in and out of the changing light from the shop windows: rose light, gold light, diamond light, shoe shop, clothes shop, jewellers. Presently the crowd thinned out and men and women became individual beings instead of the corpuscles of a mob."

The Mortimer family business was in the Strand in Julian Symons's *The Blackheath Poisonings;* while in Ngaio Marsh's *Death in Ecstasy,* Alleyn went down the Strand to a little street where the victim's solicitor, Mr. Rattisbon, had his office. It looked like a memorial to Charles Dickens, with a dingy entry smelling of cobwebs and old varnish. A dark staircase led to a landing where a frosted glass skylight let in enough light to show "Rattisbon" on the door. The atmosphere was made up of dust, leather, varnish, dry sherry, and age. Mr. Rattisbon even wore garments that looked Victorian. Like his father and grandfather before him, he dealt with the estates of the upper-middle classes. Harriet Vane's publishers Grimsby and Cole also had their offices in the Strand, where Lord Peter went to interview them in Dorothy L. Sayers's *Strong Poison.*

Walk past Exeter and Burleigh streets to Wellington Street, which runs to Waterloo Bridge. North on Wellington Street was the Lyceum Theatre, now a dance hall, where in *The Sign of Four* Sherlock Holmes, Dr. Watson, and Mary Morstan began an adventure that led to Mary and Watson's marriage.

Cross the Strand to the south side and turn right. Walk along until you see a brass marquee for the "London institution" called Simpson's-in-the-Strand. It is a restaurant that has the aura of a gentleman's club, although women are allowed to eat in the upstairs dining room. Reservations are a must. As you enter, there is a narrow, dark-wood lobby with a heavy staircase and a small open cloakroom, as well as the entrance to a ground-floor dining room. However, you may be sent upstairs to the Chandelier Room, filled with tables covered in snowy damask. There are special waiters who mind the large silver-covered carts on which the joints of roast meat are wheeled to your table; these waiters should be tipped. The decor is very eighteenth century, with paneled and painted woodwork in Wedgwood pinks and grays and a row of paintings high beneath the plaster Adam ceiling. On a weekday, even in August, the vast dining room was not crowded, so it was hard to imagine Willis wiggling about unnoticed as he jealously tried to spy on Lord Peter Wimsey and Pamela Dean at lunch in *Murder Must Advertise*.

Sherlock Holmes and Dr. Watson were great patrons of Simpson's, about which Holmes is said to have remarked, "Something nutritious at Simpson's would not be out of place." In Parker's *The Judas Goat*, Spenser was taken there by a London representative of the rich American who had hired him to wipe out the Liberty gang. The Englishman had told Spenser that Simpson's was rather a London institution, so Spenser (who had been there before) watched with a sardonic eye as he was served the native cuisine. In E.C. Bentley's *Trent's Last Case*, Trent celebrated his engagement to Mabel by taking her Uncle Burton Cupples to Sheppard's (probably Simpson's). Cupples ordered milk and soda water, appalling both Trent and the wine waiter.

Coming out of Simpson's, go left a short distance to Savoy Court, the only place in London where taxis are allowed to drive on the right-hand side of the street. Across the Court is a shining, silver-colored marquee topped by a Roman soldier. Walk to the back of the courtyard into the hotel lobby of the Savoy. It is a pleasant place to sit for a few minutes, admiring the gold and marble columns with stiff little red and gold flags.

The original Savoy, which belonged to John of Gaunt, was a handsome palace that was burned down in the Peasants'

Revolt under Wat Tyler at the time Gaunt's nephew, Richard
II, was king. The hotel was built in the grand manner by
Richard D'Oyly Carte in 1889, with a bathroom for every
bedroom. The Savoy Theatre is on the site of an earlier theater
in which D'Oyly Carte staged the Gilbert and Sullivan operet-
tas. In Anne Perry's *Resurrection Row,* Charlotte and her husband, Inspector Pitt, had been there to see *The Mikado* when
the mystery opened with a dead body in a hansom cab. The
Savoy Chapel, built in 1864 on the site of (and as a replica of)
the medieval one, is the Chapel of the Royal Victorian Order.
It is often the scene of grand weddings, with receptions next
door in the hotel. In Savoy Hill, to the south of the chapel,
were the first offices of the BBC, whose international broadcasting offices are still at Bush House, across the Strand in
Aldwych.

The Savoy is featured in many detective stories, including
the spy novels of E. Phillips Oppenheim, where his heroes
regularly seem to lunch at the Savoy Grill. One of the Crane
film family tried to take a secretary there to impress her in
Edmund Crispin's *Frequent Hearses.* In *The Unpleasantness at
the Bellona Club,* Lord Peter Wimsey took jilted heiress Ann
Dorland there and asked her if she wanted lobster and cham-
pagne. She laughed at him and said that Marjorie Phelps told
her he was an authority on food. Lord Peter obligingly com-
posed a dinner for her, while explaining to her the kind of man
who would fall for her. In John Buchan's *The Thirty-Nine
Steps,* Richard Hannay, using up time before the trap is to be
sprung on the Black Stone conspiracy, had a very good lunch
at the Savoy. He smoked the best cigar they had to offer, then
took a cab far north in London—perhaps all the way to Hack-
ney Green, where Edgar Allan Poe once went to school—and
hiked back to the West End.

But, most of all, the Savoy Hotel is Christie territory. In
The Mystery of the Blue Train, her American millionaire, Rufus
Van Aldin, always stayed there when in London. Hercule
Poirot sent Hastings to work at the Savoy as a secretary for
another rich American in *The Big Four.* In *The Secret Adversary,*
Tommy Beresford told Tuppence Cowley that it was perfectly

sickening during the war (World War I) how those brass hats drove from the War Office, to the Savoy and the Savoy to the War Office, but he seemed to enjoy Julius Hersheimer's private supper party in a private room there, where the caterers had carte blanche! Agatha Christie's own publishers threw several big parties for her at the Savoy, and in 1954 she herself hosted one for over 100 people to celebrate the opening of her mystery play, *Witness for the Prosecution.*

Leave the precincts of the Savoy and walk westward along the Strand to Adam Street. Before ending this walk at Embankment Underground Station, you are going to explore the area south of the Strand known as the Adelphi. (*Adelphi* in Greek means brothers.) This section was developed by the Adam brothers on the site of the town house of the bishops of Durham. The Adams built terraces of houses raised on arches above the Thames, but many of them no longer survive.

Turn left and walk down Adam Street, where at Nos. 7, 8, and 9 you can see how the Adelphi was meant to look, with rows of tall, plain houses built of dark brick. Looking down toward the Embankment and the Thames, you can see how high the whole development was built above the river. You are standing on the "steep streets of the Adelphi looking towards the sunset-covered river," described by G.K. Chesterton in his Father Brown story, "The Man in the Passage." In that tale, a murder occurred in a dark alley off the fictional Apollo Theatre on the Strand.

In Nicholas Blake's *End of Chapter,* the publishing firm of Wenham and Geraldine, where Nigel Strangeways investigated a mystery, had its office on fictional Angel Street, Adelphi Terrace, for which Adam Street makes the best substitute. According to Blake (a.k.a. the Poet Laureate, C. Day Lewis), Wenham and Geraldine, Publishers, occupied the last house on Angel Street. Its front faced the street, and its rear overlooked the gardens (Embankment). Angel Street was a "distinguished backwater," where the Strand traffic roared softly. Nigel Strangeways thought it would be nice to live in a top-floor flat in one of these tall, elegantly uniform houses. The firm's main door, flanked by two display windows, was set in the facade of brick. The exquisite molding and fanlight of the doorway created an impression of solidity and grace when Victorian grandees went up the shallow steps to take a glass of Madeira.

In Georgette Heyer's *Death in the Stocks,* the law firm of Carrington, Radclyffe and Carrington had its offices on the first floor of a house at the bottom of Adam Street, facing the Adelphi Terrace. The head of the firm, Giles Carrington's father, worked in a big, untidy room with a view of the Thames River through a gap in the buildings nearby.

Now walk to the end of Adam Street and turn right into the Adelphi Terrace. This is the place where John Dickson Carr's G.K. Chesterton look-alike, detective Dr. Gideon Fell, lived at No. 1, handy to Scotland Yard consultations. Turn right and walk along Adelphi Terrace until you come to Robert Street. Turn left and look for the steps down into Lower Robert Street. Lower Robert Street can give you a glimpse of one of the original Adam arches. This "basement" area was where young thieves like Oliver Twist hung out in Charles Dickens's time.

Then go back to ground level to take Robert Street to John Adam Street and turn left. No. 8 is the elegant Royal Society of Arts. Walk a short distance to Buckingham Street (the names show that this area once belonged to the Villiers dukes of Buckingham) and turn left toward the river. Buckingham Street is filled with small houses with old-fashioned door hoods and iron snuffers for linkboys' torches. No. 15 stands on the spot where Charles Dickens lived as a young journalist. He was to use it as a setting in *David Copperfield.*

At the end of Buckingham Street is the Watergate, a huge arch that marked the entrance to the Villiers palace from the Thames. Walk through and turn left on Watergate Walk to find Gordon's Wine Bar in a cellar there. Gordon's is very popular with the bureaucrats from Whitehall. It may be the model for the pub frequented by Blake's Nigel Strangeways, who found the pub filled with two types—the lower ranks of business and civil service, who had identical hideous and slovenly accents, which Strangeways felt were the product of the marriage between a dying Cockney and a degraded culture. Strangeways quoted T.S. Eliot's lines: "Unreal City/ . . . A crowd flowed over London Bridge, so many,/ I had not thought death had undone so many." But Strangeways went to another pub near the publishing house, which had a countrified feel to it, with high-backed settles and a cheerful fire, both things to be found at Gordon's Wine Bar, as well.

Walk back along Watergate Walk until you come to Villiers Street. The Players' Club, open to members only, is located here. Dorothy L. Sayers corresponded with the secretary of the club about a production of her comedy, *Love All,* but World War II made casting it impossible.

Turn left and walk to the Embankment Gardens, along the Thames. From here, you can get a good view of Cleopatra's Needle, given to Queen Victoria by the Viceroy of Egypt in 1819 and set up here in 1878. Its twin stands in Central Park, New York City. G.K. Chesterton's anarchist, Thursday, was landed here at night by a river tug in *The Man Who Was Thursday.*

Across the Thames River, you have a good view of the South Bank theater district. It includes the Royal Festival Hall, across the Hungerford Bridge footpath, and, farther east by Waterloo Bridge, the National Theatre, both built since World War II. In *Cast for Death,* Margaret Yorke's don Patrick Grant took the Hungerford footpath across the river to the Players' Theatre (a fictional mix of the National Theatre and Festival Hall), near the point where the body of his actor friend was found in the water.

Farther south on Waterloo Road is the Old Vic, famous for its Shakespearean productions. In *A Surfeit of Lampreys,* Ngaio Marsh's Alleyn stood on the Embankment near Scotland Yard one night and discussed an Old Vic production of *Macbeth* with a bobby on the beat. Marsh herself went to every production she could manage from the time she came to London in the 1920s. Walk back to Villiers Street and turn left to the Embankment Underground Station, which ends the walk.

4

BLOOMSBURY WALK

BACKGROUND

This walk takes you into Bloomsbury, the heart of intellectual London. Both the British Museum and London University are here, together with publishing houses, bookstores, art galleries, small museums, and thousands of students.

Bloomsbury is a corruption of the word *Blemonde*. In the eleventh century, the land was given by William the Conqueror to his vassal, Baron Blemonde. Today's Bloomsbury had its beginning in 1660, when the Earl of Southampton decided to lay out a square south of his house. The Duke of Montagu then built a lavish mansion on the site of the present British Museum. To the west, the dukes of Bedford and other great land-owning families established their residences. Their family names—Russell, Tavistock, Bedford, and Woburn—still label the area.

In the eighteenth and nineteenth centuries, this was an elegant neighborhood of handsome row houses and attractive squares. Gradually it became less desirable, although it has always remained respectable. Eventually, the mansions became flats, boardinghouses, and small hotels, places where students, artists, and other intellectuals could afford to live.

The well-known Bloomsbury group, which was formed in the early part of the twentieth century, lived in and around Gordon Square, located in the heart of the London University buildings. The group included Virginia Woolf; her husband, Leonard; her sister, Vanessa; and Vanessa's husband, Clive Bell; as well as Lytton Strachey, E.M. Forster, and others from the world of arts and letters, who met "for human intercourse and the enjoyment of beautiful objects."

LENGTH OF WALK: 3.2 miles.

See map on page 68 for boundaries of this walk. See list on page 240 for the books and detectives covered.

PLACES OF INTEREST

University of London: University College, Gower Street. The central range, weekdays, 9:30–5:00. The Petrie Museum of Egyptology, weekdays, 10:00 A.M.–noon; 1:15–5:00 P.M. Free.

British Museum, Great Russell Street. World's greatest collection of antiquities. Weekdays, 10:00–5:00; Sun., 2:30–6:00 P.M. Free. Reading Room. Tours precisely on the hour, weekdays, 11:00–4:00 P.M. A scholar's pass is needed for use of the library.

Percival David Foundation of Chinese Art, Gordon Square. Chinese ceramics from 960 A.D. Mon., 2:00–5:00 P.M.; Tues.–Fri., 10:30–5:00; Sat., 10:30 A.M.–1:00 P.M. Free.

Courtauld Institute Galleries, Woburn Square. Outstanding collection of Impressionist and Post-Impressionist paintings. Weekdays, 10:00–5:00; Sun., 2:00–5:00 P.M. Admission charge.

Jewish Museum, Adolph Tuck Hall, Woburn House, Tavistock Square. (Site of Tavistock House, where Dickens wrote *Bleak House.*) Mon.–Thurs., 12:30–3:00 P.M.; Sun., 10:30 A.M.–12:45 P.M. Free.

Dickens House, 48 Doughty Street. Dickens lived here from 1837 to 1839. Only surviving Dickens residence in London. Mon.–Sat., 10:00–5:00 P.M. Admission charge.

PLACES TO EAT

Lamb's, 94 Lamb's Conduit Street. A favored spot of Charles Dickens. An excellent example of authentic Victorian architecture and decoration. It has Rowlandson engravings, plus hundreds of photographs of early theatrical personalities. 01-405-0713.

Pizza Express, 30 Coptic Street. A reliable chain, has wine license.

Museum Tavern, 49 Great Russell Street. Pub across from the British Museum, where Karl Marx drank. Echoes of the Bloomsbury group can be heard among stained glass and velvet draperies. 01-242-8987.

————— BLOOMSBURY WALK —————

Begin the walk at the Euston Square Underground Station. Leave the station and take Melton Street to Euston Road. Cross Euston Road and walk right to Gower Street. Parallel with Gower Street, off to the right, is Tottenham Court Road, which has several mystery associations.

In *The Case Is Closed,* Patricia Wentworth's model, Celia, who works with Marion, the wife of convicted killer Geoffrey Grey, refused to show a "ghastly pink rag" because it was not her style, and "she wouldn't be seen dead in it in Tottenham Court Road."

Tottenham Court Road is the home of cheap bargains, especially furniture. In her stage directions for *Busman's Honeymoon,* Dorothy L. Sayers commented about this when describing certain rooms in Talboys. Sherlock Holmes bought his Stradivarius violin from a pawnbroker in Tottenham Court Road, and in Antonia Fraser's *A Splash of Red,* Jemima Shore was confronted by the querulous old stepfather of the murdered Chloe in the Tottenham Court Road Underground Station.

Edmund Crispin's Gervase Fen checked out the alibi of the suspect, novelist Evan George, in a Tottenham Court Road pub in *Frequent Hearses.* While in Dorothy L. Sayers's *Whose*

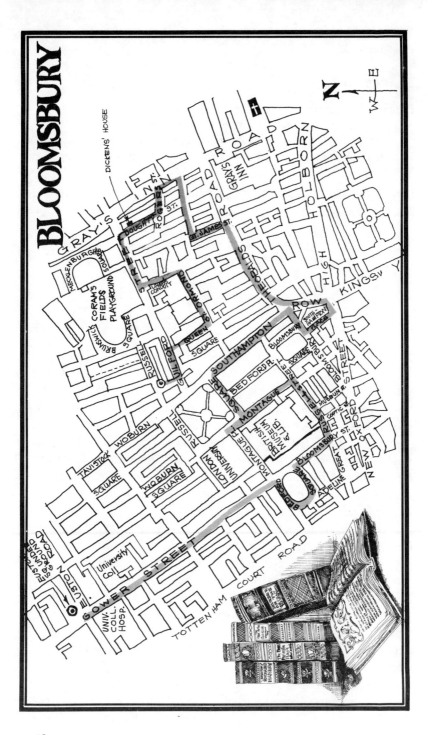

BLOOMSBURY

Body?, Mr. Thipps and his friend went into a nightclub near Tottenham Court Road and Oxford Street on the night the body was put into Thipps's bathtub. While they were there, the club was raided. And finally, in *A Splash of Red*, Sir Richard Lionnel summoned Jemima Shore to a command luncheon at Little Athens on Percy Street, just west of Tottenham Court Road, because he found the ambience attractive. He also lunched there with his wife the day his mistress, Chloe, was murdered in her penthouse apartment.

Walk south along the left-hand side of Gower Street, the main street of London University. You will pass the entrance to University College, with its neoclassic portico, high steps, and dome. It was described by G.K. Chesterton in his essay, "The Diabolist."

Mystery associations with Gower Street abound. G.K. Chesterton attended the Slade School of Art, which used to be in the north wing of the main building. There, he decided to be a writer rather than an artist.

In Fraser's *A Splash of Red*, the Queen Mother was seen at University College. A witness thought she was there to "open" Sir Richard Lionnel's Adelaide Square.

Thriller writer Helen MacInnes attended University College before marrying classics professor and World War II secret agent, Gilbert Highet.

In *Funeral Sites*, Professor Thea Crawford of University College was a college friend of the hunted Rosamund Sholto and the teacher (don) who taught archeology to Jessica Mann's female sleuth, Tamara Hoyland.

Agatha Christie's second husband, Max Mallowan, was the first professor of Western Asiatic archeology at the Institute of Archeology of London University. According to Janet Morgan in *Agatha Christie*, Christie worked as a volunteer dispenser in University College Hospital during both world wars. (Her hospital work was the source of much of her knowledge of medicines and poisons.) In Ruth Rendell's chilling *From Doom with Death*, the Prewetts' alibi was that they were at University College Hospital with Mrs. Prewett's sick mother. Dr. Watson attended medical school there before meeting Sherlock Holmes.

The west side of Gower Street, from University College south, is one of London's longest unbroken stretches of late Georgian houses.

Just past Gower Mews, turn right into Bedford Square. En route you will pass the Royal Academy of Dramatic Art, where Sayers's friend, Muriel St. Clare Byrne, lectured.

Bedford Square, a gracious square with nicely kept row houses and tall trees, was the second square to be built in Bloomsbury. It is the least altered eighteenth-century square in London.

In *A Splash of Red*, Antonia Fraser placed the fictional offices of Brighthelmet, Valentine Brighton's publishing firm, next to the actual offices of the Jonathan Cape publishing firm. William Heinemann, the publisher of many hardcover editions of mystery stories, is also located on the north side of the square in a house with a bright green door.

Bedford Square is replete with blue historical markers, making it great fun to walk around and see who lived where. There are plaques to reformers, doctors, scientists, and literary people. At No. 40, for example, Sir Anthony Hope, the author of the romantic mystery, *The Prisoner of Zenda*, lived with his beautiful, red-haired wife. They, like most of London's literary community, were friends of G.K. Chesterton.

Sandwiched between Bedford Square and Tottenham Court Road is Antonia Fraser's fictional Adelaide Square, where, in *A Splash of Red*, Jemima Shore stayed for an incognito vacation in the penthouse of her college friend, Chloe Fontaine, in order to work in the British Museum.

From her window in Adelaide Square, Jemima could look across the trees to the elegant eighteenth-century houses on the opposite side of the square; her building, designed by developer Sir Richard Lionnel, was a concrete, balconied block, in style somewhere between the Mappin Terrace at Regent's Park Zoo and the National Theatre.

Look west beyond Bedford Square, and you will see an ugly modern building rising up. It is an example of the architecture that Prince Charles has referred to as "stumps." Antonia Fraser, like P.D. James and others, often includes her aesthetic view of London buildings in her mysteries.

Two amusing American women who were sisters, as well as professors, were staying in a small hotel in Adelaide Square. They discovered the body of Brighton in the British Museum Reading Room.

Leave Bedford Square at the southeast corner and turn right into Bloomsbury Street. Walk south to Great Russell Street and turn left. At the end of Bloomsbury Street on the right-hand side is the Kenilworth Hotel. The Redgauntlet Hotel in Dorothy L. Sayers's *The Documents in the Case* very likely was modeled after the Kenilworth, as well as the "Peveril Hotel" in *Unnatural Death*. Both names are taken from the writings of Sir Walter Scott. Sayers's Paul Harrison stayed in the Redgauntlet while he tried to discover who had murdered his father.

After turning left at Great Russell Street, head east along the left-hand side of the street toward the British Museum. In *A Splash of Red*, artist Kevin John Athlone was seen in a Great Russell Street pub by a waitress from a local café. The young Sherlock Holmes consulted in the library of the Pharmaceutical Society in the offices at No. 40 Great Russell Street.

Pick out a likely looking, seedy tobacco shop near the museum, where Michael Innes's classical scholar, Meredith, who had been working on the Duke of Nesfield's medieval manuscript of Juvenal, went to buy some tobacco. By accidentally quoting from Dr. Johnson's "London, A Poem," he seemed to be saying the password, "London's going." The tobacconist promptly replied, "Rotterdam's gone," and opened a trap door to a cellar that led to the offices and showrooms of a gang of international art thieves in *From London Far*.

As you walk along the north side of Great Russell Street, you will see the entrance to Coptic Street and then Museum Street. No. 46 Great Russell Street is a little bookshop specializing in books of the Orient. It has been doing so since 1740. Turn left on Museum Street to the British Museum. Jemima

Shore, en route to the Reading Room of the British Museum, had the perfect scholar's lunch of pizza, salad, and one glass of white wine at the Piazza Perfecta. (Try Pizza Express at 30 Coptic Street, a decent chain that serves wine by the glass.)

Directly across from the British Museum is the place where Randolph Caldecott, the artist and book illustrator, once lived. He gave his name to the Caldecott Medal, which is annually awarded to an outstanding children's picture book.

Now walk through the great iron gates into the forecourt of the British Museum. Note the imposing classical frontage with intricately sculpted pediment and portico above massive pillars.

The British Museum houses the world's most extensive collection of antiquities in a series of vast halls. It certainly has not been ignored by the creators of mystery fiction.

In G.K. Chesterton's *The Man Who Was Thursday,* Gabriel Syme thought that Sunday looked like the great Mask of Memnon. Jemima Shore, upon arriving at the British Museum's Reading Room, was tempted to abandon her plans to research a book on Edwardian women philanthropists in favor of the cooler halls of the museum itself, "presided over by huge, wide-mouthed, slat-eyed Egyptian monarchs and eagle-headed Assyrian deities."

In *Cast for Death,* Margaret Yorke's don Patrick Grant knew that his Greek policeman friend, Manolakis, would want to make a sentimental trip to see the Elgin Marbles; so, he met him outside the museum after Manolakis had kept a tryst with the fragments of the Parthenon. (The government of Greece is still trying to get Britain to return these sculptures, which were brought to London by Lord Elgin in 1802.) In Sayers's *Murder Must Advertise,* Ginger Joe discovered that during Victor Dean's murder, Mr. Barrow of Pym's Publicity was in the British Museum studying Greek vases with a view to an advertising display for Klassika Corsets.

While hospitalized, Alan Grant, in Josephine Tey's *The Daughter of Time,* asked his actress friend, Marta Hallard, if she knew anyone at the British Museum who could do research for him on Richard III.

A copy of the Magna Carta is in the British Museum, which brings to mind Ngaio Marsh's *A Surfeit of Lampreys* because that is what the chroniclers of the document's signer, King John, say he died of. In *Unnatural Death*, Lord Peter Wimsey told a taxi driver to take him to the British Museum because he was going to collate a twelfth-century manuscript of *Tristan*. (Sayers herself published a translation of *Tristan* in 1929 and then did no more translating until Dante's *Divine Comedy* in the late 1940s and early 1950s.)

In *A Splash of Red*, Jemima Shore saw the Reading Room, with the sun beating on the great glass dome, as a humid temple in the midst of the sprawling castle of the museum. American private eye Spenser in Robert Parker's *The Judas Goat* went to the British Museum to look at the Elgin Marbles and the Reading Room's enormous, high-domed ceiling. There was a grand and august quality about it. He could imagine Karl Marx writing the Communist Manifesto there. G.K. Chesterton worked there on his biography of Robert Browning, often drawing cartoons to cadge the price of lunch. Chesterton's friend, George Bernard Shaw, also worked there when he was a poor, young music critic. John Munting, the biographer in Sayers's *The Documents in the Case,* also did his research there.

One real-life mystery connected with the British Museum concerns the death of Henry Symons, a sometime deputy superintendent of the Reading Room, who allegedly shot himself in the Cracherode Room. According to the story, his superior's first comment on hearing the news was, "Did he damage the book bindings?"

Another real mystery concerned the officially licensed copy of Dorothy L. Sayers's play *Love All*. The "censored" copy had been sent to the British Library from the Lord Chamberlain's office (see St. James Walk). The copy was "lost" until it was discovered that the license had not been secured until after the 1940 performance. The play was then "found," thanks to the efforts of Dr. Margaret Nickson, the assistant keeper of the Department of Manuscripts of the British Library's Reference Division.

Dr. Nickson took us on a behind-the-scenes tour of the library. From high above, we entered the vast, domed Reading Room through doors camouflaged to look like part of the rows of books circling the room. We looked down upon the scholars working diligently below, despite the late August heat. Then we made our way out through the maze of mysteriously arranged stacks.

After you leave the British Museum, walk east on Great Russell Street to Montague Street. Turn left and follow Montague Street to Russell Square. It was at No. 24 Montague Street, just around the corner from the British Museum, that young Mr. Sherlock Holmes took rooms when he first came down from Oxford. The building, a four-storey, late-Georgian house, is still standing.

At Russell Square, look left, down Montague Place. There, at No. 23, a young doctor named Arthur Conan Doyle lived when he arrived in London to practice medicine. This was London's largest square begun in 1800. But before considering the Square itself, there are a number of mystery associations and places of interest that lie just north of the boundaries of this walk.

Some of the Victorian mysteries of Anne Perry take place in this general area. In *Callander Square,* Emily (Viscountess Ashworth), sister of Anne Perry's Charlotte Pitt, lived only a carriage ride away from the fictional Callander Square (Tavistock Square), where workmen planting shrubs dug up the bodies of two babies. Charlotte, intent on sleuthing despite her husband's warnings, came upon the body of Dr. Freddie Bolsolver among the roots of last year's Michaelmas daisies.

Up Southampton Row at 34 Tavistock Chambers, Tavistock Square, was the flat of Phil Driscoll, the murder victim in John Dickson Carr's *The Mad Hatter Mystery.* It was there that Driscoll's mistress went to burn her love letters and accidentally burned the manuscript of an unknown Poe story.

Like Tavistock Square, Woburn Square is north of Russell Square. Today it has been partly torn down because of university expansion. There, Philip Boyes stayed with his lawyer cousin, Norman Urquhart. The Courtauld Institute Gallery, also in Woburn Square, is worth a full afternoon of your time. In *Innocent Blood,* P.D. James's Philippa Palfrey took her newly found, ex-convict mother there to see the Impressionist paintings after they had bumped into the Honorable Gabriel Lomas at the Royal Academy of Art in Piccadilly. (See Mayfair/Oxford Street Walk.)

Now, return your attention to Russell Square. With its uninterrupted view of the Hampstead Hills, it was once an exclusive residential area. Today it is the location of offices serving the university and the museum. Turn right off Montague Street and walk through the square, with its enormous public garden.

No. 24 was the address given the cabbie by Sir Julian Freke when he tried to share a cab with Charles Parker in Dorothy L. Sayers's *Whose Body?* As you cross the square, you will pass Bedford Place, where the Sherlockian Lonsdale Hotel is located near the Bloomsbury Square end.

At the southeast end of Russell Square is Southampton Row. Turn right and head south to Vernon Place, where you will again turn right.

Lord Peter Wimsey worked as a copywriter for Pym's Publicity in Southampton Row in Sayers's *Murder Must Advertise.* At No. 31 Southampton Row are the offices of Hughes Massie, the literary agents for Ngaio Marsh and Agatha Christie.

In Sayers's *Strong Poison,* Harriet Vane bought arsenic in a Southampton Row chemist shop to show that it could be obtained. Later, she was accused of poisoning her lover, Philip Boyes.

Turn left into Vernon Place. Bloomsbury Square on your right was laid out in 1600 by the Earl of Southampton. The diarist John Evelyn came to dine in Southampton's home there. By the late nineteenth century, the square was no longer fashionable, although it has always remained respectable.

Bloomsbury Square seems a likely location for the office where P.D. James in *Innocent Blood* placed Maurice Palfrey. It had "overflowed into an agreeable late eighteenth-century house owned by the college." Portions of Michael Caine's *Half Moon Street* were filmed here in the quiet timelessness of Bloomsbury Square.

Now turn left off Vernon Place, into Southampton Place. The Holborn restaurant, where Stamford introduced Watson to Holmes, was located here. The National Westminster Bank next door occupies a building contemporary with the Holborn. No. 6 Southampton Street (now Place) was where Dr. Watson had his surgery offices for several years.

Follow Southampton Place to High Holborn. Turn left and, after a short distance, left again into Southampton Row. Follow Southampton Row to Theobald's Road (pronounced Tibbald's) and turn right. You will be walking east.

In *End of Chapter* by Nicholas Blake, the senior editor for Wenham and Geraldine, Stephen Prothero lived in a Holborn flat where he had Nigel Strangeways to tea. The gym at which interior designer Denton Westbury, the gay son of Lord Charlton, studied karate in Patricia Moyes's *Who Is Simon Warwick?* was also located on High Holborn.

Walk east along Theobald's Road. In Sayers's *Strong Poison*, Philip Boyes stood about in Theobald's Road for some time looking for a stray taxi after his last visit with Harriet Vane.

Follow Theobald's Road to Great James Street and turn left. Dorothy L. Sayers and her husband Atherton Fleming lived in No. 24, a neat, two-storeyed, yellow-brick maisonette. Great James Street was "the mean street" in the Lord Peter Wimsey story, "The Footsteps That Ran."

Turn right off Great James Street into Northington Street, which will take you past several mews, as well as John Street, to Gray's Inn Road. Philip Boyes staggered into the fictitious Nine Rings Pub in Gray's Inn Road after his final visit with Harriet Vane in *Strong Poison*.

Go left on Gray's Inn Road to Roger Street. Reginald Colby, a lawyer in *Who Is Simon Warwick?* had his offices here, on the northern edge of legal London. (See Inns of Court/ Fleet Street Walk.)

In *Forfeit,* Dick Francis's reporter, Tyrone, lived with his crippled wife, Elizabeth, in a mews off Gray's Inn Road, perhaps King's Mews. In real life, Dick Francis's wife had polio but fortunately was not so badly paralyzed. Jemima Shore, in Antonia Fraser's *Quiet as a Nun,* saw the photo of her lover, M.P. Tom Amyas, on the front page of the London *Times,* which had its editorial offices in New Printing House Square on Gray's Inn Road. Since 1986, its new offices are in the East End at Wapping. And finally, author Nicholas Freeling, creator of Inspector Van der Valk, was born in Gray's Inn Road, and it is also the home of the Crime Writers' Association's member, Marian Babson.

Now turn right off Roger Street, into Doughty Street. Dickens House, where he lived early in his married life and wrote *The Pickwick Papers* and *Oliver Twist,* is there at No. 48. One of a long row of dark brick houses with bright blue doors, it is, again, the only one of Dickens's London residences that remains. Today it is the site of a Dickens museum that is well worth a visit.

Originally, Harriet Vane had a flat at 100 Doughty Street. (Hers was a fictitious number; Numbers 29, 30, or 31 seem to be reasonable substitutes.) Then she moved to a flat which overlooked the tennis court in Mecklenburgh Square. There, in *Gaudy Night,* she sat at a writing table and looked out into the square. She watched a group of tennis players and then turned her attention to the invitation to attend the Gaudy at her old Oxford college, Shrewsbury. Suddenly she decided to go. Before she could change her mind, she ran quickly to drop her acceptance in the pillar box. In *Strong Poison,* the police hunted in Mecklenburgh Square for a small white packet of arsenic that Harriet's lover, Philip Boyes, might have lost there.

Sayers herself lived in a flat at 44 Mecklenburgh Square, next to Coram Fields where Thomas Coram set up a Foundling Hospital in 1739. The Woolfs moved their Hogarth Press to Mecklenburgh Square after being bombed out of Tavistock Square.

Turn left at the end of Doughty Street and walk along the

south side of Mecklenburgh Square past Mecklenburgh Place
to Guilford Street. Continue along Guilford Street until you
come to Lamb's Conduit Street, where you will turn left. The
Lamb, a late Victorian pub complete with settles, cast-iron
tables, and boxed-in bar, is at No. 94.

In *Strong Poison,* Philip Boyes, who had been staggering all
about the area, finally found a taxi in Guilford Street. In Argyle
Square, north of Coram's Fields on the edge of Bloomsbury, a
terrorist group called Magma had buried an atomic bomb that
Magma member, sociology professor Julian Despard, desper-
ately tried to locate in Geoffrey Household's *Hostage: London.*

Mecklenburgh and Brunswick squares (at either end of
Coram's Fields) are the two remaining squares that were built
for the prosperous bourgeois. They are the best places to locate
the large and tomblike house of Mrs. Manderson's Uncle Cupples, a retired banker. There, E.C. Bentley's Trent listened to
the conversation of a retired Egyptologist, while gazing at
Mabel Manderson in *Trent's Last Case.* Somewhere near here,
too, may have been the flat Margery Allingham lived in, over
the studio of George du Maurier, the artist, author of *Trilby,*
father of actor Gerald du Maurier, and grandfather of author
Daphne du Maurier. In Julian Symons's *The Blackheath Poisonings,* Paul Mortimer had a flat in Guilford Street.

Follow Lamb's Conduit Street to Great Ormond Street,
where you will turn right. The Hospital for Sick Children, on
the north side of Great Ormond Street, was combined with
the Foundling Hospital in Patricia Moyes's *Who Is Simon Warwick?* The infant Simon Warwick was taken there when his
parents were killed by a World War II buzz bomb.

Charles and Lady Mary Parker lived at 12A Great Ormond
Street, as did Lord Peter when he was masquerading as Death
Bredon in *Murder Must Advertise.*

Follow Great Ormond Street to Queen Square (now Hospital Square), on your right behind the hospital. It was built in
the days of Good Queen Anne. At the north end of the Square
is a garden with a statue, not of Anne, but of George III's
queen, Charlotte. Queen Square offers another choice for Callander Square, where Charlotte Pitt investigated the deaths of

the two babies. Today, instead of upper-class homes, Queen Square is the site of hospital buildings and offices.

Walk to your right through Queen Square to Queen Anne's Walk. Turn left and take Guilford Street to Herbrand Street, where you will find the Russell Square Underground Station. In *The Judas Goat,* Parker's private eye, Spenser, took the tube from Russell Square to Regent's Park Zoo. You may follow his example or end the walk here.

5

SOHO
WALK

BACKGROUND

The neighborhood's odd name of Soho probably came from the hunting call "so-hoe." It was used as a battle cry by the Protestant followers of the Duke of Monmouth. He was the ill-fated illegitimate son of Charles II, who once lived in the area. Soho became London's chief foreign quarter in 1685, when the French King Louis XIV revoked the Edict of Nantes, sending thousands of Huguenots fleeing across the Channel. Soho is still known for its foreign shops and restaurants, as well as the cosmopolitan, rather seedy atmosphere found in its narrow streets. Today Soho is London's Chinatown, but other nationalities—French, Italian, and Swiss—are still there, too. Most people think of Soho as the place to go for foreign food, especially after the theater, for Shaftesbury Avenue is the western curve of the West End theater district. Soho is also London's red light district, scene of sleazy or vicious crime, and this atmosphere is faithfully duplicated in detective fiction.

LENGTH OF WALK: **3 miles**

See map on page 83 for boundaries of the walk and page 244 for a list of the detectives and their stories covered.

PLACES OF INTEREST

Statue of Eros, Piccadilly Circus.

Leicester Square: Movie houses, half-price ticket office.

National Gallery, Trafalgar Square. Free. Daily, 10:00–6:00; Sun., 2:00–6:00 P.M. Ground-floor restaurant.

National Portrait Gallery, St. Martin's Place. Free. Mon.–Fri., 10:00–5:00; Sat., 10:00–6:00 P.M.; Sun., 2:00–6:00 P.M.

Carnaby Street: Fashions.

Charing Cross Road: Bookstores.

Shaftesbury Avenue: Theaters.

Palladium Music Hall, 8 Argyll.

House of St. Barnabas, 1 Greek Street, Soho Square. Eighteenth-century mansion. Open by written appointment only.

Guinness World of Records, Trocadero Centre, Coventry Street. Admission charge. Open daily 10:00–9:30 P.M.

PLACES TO EAT

Soho is a neighborhood in which you can eat well or cheaply. It abounds in restaurants, although we are listing only a few, most mentioned in detective stories. Many Soho restaurants are closed on Sundays, but those in Chinatown, near Gerrard Street, are open.

Quality Inn (inexpensive chain), Coventry Street and Rupert Street.

Manzi's, 1-2 Leicester Street. Fish and seafood. Reservations needed. 01-734-0224. Open until 11:30 P.M. Closed Sundays.

Au Jardin des Gourmets, 5 Greek Street. French, famous for its wine cellar's old claret. Reservations needed. 01-437-1816. Open to 11:30 P.M. Closed Sundays.

National Gallery, Cafeteria. Mon.–Sat., 10:00–5:00; Sun., 2:30–5:00 P.M.

Tom Cribb (pub), Panton Street (behind Haymarket).

Red Lion (pub), 14 Kingly Street.

La Terrazza, 19 Romilly Street. Reservations needed. Open daily to 11:30 P.M. 01-734-2504.

Regent Palace Hotel, Sherwood Street. Coffee shop, pub, and
   English carvery in main dining room off hotel lounge.
Pizzaland (the "green and white" chain), Leicester Square.
Loon Fung, 37 Gerrard Street (near Detection Club rooms).
   Popular with Chinese. 01-437-5429. Open to 1:00 A.M.

───────────── **SOHO WALK** ─────────────

Begin this walk at the Shaftesbury Avenue exit of the Piccadilly
Circus Underground Station. (This is a big station with many
exits; so be sure you take the right one.) As you come up into
Piccadilly Circus, you will see a Boots the Chemist store. According to Julian Symons in *Mortal Consequences,* it was the
lending libraries of this British chain and those in the W.H.
Smith bookstores that created the wide public demand for
detective stories. (These stores are still the best places to find a
selection of paperbacked mysteries, although the libraries no
longer operate.)

   Here at Piccadilly Circus you are at the hub of the British
Empire, the very name, according to New Zealander Ngaio
Marsh, brings a lump to the throat of someone from the Anti-
podes. It is a place where some people loiter and others rendezvous at the base of the memorial to philanthropist Lord
Shaftesbury, a tiny, Art Nouveau aluminum statue of the Angel of Christian Charity, known as Eros. In *A Surfeit of Lampreys,* Ngaio Marsh's New Zealander Roberta Grey knew that
to British colonials, the symbol of London is homely, "a small
figure perched slantwise above a traffic roundabout, an elegant
Victorian god with a Grecian name."

   Historically, Piccadilly Circus was deliberately created
from existing streets and alleyways by John Nash to make a
grand sweep from the Prince Regent's Carlton House to Regent's Park. If the construction work is finished and the statue
is back in place, you may catch a glimpse of Eros if the eternal
traffic jam will let you. (The present construction is intended
to solve the traffic problem.)

   In *The Dirty Duck,* Martha Grimes's Superintendent Jury,

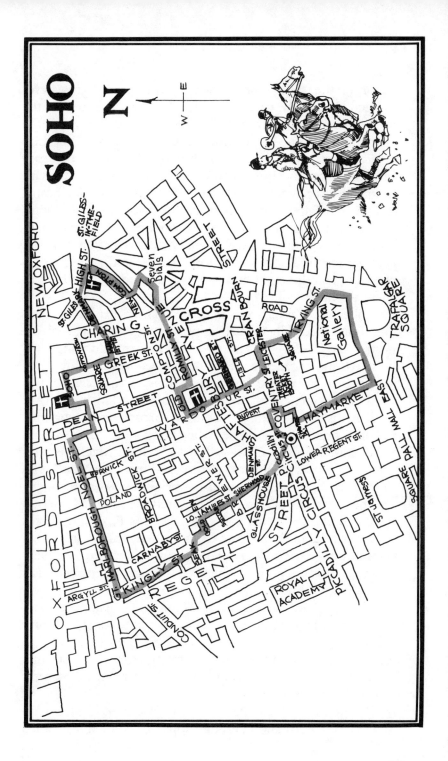

SOHO

N

W ——— E

NEW OXFORD

ST. GILES-
IN-THE-
FIELD

ST. GILES HIGH ST.

MONMOUTH ST.

Seven
Dials

STREET

CHARING G

CROSS

CRANBOURN

ROAD

IRVING ST.

TRAFALGAR
SQUARE

GREEK ST.

OLD COMPTON

ROMILLY ST.

DEAN

STREET

WARDOUR

LISLE ST.

COVENTRY ST.

National
Gallery

National
Gallery

SHAFTESBURY

RUPERT
ST.

LEICESTER
SQUARE

TICHBORN
COURT

HAYMARKET

BERWICK

POLAND

BROADWICK ST.

LEXINGTON ST.

OLD
JAMES ST.

SHERWOOD ST.

DENMAN ST.

GLASSHOUSE ST.

PICCADILLY CIRCUS

LOWER REGENT ST.

PALL MALL EAST

ST JAMES

MARLBOROUGH

NOEL ST.

CARNABY ST.

KINGLY ST.

REGENT

STREET

ROYAL
ACADEMY

SQUARE PALL MALL

OXFORD

STREET

ARGYLL ST.

CONDUIT ST.

83

deploring the traffic mess, thought the green lights never changed. Piccadilly Circus by the Shaftesbury Exit was the place where Simon Brett's Charles Paris met "Henry," the aristocratic ingénue he promised to take to a musical audition in *Not Dead, Only Resting*. In Agatha Christie's *The Secret Adversary*, after meeting for the first time since the war with shouts of "Tuppence, old thing," and "Tommy, old bean," Tommy told Tuppence, "What an awful place Piccadilly Circus is, there's a huge bus bearing down on us." Dorothy L. Sayers's Lord Peter Wimsey entered detective fiction in *Whose Body?* sitting in a taxi at Piccadilly Circus and saying to his infuriated taxi driver, "Oh damn, d'you mind putting back to where we came from?"

Robert B. Parker's private eye, Spenser, exploring London, found Piccadilly Circus "implacably ordinary with movie theatres and fast foods," but in *Frequent Hearses* Edmund Crispin's Oxford don, Gervase Fen, recognized its centrality when he said that, by taking Piccadilly Circus as your center, you could draw a circle with an 18-mile radius and include all the major British film studios. Piccadilly Circus's garish charm is probably best seen at night, when its gigantic electric billboards glitter, but in *Cloak of Darkness* Helen MacInnes's secret agent, Robert Renwick, commented that, like New York's Times Square, Piccadilly was just as bright by day as by night.

The famous Criterion Long Bar used to be in the Criterion Theatre Building, which you can see across Piccadilly Circus on Lower Regent Street. The Criterion Bar was the site of the meeting between Dr. Watson and young Stamford in Conan Doyle's *A Study in Scarlet,* which led to Watson's introduction to Sherlock Holmes.

Turn left and walk east, as Tommy and Tuppence did. Leave Piccadilly Circus on Piccadilly. It will become Coventry Street as it crosses the Haymarket. This is an easy place to become confused and follow the wrong street; so note that Shaftesbury Avenue is on your left and Lower Regent Street is on your far right.

On the left, you will pass the new Trocadero Centre, with bookstores, record and clothing shops, the three-dimensional

Guinness World of Records Museum, and several restaurants. This complex is on the site of three restaurants: the old Trocadero, Scotts, and the original Lyons Corner House, toward which Tommy and Tuppence were heading for tea in *The Secret Adversary*. In Georgette Heyer's *Death in the Stocks,* Roger Vereker, the family black sheep, who appeared to claim his murdered brother's money, dined at the Trocadero the night Arnold Vereker was murdered in the stocks.

The old Lyons Corner House was also the place at which the Canadian Mr. Cropper ate breakfast and fell in love with one of the Dawson maids in Dorothy L. Sayers's *Unnatural Death*. Sayers herself left her college friend, ·Muriel St. Clare Byrne, one afternoon and went to the Lyons Corner House for supper, during which she dreamed up the murder method used in their play, *Busman's Honeymoon*. In *The Man in the Queue,* Josephine Tey's suspect, Jerry Lamont, and his murdered bookie boss, Bert Sorrell, had lunched in the Coventry Street Lyons. In Dorothy L. Sayers's *Murder Must Advertise,* coming out of Lyons Corner House, two of Pym's Publicity's secretaries first met copywriter Death Bredon in evening dress and then saw him apparently arrested in front of the Criterion Bar. If you are ready for refreshments, since the Lyons Corner House is gone, try the Trocadero or the Quality Inn (one of a chain, like the Lyons Tea Shops) on the north side of Coventry Street at Rupert Street. Then cross Coventry Street at Rupert Street and turn right to walk back along Coventry Street to Shavers Place. It is a tiny, angular alleyway that leads to the Haymarket. It is the nearest thing in the vicinity to the unnamed cul-de-sac where Ngaio Marsh's detective Roderick Alleyn lived before his marriage to Agatha Troy. In his flat, he had Troy's painting of Suva Harbor—which Troy was painting on shipboard when they first met in *Artists in Crime*—and he was waited upon by Vasily, an old Russian from his first case, *A Man Lay Dead*.

Walk through Shavers Place into the Haymarket and turn left to go south toward Trafalgar Square. As its name suggests, the Haymarket was the site of London's market for hay and straw. It was associated with the theater world, also, and has two theaters: Her Majesty's Theatre (which changes its name with each sovereign), where the Haymarket Opera House once stood, and the pillared Haymarket Theatre, just beyond the main offices of American Express.

During Victorian times, the Haymarket was also the center for prostitution, as young Paul Mortimer discovered in Julian Symons's *The Blackheath Poisonings.* In Anne Perry's *The Devil's Acre,* the fastidious upper-class blades preferred Haymarket prostitutes to those in Devil's Acre. In Josephine Tey's *The Man in the Queue,* murder suspect Lamont went to a movie and then meant to duck into the Haymarket to hide, but he saw Inspector Grant shadowing him and ran (all the way to Scotland).

As you walk south on the Haymarket, you will pass Panton Street on your left, with a pub called the Tom Cribb. It was known as the Union Arms when Regency ex-prize fighter Tom Cribb took it over in 1811, and it appeared as the Union Arms in John Dickson Carr's Regency detective story, *The Bride of Newgate.* Although it is not about to be displaced by a modern development, the Tom Cribb is in about the right area to double as Simon Brett's pub, the Montrose, tucked away in a basement behind the Haymarket, where actor Charles Paris drank large amounts of Bell's Scotch.

Keep going down the Haymarket to the corner of Pall Mall. Turn left there to go into the northern end of Trafalgar Square, where you will find yourself standing in front of the imposing National Gallery. It opened in 1824, built high above Trafalgar Square like a ship's deck, with a spectacular view down Whitehall to Parliament. The Gallery is adorned with a Grecian portico that made use of some of the marble columns from the Prince Regent's Carlton House. The National Gallery contains the major collection of paintings in England.

In Ngaio Marsh's *A Surfeit of Lampreys,* Henry and Frith Lamprey drove New Zealander Roberta Grey westward from the docks in the East End, following the route Ngaio Marsh herself took on her first trip to London. The Lampreys kept pointing out the major sights but mixed them up. For example, Frith said, "That's the Tate." "She means the National Gallery," corrected Henry.

In *An Unsuitable Job for a Woman*, P.D. James's detective, Cordelia Gray, depressed by the suicide of her partner, left their Kingly Street office and walked to Trafalgar Square. There, she sought consolation in the National Gallery. (P.D. James's characters tend to be fond of and knowledgeable about paintings.) In *The Secret Adversary*, Tuppence met Tommy there promptly at 10 o'clock. Waiting for him to come to their first business meeting as Young Adventurers, Tuppence had ensconced herself on a red velvet seat and gazed at the Turners with an unseeing eye. (Turner's paintings are at the Tate Gallery, south of Parliament, and the red plush seats are around the corner at the National Portrait Gallery.) Because terrorist attacks and art snatches are not limited to fiction, you will have your bags and cameras checked very thoroughly by security personnel.

Walk past the National Gallery, unless you want to take the time to see some of its vast collection, eat in its attractive ground-floor restaurant, or use its restroom facilities or public telephones. Turn left at St. Martin's Place and stop at the National Portrait Gallery, tucked in behind the National Gallery.

In the tiny square opposite the National Portrait Gallery, there is a statue of Nurse Edith Cavell, who was shot in World War I. This gallery is very popular with detectives, and its collection includes a number of mystery-associated portraits.

In Robert B. Parker's *The Judas Goat*, Spenser spent an afternoon there, staring at portraits of people from another time. Actress Marta Hallard brought the hospitalized Inspector Grant a copy of the portrait of Richard III from the National Portrait Gallery. This led him to investigate the murder of the princes in the Tower in Josephine Tey's *The Daughter of Time*. Though the gallery has several portraits of Ngaio Marsh's real hero, William Shakespeare, it does not have the Grafton portrait, which Marcus Knight, who played Shakespeare in *Killer Dolphin*, resembled.

Except for the Royal Family, the collection contains no

portraits of living persons. Paintings are chosen for their historical interest and are hung chronologically, with the oldest ones on the top floor. There, you can find both Richard III and Henry VII, as well as the More family portrait including Sir Thomas More, whose *Historie of Richard III* gave Shakespeare his material.

There are also portraits of a number of mystery writers, beginning with Grand Masters Charles Dickens and Robert Louis Stevenson. In the first floor's 20th Century Gallery, you will see, among others, G.K. Chesterton, Graham Greene, E.C. Bentley and, high up near the ceiling, Dorothy L. Sayers. A copy of this Sayers portrait presented by the Dorothy L. Sayers Society hangs in the Sayers Room in the tower of St. Anne's Soho.

The National Portrait Gallery has an excellent bookstore on the ground floor. (It is matched only by the gift shops at the British Museum and the Victoria and Albert Museums. See Bloomsbury Walk and Brompton/Hyde Park Walk.) In it you can find books about the real-life mystery of Richard III, badges with his portrait, postcards of the portraits of detective story writers, and some marvelously colorful tea towel portraits of the Tudors. This evidence of a "Richard III industry" should remind you that detective writer Catherine Aird, writing about Josephine Tey in *Murderess Ink,* said that Tey had single-handedly kept alive that historical controversy.

Outside the National Portrait Gallery, turn to your left and follow curving Irving Street into Leicester Square. Famous now for its movie theaters, the square dates from 1670, when it was laid out on the site of Leicester House, home of the family of Sir Philip Sidney, the Elizabethan soldier-poet. Both the painter Sir Joshua Reynolds and the satiric writer Dean Swift lived here during the eighteenth century, as did caricaturist and painter William Hogarth. The square then became the site of nineteenth-century music halls like the Alhambra (now the Odeon).

Today Leicester Square is a major meeting place for tourists, especially the young. It has public lavatories and many fast-food restaurants. It is closed to traffic, making it attractive to the crowds who loiter under its tall plane trees or stand in line at the half-price ticket kiosk near the northwest corner, where same-day tickets are sold for West End shows.

In Robert Louis Stevenson's *The New Arabian Nights,* the disguised Prince Florizel of Bohemia and his Master of Horse went looking for adventure in the streets of London. They were driven by sleet into an oyster bar in the vicinity of Leicester Square, where suddenly a young man entered with a tray of cream tarts, which he offered to everyone. The young man then invited Prince Florizel to join the Suicide Club. This Stevenson tale was recalled by Lord Peter Wimsey when he and Charles Parker ate snails in a Soho restaurant at the opening of *Unnatural Death.* (There is no oyster bar in Leicester Square, but there is a fish and chips place on the south side of the square. If you want a more distinguished fish meal, make a reservation at Manzi's, No. 1-2 Leicester Street.)

In Sayers's *Busman's Honeymoon,* Lord and Lady Peter Wimsey killed time with an educational film and a Mickey Mouse cartoon at one of the Leicester Square movie houses, while waiting for the House of Commons to adjourn, so they could meet with barrister and M.P. Sir Impey Biggs. In Julian Symons's *The Blackheath Poisonings,* young Paul Mortimer of the toy manufacturing family walked north to Leicester Square from the family factory on the Strand to eat his baker's pie among the grass and flowers and dream of being a great reporter. Later, when his cousin Isabel was being tried for the murder of his father, Paul stumbled by night into the Caravanserai, one of Leicester Square's Victorian brothels. In Anne Perry's *Resurrection Row,* Sir Desmond and Lady Cantlay were heading toward Leicester Square after seeing a production of Gilbert and Sullivan's *The Mikado* when they hailed a hansom cab with a dead cabbie.

The most fantastic detective scene set in Leicester Square occurred in G.K. Chesterton's *The Man Who Was Thursday.* The band of anarchists met in Leicester Square for Sunday breakfast. They sat on a hotel balcony that overlooked the Square, "with its sunlit leaves and the Saracenic outline of the Alhambra." The most likely candidate for Chesterton's hotel is

the Victorian sandstone hotel at the northeast corner of
Leicester Square and Leicester Place, which has a balcony
above a bright green Pizzaland.

Leave Leicester Square on Leicester Street (at the north-
western corner). Go north on Leicester Street past Manzi's to
the next street, which is Lisle Street. You will find yourself in
an area of narrow, rather dirty streets with small food shops
and cafés. It was "off Lisle Street" that Sonny Haliwell ran
Contemporary Books, an adult bookstore, for a crime syndi-
cate. He became the third victim of the karate-chop killer in
Julian Symons's *A Three Pipe Problem*.

Turn left on Lisle Street and walk to Wardour Street; then
turn right and walk up Wardour Street one block to Gerrard
Street, where you will turn right again. This street, which is the
heart of London's Chinatown, is closed to traffic. Restaurants,
strip joints, and shops abound here. Gerrard Street has many
detective-story associations, none of them, however, with that
notorious Yellow Peril, Fu Manchu. This must be the vicinity
into which Martha Grimes's Amelia Blue Farraday wandered
in *The Dirty Duck*. She became bored with the strip joints,
blue-movie houses, and cheap Chinese restaurants and went
back to Berkeley Square to her death.

Walking along Gerrard Street, look for No. 31, the site of
the first club rooms rented by the Detection Club and furnished with secondhand furniture found by Helen Simpson,
Sayers's friend who wrote the mystery *Enter Sir John*. It was
also the site of Dorothy L. Sayers's fictitious Soviet Club in
Clouds of Witness. The Soviet Club was the place, filled with
smoke and din and dreadful food, where Lady Mary's leftist
friend, Miss Tarrant, took Lord Peter to dine and kept dipping
her beads in the soup. Lord Peter also met and was shot at by
Lady Mary's former lover, Goyles, an incident that helped
start the romance between Lady Mary and detective Charles
Parker. Today No. 31 houses a shop called Loon Fung China
Crafts. The street was also the home of John Dryden. At the
Turk's Head, a long-gone pub, Dr. Samuel Johnson (whom
Chesterton loved to portray) and Sir Joshua Reynolds found-
ed their famous Literary Club. In *Great Expectations*, Charles

Dickens's Mr. Jaggers lived in a "stately" house in Gerrard Street, a fact difficult to imagine now.

The Detection Club was founded in the late 1920s by Anthony Berkeley (a.k.a. Francis Iles, whose real name was A.B. Cox) as a place for mystery writers to meet and eat and talk crime. Berkeley described their monthly meetings in *The Poisoned Chocolates Case,* in which the Crimes Circle members try to solve a real crime for Scotland Yard.

G.K. Chesterton, as the Detection Club's first Ruler (or president), presided over the yearly initiation banquets. Chesterton wore a magnificent Mandarin robe and Fu Manchu pillbox hat, both of which Dorothy L. Sayers found fitted her perfectly when she, too, became Ruler. Both Sayers and Chesterton took these amusing ceremonies very seriously, to the great annoyance of some of the other members, like Christianna Brand, who felt they were too childish.

Other detective story writers found the occasion fascinating. John Dickson Carr, who idolized Chesterton (and made his Dr. Gideon Fell a Chesterton look-alike), was very disappointed when he, the only American member, was not inducted by Chesterton, who at the time was in bad health. Gladys Mitchell fondly remembered being thrilled at her candlelight initiation, performed by G.K.C. himself, at the Northumberland Hotel, which was across the street from the Sherlock Holmes Pub. (See Westminster Walk.) Ngaio Marsh was in and out of England too much to be made a member until, near her death, the Club made an exception in her honor. But she remembered being a guest at an annual dinner in the 1950s at which Dorothy L. Sayers presided in "full academic regalia." At this ceremony, she saw John Dickson Carr, Freeman Wills Crofts, John Rhode, and Anthony Gilbert acting as wardens and carrying their ritual weapons. Marsh wrote that she thought they seemed rather elderly to be indulging in these capers, but it was great fun meeting them all.

At the annual banquet, the Ruler presided over the Rite of Initiation for new members. Written by Dorothy L. Sayers, it was a delightful parody of *The Book of Common Prayer.* Surrounded by Club Wardens (members) bearing the tools of their trade, the Candidate had to place his hand on Eric, a lighted skull, and solemnly swear not to place undue reliance on "Divine Revelation, Feminine Intuition, Mumbo-Jumbo, Jiggery-Pokery, Coincidence or the Act of God." Having so sworn, he or she then promised to observe a seemly moderation in the use of "Gangs, conspiracies, Death-rays, Ghosts, . . . trap-doors, Chinamen . . . and utterly forswear Mysterious Poisons unknown to Science." The Ruler then declared the Candidate a Member, but warned him that if he failed to keep his promises, other members would steal his plots, his publishers would "do him down" in his contracts, strangers would sue him for libel, and his pages would swarm with misprints.

Many of our detective-story writers belonged to the Detection Club. Its Rulers have been G.K. Chesterton, E.C. Bentley, Dorothy L. Sayers, Agatha Christie, Julian Symons, and H.R.F. Keating. In order to defray the expenses of club rooms, Detection Club members put together such collections of stories as *Verdict of 13,* collaborated on such mysteries as *The Floating Admiral* and *Crime on the Coast,* and wrote and produced two radio serials for the fledgling BBC, "The Scoop" and "Behind the Screen."

After World War II, the club moved to a room in Kingly Street, which it arranged to use for a small fee through Sayers's church connections. Now, according to President Keating (a.k.a. Evelyn Hervey), the club meets only twice a year at the Garrick Club on Garrick Street (see Covent Garden/The Strand Walk) but still dines once a year at the Café Royal on Regent Street. (See Mayfair/Oxford Street Walk.)

Turn around and go back to Wardour Street, where you will turn right and walk past Dansey Place to Shaftesbury Avenue. The name of Wardour Street is synonymous with the British film industry, which started here, although the studios themselves now are located outside the city. Shaftesbury Avenue was named for the nineteenth-century philanthropist, Lord Shaftesbury. The avenue, cut through Soho in 1886 to connect Holborn and Piccadilly, is one of London's principal theater streets. The Queen's Theatre, visible at the corner of

Shaftesbury Avenue and Wardour Street, is one of several that may have been the theater patronized by Agatha Christie's Lady Eileen (Bundle) when she came to Town in *The Seven Dials Mystery.*

In *From London Far,* Michael Innes's amateur detective, Meredith, set out to walk from the British Museum in Bloomsbury by way of Shaftesbury Avenue to Piccadilly and the Athenaeum for a couple of hours of "light reading" in scholarly journals. In John Creasey's *The Toff and the Deadly Parson,* fictitious Pond Street was described as a dingy thoroughfare off Shaftesbury Avenue, where the Toff went to find the disreputable Daisy Club. Prolific John Creasey wrote under a number of aliases, but detective writer Margaret Truman, daughter of the former American president, reported that when she met Creasey he looked just like Inspector Gideon (J.J. Marric).

Cross Shaftesbury Avenue and continue north on Wardour Street. On your right, you will come to the open churchyard of St. Anne's Soho. Bombs in World War II destroyed all but its bulbous, Russian-looking church tower by Cockerill. The essayist William Hazlitt is buried somewhere here, but of more interest to mystery buffs is the fact that, inside the tower and beneath the floor of the Sayers Room, lie the ashes of Dorothy L. Sayers. A copy of her portrait, presented to St. Anne's by the D.L. Sayers Historical and Literary Society, hangs in the room. From 1952 to her death in 1957, Sayers was vicar's warden of the parish of Soho, which also included St. Thomas Regent's Street, demolished, and St. Paul's Covent Garden, the actors' church. You need to be about six feet tall to see in the tower window, but St. Anne's services are held at 57 Dean Street, and you can ask there for the key to the tower.

Return to Wardour Street and turn right to walk north. No. 17 used to be Pinoli's, the restaurant where the Junior Debating Society (the JDC), the schoolboy literary club to which G.K. Chesterton and E.C. Bentley belonged, held a famous stag party on the eve of the Boer War. Keep walking until you reach Old Compton Street, where Simon Brett's actor, Charles Paris, met his Cockney-talking pal, Stan, the decorator, at the Patisserie Valerie in *Not Dead, Only Resting.*

Turn right on Old Compton Street and walk east to Dean Street, where you will turn right. In Charles Dickens's *A Tale of Two Cities,* Dr. Manette lived at No. 10 Dean Street. At this point, you are in the heart of the Soho restaurant area. Many detective stories have characters eat at a restaurant "in Soho" without being more specific. This area is the probable site of the fictitious Reeder Street's Moulin Gris, where Thalia Drummond was taken by one of the Crimson Circle in Edgar Wallace's *The Crimson Circle.* In Christie's *The Big Four,* there was a small foreign restaurant in Soho where Poirot and Hastings often dined and observed Inspector Japp at an adjacent table. Somewhere nearby should be the small restaurant on fictitious Mervyn Street, where the Thursday Club met in John Buchan's *The Three Hostages.* Started by some people who had queer jobs and wanted to keep in touch after World War I, the club met on the second floor in a pleasant room, paneled in white, with big fires burning at each end. You may also be walking by Veglio's, a fictitious Soho restaurant to which racist M.P. Sir Pountney took the actress playing the TV Irene Adler in Symons's *A Three Pipe Problem,* or Pesquero's, the restaurant in Soho to which Dame Beatrice's secretary, Laura, is taken by her Scotland Yard fiance in Gladys Mitchell's *Watson's Choice.*

Somewhere on Dean Street, above a pizza restaurant, Oxford don Patrick Grant went to see the agent of his dead actor friend in Margaret Yorke's *Cast for Death.* Edmund Crispin in *Swan Song* had operatic tenor Adam Langley take Elizabeth Harding to dinner in a restaurant in Dean Street, where they sat at a table with a red-shaded lamp and were waited on by a garrulous Cypriot. Langley ordered an especially good claret as he proposed to Elizabeth, who accepted.

In one of these streets must be Chang's Club. Inspector Gideon went there to find the hit-and-run murderer of renegade Constable Foster in J.J. Marric's (John Creasey's) *Gideon's Wrath.* Marric's fictional Winter Street, the worst street in Soho, may be near here, too.

Follow Dean Street south to Romilly Street and turn left.

At this point, you are just opposite the parking lot behind St. Anne's. (Dorothy Sayers had tried hard to get a multimedia chapel-cum-theater built on the site of St. Anne's Church, but the parking lot was built instead.) No. 27 Romilly Street was the site of the Moulin d'Or, a restaurant at which Dorothy Sayers liked to eat and on which she based the Au Bon Bourgeois in *Unnatural Death*. There, a young doctor started to tell Lord Peter and Charles Parker about the mysterious death of Agatha Dawson. A possible Romilly Street substitute for Sayers's favorite French restaurant might be the Italian La Terrazza, with a white facade, at 19 Romilly Street. There are no French restaurants left on this street.

When you walk east along Romilly Street, the first crossing you will come to is Frith Street, where Mozart once stayed, with his father and sister (reminding detective-story buffs of Ellis Peters's delightful mystery, *The Funeral of Figaro*, built around a production of that opera).

Next, cross Greek Street. In *Unnatural Causes*, P.D. James's Adam Dalgleish came to the Cortez Club, a pseudo-Spanish disco near Greek Street. He had to interview its owner, who had shot his partner and gotten away with it, but now was implicated in the Suffolk murder of mystery writer Maurice Seeton. At No. 5 Greek Street, there is still a French restaurant called Au Jardin des Gourmets, known for its old claret, making it another good substitute for Sayers's Moulin d'Or. In Gladys Mitchell's *Watson's Choice*, murder suspect and lawyer Toby Dance told Scotland Yard that he usually lunched at the Jardin des Gourmets near his office, where "nobody hurries over lunch. It'ud be a sin."

At the end of Romilly Street, you will come to Cambridge Circus, the crossroads of Shaftesbury Avenue and Charing Cross Road. Here, in *The Man in the Queue*, Tey's Inspector Grant found the palatial offices of Laurence Murray, "Lucky-Folk-Bet-With-Laury Murray," one of the biggest bookmakers in London. This rather nondescript traffic center is also the site of the mysterious Circus from which the secret work of Smiley's people was orchestrated in such cold-war thrillers of John Le Carré as *Tinker, Tailor, Soldier, Spy*. (You will notice, however, that British espionage seems to have many different locales, depending on which author you read.)

Cross Cambridge Circus to Earlham Street, directly opposite you. Walk down Earlham Street to the next circle, which is the infamous Seven Dials. It was (and is) the meeting place of seven narrow alleys. In the eighteenth and nineteenth centuries, it was a well-known hangout for thieves. Hogarth used it for his illustrations of "Gin Lane." It was then made famous by Charles Dickens in *Sketches by Boz*. Dickens said of the slums about "the Dials," "The streets and courts dart in all directions [and] unwholesome vapour hangs over the house-tops." A pillar topped by a clock with seven dials once stood here, until it was torn down in a hunt for "hearsay" hidden treasure.

The idea of Seven Dials as a dangerous and mysterious place has persisted. In Anne Perry's Victorian mystery, *Bluegate Fields,* Inspector Pitt went there searching for evidence and interviewed a nervous little woman who rented rooms only to men "of the very best character." Agatha Christie used it for the Seven Dials Club at the fictitious No. 14 Hunstanton Street, which served fish and chips amidst general squalor, in what Bill Eversleigh called a "kind of East End-slumming-stunt." This club, where the walls were covered with rough charcoal sketches, was patronized by the Bright Young Things, prostitutes, and rich Jews. It was the meeting place of the secret Seven Dials organization, spied upon by Lady Eileen (Bundle) in *The Seven Dials Mystery.* In Julian Symons's *The Blackheath Poisonings,* Paul Mortimer wandered into this den of thieves with a drinking crony who took him to a vicious dog/rat fight. In *Death in Ecstasy,* Ngaio Marsh's phony Father Garnette got his heroin from an agent in Seven Dials.

Take Mercer Street, which is to your left, and walk west out of Seven Dials. As you cross Shaftesbury Avenue again, Mercer Street becomes St. Giles Passage. Follow St. Giles to New Compton Street and turn right on New Compton Street to St. Giles High Street. Turn left on St. Giles High and follow it around the south side of St. Giles-in-the-Fields.

St. Giles is one of the lost villages of London, swallowed up by urban growth. The original village church was a lazar house in Henry I's time, and it has the tomb of Richard Penderell, who guided Charles II to safety after the Battle of Worcester. For mystery readers, however, the chief interest of St. Giles-in-the-Fields is that it was customary for condemned felons on their way to the gallows to stop here at Bow Tavern, one of the foulest London rookeries. Wearing their Sunday best, they were cheered on with a cup of ale on their way to Tyburn at Marble Arch. St. Giles's churchyard contains graves of many of Tyburn's victims, too. A superb description of the place and time can be found in John Creasey's *The Masters of Bow Street,* a fictionalized history of the foundation of Scotland Yard. (See Brompton/Hyde Park Walk.)

Turn to your left off St. Giles High Street into nondescript-looking Denmark Street and follow it back to Charing Cross Road. Denmark Street is London's Tin Pan Alley, the mecca for all would-be pop singers. Walking along Denmark, you will soon reach Charing Cross Road, which once was the home of most of London's famous secondhand bookstores, including the one made famous by Helene Hanff in *Eighty-Four Charing Cross Road.* In *The Man in the Queue,* Inspector Grant found the bookmaker's offices of Albert Sorrell at 32 Minley Street, off Charing Cross Road. Then, in Tey's *The Daughter of Time,* the hospitalized Grant asked actress Marta Hallard to get someone to go to Charing Cross and buy him a copy of Sir Thomas More's *Historie of Richard III.* In Dorothy L. Sayers's short story, "The Learned Adventure of the Dragon's Head," Lord Peter Wimsey, babysitting his nephew St. George, took him shopping at Ffolliott's dark bookstore, where Lord St. George purchased a battered copy of Münster's *Cosmographia universalis.*

There are far fewer bookstores here today, but across Charing Cross Road at Manette Street stands Foyles, a London institution. Unfortunately, its selection is no longer extensive, it has virtually no secondhand books, its wares are displayed by publisher, and its system of selling books is cumbersome. For current mystery titles, you will do better to head for the nearest W.H. Smith or go to Hatchard's on Piccadilly. (See St. James Walk.)

Cross Charing Cross Road and walk west on Manette Street past Foyles, back to the head of Greek Street. Turn right on Greek Street and walk north to Soho Square. At the corner of Greek Street and Soho Square is the handsome eighteenth-century House of St. Barnabas, now open by appointment only. At this corner in Margery Allingham's *Tiger in the Smoke*, there was a street fight between "Duds" Morrison and another man, which sent Duds, one of Havoc's men, to prison.

Soho Square is very built up with modern office buildings, but it still has a green park in the center with a weathered statue of Charles II. The square took its name from Charles's illegitimate son, James, the Protestant Duke of Monmouth, whose mansion was here. He used the hunting call "so-hoe" as his battle cry at Sedgemoor when he fought for the crown against his Roman Catholic and unpopular uncle, James II. There is also a French Huguenot Church at the corner of the square, a reminder of the Huguenots who came to Soho as refugees in the seventeenth century.

In Agatha Christie's *The Secret Adversary*, intrepid Tommy Beresford followed a gang member from South Audley Street up Shaftesbury Avenue to the maze of mean streets around Soho until he reached a small dilapidated square. Tommy followed Boris up the steps of an evil-looking house, at whose door Boris rapped sharply with a peculiar rhythm. Then Tommy lost his head, rapped the same way, asked for "Mr. Brown," and was admitted, too. Tommy overheard the crooks' plans and then was knocked on the head, but he eventually escaped, in the best traditions of the intrepid detective. On the west side of Soho Square, there still are several decayed-looking houses, waiting to be torn down, that look suitable for Tommy's adventure.

Now take Carlisle Street to the west, out of Soho Square. Go across Dean Street on Carlisle to Great Chapel Street. Turn right on Great Chapel Street to Hollen Street. Turn left on Hollen Street, which soon becomes Noel Street, and walk along Noel Street, which crosses Wardour Street again at the northern boundary of Soho. Noel Street is an old Cockney-Jewish neighborhood with a street market south on Berwick

Street. At Poland Street, Noel Street becomes Great Marlborough Street, which runs all the way to Regent Street.

As you go along Great Marlborough Street, you pass many small shops connected with clothing manufacturing. Then, on your left, you will pass a very large round sign that marks this end of Carnaby Street, which was the clothes center of the 1960s youth culture in London—and the world. In Mary Stewart's thriller *The Gabriel Hounds,* her heroine asks her cousin Charles, who, disguised as an Arab, has just rescued her from a harem, "Where did you get that Carnaby Street rig anyway?" Much Mod, New Wave, pop fashion has now moved to the King's Road in Chelsea. (See Brompton/Hyde Park Walk.) In P.D. James's *The Skull Beneath the Skin,* Cordelia Gray sent her office helper, Bevis, to a Carnaby Street deli to get them lunch.

As you continue west, on the other side of Great Marlborough Street, you will pass Argyll Street, which runs north to Oxford Street, just before Oxford Circus. Argyll Street is the site of the world-famous Palladium Music Hall. In Sayers's *The Unpleasantness at the Bellona Club,* Robert Fentiman booked to take Ann Dorland there for an evening's entertainment, proving that she would attract strong, silent men, just as Lord Peter Wimsey had predicted. In Sax Rohmer's *The Trail of Fu Manchu,* during one of Fu Manchu's efforts to subvert Western Civilization with Eastern magic, a Limehouse landlady was given tickets to the Palladium by an undercover Scotland Yard man so that he could gain access to her building in the East End.

Beyond Carnaby Street, on the south side of Great Marlborough Street, you will reach Kingly Street. At its far corner is the Tudor-timbered back of Liberty's, a department store famous for its cashmere sweaters and print scarves. Lord Peter borrowed some of his wife's Liberty ties for his costume the night his son Bredon was born, when he helped solve the case of "The Haunted Policeman."

Turn left behind Liberty's and walk down Kingly Street. You are retracing the workaday steps of P.D. James's Cordelia Gray in *An Unsuitable Job for a Woman.* Gray came up from the Oxford Circus Underground and plunged into the "cacophony" of Kingly Street "between the blocked pavement and shining mass of cars and vans which packed the narrow street." She saw the bronze plaque that read "Pryde's Detective Agency, Props. Bernard G. Pryde, Cordelia Gray." Later, in *The Skull Beneath the Skin,* Gray stood looking at a new plaque that Bevis had put up crookedly, while their office cat dived under trucks. Kingly Street also was the postwar site of the Detection Club rooms that Dorothy L. Sayers got cheaply through her Church of England connections.

Farther along, you will pass the Red Lion pub at 14 Kingly Street, which is about the right location for James's The Golden Pheasant, where Bernie and Cordelia lunched, presided over by Mavis, "who changed her dress three times a day and her hair style once a year and her smile never."

Kingly Street runs into Beak Street. The famous Italian painter Canaletto lived there at No. 41, painting his scenes of London spires under a Venetian blue sky. Turn left (or east) along Beak Street to Upper John Street and then turn left along Upper John Street to reach Golden Square. Created in 1681, this is the very first Soho square. Most of its buildings are modern and contrast oddly with the park's statue of George II in a Roman toga. On the west side of the square, there still are two eighteenth-century houses that were once combined into the Portuguese Embassy. They are similar to those invented by Margery Allingham for her fictional Ivory Art Gallery at Nos. 38 and 39 Sallet Square, near Regent Street and the Café Royal in *Black Plumes*. (Another suggestion is St. James's Square. See St. James Walk.)

Walk across Golden Square to the east and turn right to take Lower James Street south to Brewer Street. Turn left on Brewer Street and go as far as Bridle Lane. Somewhere nearby is fictional Grace Street, where Helen MacInnes's superspy Robert Renwick's Interintell had its offices on the top floors of J.P. Merriman & Co., Consultant Engineers. In *Cloak of Darkness,* Renwick was asked to rendezvous at the Red Lion in Bridle Lane, which was not far from his office.

Turn right and walk back along Brewer Street; then turn

left at Sherwood Street and go south toward Piccadilly Circus. On your left, you will pass Denman Street with the Piccadilly Theatre on the corner, across the street from the Regent Palace Hotel. Cross Sherwood Street and look in the small, dark gateway that leads into tiny Ham Yard behind the theater. It is suspiciously like Goff Place in Margery Allingham's *Tether's End*. Allingham described Goff Place as a cul-de-sac off Deban (Denman) Street, near the Avenue (Shaftesbury, which is just beyond you to the south). On a dark and rainy night, Goff Place was the scene of a murder by "Major" Gerry Hawker, who made his getaway in a bus with two museum figures in it.

If you continue to walk down Sherwood Street, you will come back to Shaftesbury Avenue and the Piccadilly Circus Underground Station. Or, if you are ready for afternoon tea, this might be the perfect time to have it in the Regent Palace Hotel.

The decor of the main dining room is very like that in Anthony Berkeley's Piccadilly Palace Hotel Lounge in *The Piccadilly Murder*. It has imitation marble columns trimmed with 1920s metal and pink shell-like ceiling fixtures with a vaguely Hollywood look. Berkeley wrote that "the lounge of the Piccadilly Palace is what Monte Carlo is to Europe's new rich . . . our mecca and our rendezvous. The vastness of its gilt and synthetic-marble interior . . . the hum and buzz and heat and smoke of its almost palpable atmosphere—makes us look round with sober pride and reflect that now at last we are seeing life." Berkeley's Ambrose Chitterwick, of course, saw murder take place here, but you will probably only observe the tea and drinking customs of an international range of tourists at the end of this walk.

6

MAYFAIR/ OXFORD STREET WALK

BACKGROUND

Throughout the world, Mayfair, London's most glamorous neighborhood, is synonymous with elegance, high living, and wealth. A Mayfair address is just about the best you can have. As a London friend explained, "It's smart, terribly smart." To be called "Fair and Mayfair" means that you are one of the beautiful people.

This was not always the case. Originally, the May Fair was an annual event that took place in an open area between Berkeley Street and Park Lane. In George III's time, it was suppressed because the goings-on there created a public nuisance. The area around Shepherd Market was especially despicable. That was Mayfair before the aristocrats arrived.

First came the townhouses of the landed gentry, some of whom still maintain residences there. Next came the hotels for the aristocrats who couldn't or wouldn't maintain a house in town but demanded all the amenities of one. Many of the townhouses are gone or have been divided into elegant flats, but the fine hotels are still there to provide, on a London visit, all the comforts one would expect to find in a country manor.

Mayfair is also noted for shopping. Fine fashions and other expensive goods abound. If you are determined to shop, you do not have to forgo seeing the city, because shopping is interwoven with London's fabric. This is especially true in Mayfair.

The Mayfair walk is a long one, but it can be divided into two or more sessions. If you choose to do it as one walk, it will take a full day. Normally we say little about dress, except to suggest that you wear comfortable walking shoes, but on this elegant jaunt let us remind you that if you plan to stop, you should dress accordingly. This is not the day for your University of Illinois sweatshirt and running shoes. If you are taking tea, lunch, or dinner at the Ritz or Brown's Hotel or a similar spot, ties and jackets are *de rigeur* for men, as is comparable attire for women.

LENGTH OF WALK: 6.2 miles

See text for shorter segments. See map on page 105 for the boundaries of this walk, and page 249 for a list of detectives and stories.

PLACES OF INTEREST

Sotheby's, 34-35 New Bond Street. The world's largest auction house. Open for previews and auctions. Mon.–Fri., 9:00–4:30 P.M. Closed Aug., Sept.

Marlborough Fine Art, Ltd., 39 Bond Street. Open Mon.–Fri., 10:00–5:30; Sat., 10:00 A.M.–12:30 P.M. Free.

Museum of Mankind, 6 Burlington Gardens. Mon.–Fri., 10:00–5:00; Sun., 2:30–6:00 P.M. Free.

U.S. Embassy, Grosvenor Square.

The Royal Academy of Arts, Burlington House. Piccadilly. Open daily, 10:00–6:00 P.M. Free, except for major exhibitions.

PLACES TO EAT

Café Royal, 68 Regent Street. Grill and Le Relais restaurant. Continental food. Ornate rococo decor from the days of Oscar Wilde. Open daily, noon–11:00 P.M. Reservations. 01-429-6320, -6082.

The Connaught Hotel, Carlos Place. Grill and restaurant. English and French food in elegant continental dining room. Open 12:30–10:30 P.M. Closed Sat. and Sun. Reservations. 01-492-0668.

Brown's Hotel Restaurant, 21-24 Dover Street. Genuine English ambience in dark-paneled dining room. Open 12:30–10:00 P.M. Afternoon tea in the lounge. Reservations. 01-499-6122.

Shepherd's Tavern, 50 Hertford Street. A 300-year-old pub with a paneled bar. Serves real ale. 01-499-3017.

Claridge's Hotel, Brook Street. Elegant 1930s-style restaurant with orchestra. Huge menu. Causerie-cold buffet. Open to 11:00 P.M. Reservations. 01-629-8860.

——— MAYFAIR/OXFORD STREET WALK ———

Begin this walk by exiting from the Piccadilly Circus Underground Station and following the sign that says Piccadilly North side, Regent Street South side. As you emerge from the station, stop to admire the elegant sweep of Regency buildings on your left. They are part of the graceful crescents that once stretched all the way north to Regent's Park.

Across the street, the Café Royal at 68 Regent Street is on your right. On September 8, 1902, Sherlock Holmes was attacked here, but escaped his attacker by running through the restaurant in Sir Arthur Conan Doyle's "The Adventure of the Illustrious Client." This is probably why the Café Royal is the site of the Detection Club's annual initiation rites, which have been presided over, in turn, by G.K. Chesterton, E.C. Bentley, Dorothy L. Sayers, Agatha Christie, Julian Symons, and H.R.F. Keating. (See Soho Walk.)

In *Black Plumes* by Margery Allingham, painter David

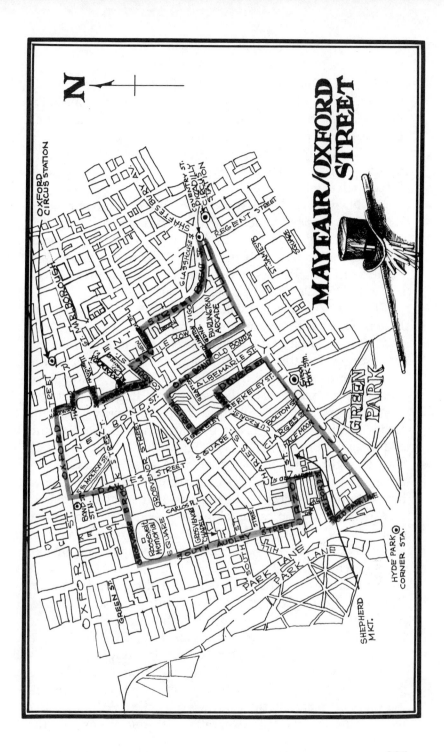

Field took Frances Ivory to the Café Royal to have an ice cream sundae and talk over the strange things happening at the Ivory Gallery at 39 Sallet Square, just off Regent Street. At 60 Regent Street, there once was a restaurant called Oddenino's, where Lord Peter Wimsey thought of taking Marjorie Phelps, the sculptress in Dorothy L. Sayers's *The Unpleasantness at the Bellona Club.*

In Ngaio Marsh's *A Wreath for Rivera,* the Metronome Restaurant, a fashionable nightclub that featured Breezy Bellairs's Band, was somewhere around Regent Street and Piccadilly. Lord Pastern and Baggot played the drums there. One night, Lord Pastern appeared to murder Carlos Rivera in front of the CID's Alleyn and his wife, Troy.

There's no longer a Lyons Tea shop along this stretch of Regent Street as there was when Baroness Orczy's Lady Molly and her friend Mary Granard stopped for a bit of refreshment after seeing a matinee of du Maurier's *Trilby.* Perhaps you would like to substitute the coffee shop in the Austin Reed store that you will pass on the west side of Regent Street, just before Vigo Street. It is perhaps a bit more pricey than the Lyons would have been, but the surroundings are pleasant, and imagination can place Lady Molly there. Lady Molly always thought that, had they gone to Mathis Vienna Café just across the street, the murder of Mark Culledon would never have occurred. To deepen the impression that mystery characters spent their time eating along Regent Street, here is one more. Dorothy Sayers's Mrs. Forrest lunched in the Cafe Verrey with her friend in *Unnatural Death,* giving herself an alibi for murder.

Several mystery characters shopped along Regent Street. In H.R.F. Keating's *Inspector Ghote Hunts the Peacock,* Inspector Ghote went into a china store, but finding it too expensive for his budget, he went into a seconds shop. There he was too humiliated to buy his wife her real English teapot.

On her way to work, where she discovered the body of her partner, Bernie Pryde, Cordelia Gray sped past the early morning shoppers scanning the windows of Dickens & Jones. Later in P.D. James's *An Unsuitable Job for a Woman,* after seeing the undertakers about her partner's funeral, she treated herself to tea at Dickens & Jones. Continue walking past the Burberry store, Heddon Street, and New Burlington Mews and turn left into New Burlington Street on your way to Savile Row. Turn right into Savile Row, across the street from the West Central Police Station. World famous for its gentlemen's bespoke tailoring, Savile Row is not a street for window shopping, since most of the displays are bolts of fabric.

At 3 Savile Row, the Beatles' company, Apple, had its headquarters. John, Paul, George, and Ringo conducted their business there, and on January 30, 1969, the final public performance of the Beatles was held on the roof of No. 3. R.B. Sheridan, the eighteenth-century playwright, lived at 14 Savile Row, but he died in 1816 in the front bedroom of No. 17. The Fortress House is on the right as you continue down the street. It is the large, gray, official-looking building, which contains, among other departments, the Royal Commission on Historical Monuments, as well as a department of British Intelligence. Jessica Mann's sleuth, Tamara Hoyland, officially works there as an archeologist. She bicycled there from her flat in Kensington in *Funeral Sites*. She became a spy recruit when her lover was blown up in *No Man's Island*.

Follow Savile Row to Conduit Street, the site of Weston's, a tailoring establishment mentioned in a number of Regency novels, including *Regency Buck* by Georgette Heyer. Cross Conduit Street and turn left to walk along Conduit to St. George Street. Turn right and walk north until you come to Maddox Street. There, at the southeast corner of St. George Street and Maddox Street, is the famous society church, St. George's, Hanover Square.

St. George's is considered to be the West End's most impressive church. It was built in 1713–24 by John James, a follower of Christopher Wren. The church has a large Corinthian portico and a baroque tower. The interior resembles St. James's Piccadilly. On either side of the entrance porch sit twentieth-century cast-iron Landseer dogs, waiting for their master. St. George's best known parishioner, the composer George Frederick Handel, had his own pew there. For 35 years, Handel's home was nearby, at 25 Brook Street, where he wrote *The Messiah* and where he died in 1759.

St. George's has been the scene of fashionable weddings of both the known and the unknown, the real and the fictional. The register records the marriages of Sir William Hamilton and Emma Hart (Lord Nelson's "Dearest Emma") in 1791; Benjamin Disraeli and Mrs. Wyndham Lewis were married there in 1839; J.W. Cross, a New York banker, and Mary Ann Evans (George Eliot) in 1880; and Theodore Roosevelt and Edith Carow in 1886. P.B. Shelley and Harriet Westbrook were remarried at St. George's in 1814 to validate their Scottish wedding vows. In 1907, thriller writer John Buchan was married there.

Many of Georgette Heyer's Regency characters also were married there, and the sharp-tongued Helen, Duchess of Denver, thought it was a suitable spot for Harriet and Lord Peter's wedding in Dorothy Sayers's *Busman's Honeymoon*.

Walk up St. George Street to Hanover Square. The bronze statue at the south end of the square is of William Pitt the Younger, prime minister in the days of Napoleon. The Hanover Square Rooms, the principal concert hall in London during the late eighteenth century, stood on the east side of the square, at the corner of Hanover Street. Turn right and follow the square around to Harewood Street and exit to Oxford Street. You have walked 2.2 miles and can stop here for refreshments or shopping or you may continue the walk.

Oxford Street is London's longest shopping thoroughfare. Although you will not walk its entire length today (see Marylebone/Regent's Park Walk), it runs eastward from Marble Arch to Tottenham Court Road, where it continues as New Oxford Street. The road was laid out in Roman times, possibly even earlier. Until the eighteenth century, it was known as Tyburn Road because it was the route from Newgate Prison to Tyburn Hill at Marble Arch. Oxford Street today is the site of many large department stores. This walk takes you along Oxford Street, across from several well-known stores.

In John Mortimer's *Rumpole of the Bailey,* one of Rumpole's clients, the Rev. Mortimer Skinner, had gone to the

Oxford Street summer sales, where he was arrested for shoplifting. In *Find Me a Villain,* Margaret Yorke's Nina Crowther was in a highly upset state over the breakup of her marriage. After following her husband and "the other woman," she found herself in Oxford Street. She went into John Lewis and then into Woolworth's, where she bought a cheap china cat that reminded her of her husband's mistress. In *Quiet as a Nun,* Antonia Fraser's Jemima Shore and her classmate Sister Miriam of Blessed Eleanor's Tower lunched at D.H. Evans because it was cheaper than Fortnum & Mason. Sister Miriam was later murdered for control of her great wealth.

In Jessica Mann's *Funeral Sites,* Tamara Hoyland spent an afternoon shopping at Marks and Spencers. She was buying a different style of clothing for the fugitive Rosamund Sholto in which to smuggle her out of London.

Unless you want to stop and shop, turn left off Oxford at Davies Street, which comes after New Bond Street, Woodstock, and Sedley streets. Walk down Davies Street to Brook Street, passing Weighhouse Street and St. Anselm's Place. At the corner of Davies and Brook Street is Claridge's Hotel, a favored spot with the likes of Agatha Christie and Patricia Wentworth. Claridge's is a luxury-class hotel that is practically a British institution. The columned doorway is ruled over by a top-hatted, epauletted commissionaire, like the one at Agatha Christie's Bertram's Hotel. The rumor that to get a room at Claridge's you must have a recommendation from a long-time client is not true, but when you step into the elegant lobby, with its crystal chandeliers and striking art deco interior, you will think that it might be. The restaurant is decorated in pastels, a string quartet plays dinner music, and an excellent selection of French cuisine is served.

In mystery stories, Claridge's has been featured over and over again as a rendezvous. When John Buchan's Sir Richard Hannay was trying to solve a triple kidnapping, he was summoned to Claridge's by the sinister Medina to meet a great master of Eastern lore. Hannay found the hotel to be bright and commonplace, with people dancing and dining. Then a turbaned Indian led him into a small anteroom furnished with vulgar copies of French furniture. There, in *The Three Hostages,* he met the intriguing Kharama.

A letter sent to the Director of the Ministry of Morale directed him to ring up his missing brother-in-law, Charles Kennington, at Claridge's in Nicholas Blake's *Minute for Murder.* In *Spotlight* by Patricia Wentworth, Dorinda Brown went to Claridge's to apply for a job as secretary to the wife of a wealthy businessman. In *The Skeleton in the Clock,* John Dickson Carr has the Dowager Countess insist that her granddaughter, Jenny, meet her at Claridge's for lunch, despite the fact that Jenny had just met again her lost wartime love, artist Martin Drake.

Of all the writers included in this guide, none was fonder of Claridge's than Agatha Christie. Usually, she called it by name; sometimes she referred to it as Harridge's, as she does in *The Golden Ball:* "Who in England did not know Harridge's, where notables and royalties arrived and departed as a matter of course." As a matter of fact, Claridge's does fly the flag of any "resident" prince, king, or president.

In *The Secret of Chimneys,* adventurer Anthony Cade met Baron Lolopretzyl of Herzoslovakia at Claridge's to talk to him about possible kings for Herzoslovakia. In *The Secret Adversary,* the Russian conspirator, Kramenin, had a suite at Claridge's where he dictated to his secretary in sibilant Russian. Agatha Christie's scientific Mr. Parker Pyne, who advertised his business by asking, "Are you Happy?" had one client, an unhappy, middle-aged wife, meet her gigolo, Claude, at Claridge's to dine and dance in *Mr. Parker Pyne, Detective.*

Agatha Christie was not the only writer to play with the name of this hotel. Anthony Berkeley placed the murdered Miss Sinclair in a hotel in which "the air cost several pounds an hour to breathe," a place he called Alridge's in *The Piccadilly Murder.*

After you have people-watched in front of Claridge's for a few minutes and perhaps looked inside, turn and walk west along Brook Street until you reach Grosvenor Square. Brook Street also has its mystery associations. The townhouse belonging to the timid Lord Caterham, where his daughter Lady

Bundle stayed in Christie's *The Secret of Chimneys,* was located at the west end of Brook Street. In *Regency Buck,* Georgette Heyer's Lord Worth rented a house in Brook Street for his wards, the Taveners.

Grosvenor Square is the site of the American Embassy. Known as Little America, it is the largest of Mayfair's squares, occupying six acres. It has a large and beautiful central park, adorned with a statue of President Franklin D. Roosevelt. The American Embassy occupies the entire west side of the square. The roof of the Embassy is surmounted by a huge eagle that has a wing span of 35 feet. Lord Peter Wimsey went to the American Embassy to get his papers so that he could chase off to New York after the mysterious mistress of the dead Denis Cathcart. Lord Peter was striving to clear the name of his brother, the Duke of Denver, in Dorothy L. Sayers's *Clouds of Witness.* It was also the home of Julius Ricardo, the "Dr. Watson" of A.E.W. Mason's French detective, M. Hannaud. At 20 Grosvenor Square, a plaque to the left of the first door marks the location of General Eisenhower's World War II European Headquarters. No. 9 Grosvenor Square was the home of John Adams, the second U.S. President, when he was the first American minister to Great Britain from 1785 to 1788.

Just off Grosvenor Square in Carlos Place is the elegant Connaught Hotel, which has a longstanding reputation for outstanding international cuisine. Tea is served there in Victorian splendor. According to Antonia Fraser's Jemima Shore in *Cool Repentance,* her boss, Cy Fredericks, who ran Megalithic House, lunched there regularly at what was "arguably the most expensive restaurant in London." It also must be a regular hangout of television bigwigs, for, according to Julian Symons in *A Three Pipe Problem,* the grill room at the Connaught was where the idea of a Sherlock Holmes TV series was sold to the BBC's director of programmes. It is also a likely location for the place where Patricia Moyes's Sir Percy Crumble lunched, a stone's throw away from his office in Berkeley Square in *Who Is Simon Warwick?*

Leave Grosvenor Square by its southwest corner. You

should now be walking south on South Audley Street. This is and was a smart address. Two French kings lived here—Louis XVIII and Charles X—and Queen Caroline lodged here while awaiting her divorce by George IV (the former Prince Regent). In John Creasey's *The Toff and the Deadly Parson,* the wealthy church warden, Mr. Straker, lived in South Audley Street. The Alpine Club at 74 South Audley Street was one of the clubs to which Sir Julian Freke belonged. His club membership gave Lord Peter a vital clue to the murder in Dorothy Sayers's *Whose Body?*

As you continue along South Audley Street, you will pass Grosvenor Chapel. It was in this chapel that the U.S. armed forces held services during World War II.

In Sayers's *Unnatural Death,* Miss Climpson trailed Mrs. Forrest up South Audley Street past a chemist's, a florist's, and a café to her flat. Then Miss Climpson, a daughter of the Rectory, pretended to conduct a canvass to locate the exact apartment. Lord Peter later scaled a drainpipe to Mrs. Forrest's bathroom window in order to retrieve a glass with her fingerprints on it. (Feel free to peer behind a building in search of a drainpipe sturdy enough to climb. Sayers was very careful about details.)

The flat of Mrs. Rita Vandermeyer was in Audley Mansions, at 20 South Audley Street. She was part of the gang that kidnapped Jane Finn in Agatha Christie's *The Secret Adversary.*

Continue on South Audley Street past Hill Street to Audley Square. No. 2 Audley Square was the Belchester townhouse that Lord Peter Wimsey and his wife Harriet rented for their town home after their wedding in *Busman's Honeymoon.* The attractive brick and stone mansion is now the site of the University Women's Club, but try to imagine it as it was on the night Lord Peter helped the Haunted Policeman solve a mystery, after his son and heir, Bredon, was born.

Follow South Audley to Curzon Street, where you will turn left. Curzon was an elegant street in the eighteenth century, but only one mansion, Crewe House, remains among the offices, shops, and restaurants. Many of Georgette Heyer's characters lived on Curzon Street. In Agatha Christie's *The*

Mystery of the Blue Train, 160 Curzon Street was the mansion of the American Ruth Kettering and her husband, Derek, who was accused of murdering her.

North of Curzon Street off Chesterfield Street, where Somerset Maugham's Ashenden lived at No. 36, is Charles Street. Social climber Mrs. Haddington and her debutante daughter, Cynthia, rented a house there for the season and "Terrible Timothy" Harte's fiancée, Beulah Birtley, worked there as a secretary in Georgette Heyer's *Duplicate Death.*

Turn right when you reach Hertford Street, passing in front of the Curzon Theatre, one of London's most comfortable cinemas, and plunge into the maze of Shepherd Market. In 1688, James II decreed that a fair that was then held in Haymarket should be transferred to this wasteland. The plaque at the corner of Trebeck Street and Shepherd Market commemorates the fair. Shepherd Market is still a tiny village quarter of narrow streets and alleys, with an open marketplace. Today it is filled with small shops, cafés, and pubs that make it a shoppers' delight.

Robert Parker's private eye, Spenser, had lunch in a place called Shepherd Market Pub, which could be Shepherd's Tavern, at 50 Hertford Street. It is a 300-year-old pub, with a bow window, leather seats, and a telephone booth fashioned from an eighteenth-century sedan chair on its first floor landing. Cara Quayne, who was murdered in the House of the Sacred Flame in Ngaio Marsh's *Death in Ecstasy,* lived in a small, expensive house at 101 Shepherd Market. Dmitri, who catered the debutante balls in Marsh's *Death in a White Tie,* had his business in Shepherd Market.

In Michael Gilbert's *Death Has Deep Roots,* the Leopard was a pub in Shepherd Market where Nap Rumbold, the junior member of the solicitor's firm of Markby, Wragge and Rumbold, went to enlist the help of Major McCann to create a new defense for Victoria Lamartine. They held a council of war upstairs in the landlord's parlor. His description sounds like Ye Olde Bunch of Grapes at 16 Shepherd Market.

You have now walked 3.7 miles. If you wish to end your walk at this point, take White Horse Street, which leads off

Shepherd Market Street, to the right, as a passage to Piccadilly. When you reach Piccadilly, turn left and walk up Piccadilly to the Green Park Underground Station at Queen's Walk.

Continue your walk by leaving the Shepherd Market area. Go right (south) on Hertford Street; you will be walking slightly uphill. Hertford Street turns left (west) at an angle after it crosses Shepherd Street. At 10 Hertford Street, there are two blue historical markers. One notes that this was the residence from 1722 to 1792 of General John Burgoyne, whose defeat helped the Colonials win the American Revolution; the other marks the residence of Richard Brinsley Sheridan from 1795 to 1802. Continue along Hertford until you reach Old Park Lane.

Turn left into Old Park Lane. A double roadway, Park Lane, which lies to your right, runs along Hyde Park and affords an unequaled view across the Park. If the day is pleasant, you may wish to walk north along Park Lane on a side jaunt in the Park. (See Brompton/Hyde Park Walk.)

In the fifteenth century, Park Lane was called Westminster Lane; later, it was called Tyburn Lane because it led directly to the dreaded gallows at Tyburn (presently Marble Arch). Although once lined with opulent mansions, which gave it its nickname of "Millionaires Row," Park Lane is now known for its luxury hotels. Starting at the north end and working south, they are Grosvenor House, the Dorchester, the London Hilton, the Londoner, the Inn on the Park, and the Intercontinental. One other luxury hotel, the Park Lane, is not located on Park Lane, but on Piccadilly.

In the Regency period, this was a very fashionable street. Some vestiges of that period remain. The best surviving Regency houses are Nos. 93 to 99. They were built around 1820.

According to *Murder Ink*, Whitehaven Mansions was on Park Lane. This was where Hercule Poirot lived in a block of modern flats with his secretary, Miss Felicity Lemon, and his manservant, Georges. The townhouse of the Marquis of Wutherwood, the murdered older brother of Lord Charles Lamprey, was located at 24 Brummel, Park Lane. Roberta Grey and Henry Lamprey went there one night to stay with

Charles's widow in *A Surfeit of Lampreys*. Ngaio Marsh described it as one of a "row of great uniform houses [that] seemed fast asleep . . . [as] a fairy tale was unfolding."

In *Whose Body?* Dorothy Sayers's Sir Reuben Levy lived at 9a Park Lane. His murderer impersonated him for a night very much the way Sigsbee Manderson's supposed murderer impersonated him in E.C. Bentley's *Trent's Last Case*.

The Duchess of Medway's townhouse was on Park Lane. Her lady's maid turned out to be a male jewel thief in disguise, uncovered by Lord Peter Wimsey in Sayers's "The Article in Question."

Greek millionaire Conducis lived in a sumptuous mansion at fictional Drury Place off Park Lane. He pulled Peregrine Jay out of a bomb site at the Dolphin Theatre on the Southbank, took him home to bathe, gave him a complete set of clothes, and showed him the glove made for Hamet Shakespeare by his grandfather in Ngaio Marsh's *Killer Dolphin*.

Sleuth Albert Campion's sister, Valentine, was the head designer at Papendeik's fashion house, located in Park Lane, in Margery Allingham's *The Fashion in Shrouds*.

Old Park Lane brings us to Piccadilly, but, just before you leave it to turn onto Piccadilly, you will pass the Hard Rock Café, a favorite spot with teens because of its rock music associations and its good, American-style hamburgers. We queued in the rain one summer afternoon with an assorted group of young people in various styles of "in" dress, mothers and grandmothers, and harried-looking fathers—all determined, as we were, to secure one of the prized T-shirts for someone back home.

If you want to find an underground station and leave the walk at this point, turn right at Piccadilly and take the underpass to the Hyde Park Corner Underground.

If you plan to complete the Piccadilly leg of the walk, turn left off Old Park Lane onto Piccadilly. Green Park will be across the street from you, on the right. You will pass Down Street, Brick Street, and then White Horse Street on your left before you come to Half Moon Street.

As you pass Half Moon Street, note that it was once a

fashionable Regency address that has figured in both past and present writing. Recently, it gave its name to a Michael Caine movie, which we saw being filmed in Bloomsbury Square. Travel writer and novelist Paul Theroux wrote a book of short fiction called *Half Moon Street,* which is also the title of the first story in the volume. P.G. Wodehouse's Bertie Wooster lived on Half Moon Street with his perfect butler, Jeeves. Both characters are said to have been models for Dorothy L. Sayers's Lord Peter Wimsey and his man Bunter. In *Murder Must Advertise,* Lord Peter was described as "a Bertie Wooster with horned rims." Interestingly enough, Dorothy Sayers was one of the first to come to Wodehouse's defense when, as a Nazi prisoner in World War II, he was branded a traitor for making broadcasts abroad. In Edmund Crispin's *Frequent Hearses,* a member of the theatrical Crane family had a party on Half Moon Street after which the ingénue Gloria Scott threw herself off Westminster Bridge.

The next street you will come to is Clarges Street. Edgar Wallace in *The Crimson Circle* placed his fictitious Steyne Square at a corner of Clarges Street. This was where the dark limousine belonging to the head of the Crimson Circle waited for potential members to come and be given orders. As Wallace described it, it was a square of big, old-fashioned houses with iron railings and many trees. Flemings Hotel on Clarges Street was probably at least a partial model (along with Brown's) for the fictitious Bertram's in Agatha Christie's *At Bertram's Hotel,* a prewar hotel that cleverly prided itself on providing the "perfect" English atmosphere. "By 1955 it looked precisely as it had looked in 1939—dignified, unostentatious, and quietly expensive." Bertram's, in a quiet street of Georgian homes, had been patronized for years by the aristocracy, higher echelons of the Church of England, and young girls on their way to and from boarding school. Wise Miss Marple, there on a sentimental trip to London, suspected the hotel was all a facade.

Continue the walk along Piccadilly, where Ruth Callice, who joined Martin Drake in an adventure seeking prison ghosts, ran a bookshop in John Dickson Carr's *The Skeleton in the Clock.* The Toff, John Creasey's West-Ender who was equally at home in the East End, lived in Gresham Terrace on Piccadilly. In Stratton Street, on your left, was a car rental place called Hire Car Lucullus. In *Forfeit* by Dick Francis, it was "a small, plushy office off Piccadilly," where a black Rolls-Royce was rented to someone living in Radnor Mews—a South African who was being investigated by sports reporter James Tyrone.

Continue going east to Berkeley Street. In Anthony Berkeley's *The Poisoned Chocolates Case,* the Rainbow Club was "in Piccadilly, just around the corner from Sir Eustace Pennefather's rooms in Berkeley Street." It was a fictitious club that descended from the Rainbow Coffee House, founded in 1734. Its members included Graham Bendix, whose wife's murder was under investigation by the Crimes Circle.

Follow Piccadilly until you reach Dover Street, turn left, and go to Berkeley Square. (As you turn on Dover Street, you will notice a contemporary statue of a horse and rider, which was put up in 1975.) In Dorothy Sayers's *The Unpleasantness at the Bellona Club,* old General Fentiman, who was found dead in the Bellona Club on November 11, always walked along Dover Street, where he had his rooms, to the Club, which was just east on Piccadilly, at No. 49. (See St. James Walk.)

Oxford University Press is at 37 Dover Street. It brings many writers to mind, but particularly Charles Williams, whose first murder mystery, *War in Heaven,* opened in a publisher's office. (See City Walk.) This is a street of shops, small galleries, and pleasant pubs. At the head of Dover Street, just past No. 37 across the street, you will see Brown's Hotel, which figures in a number of mystery stories, but particularly in Agatha Christie's. As already noted, she probably combined Brown's with Fleming's to produce her Bertram's Hotel. Brown's Hotel, which was founded by Lord Byron's valet, is the quintessence of English hotels. As you walk into the hotel through the white double doorway of the brown Georgian building, with its window boxes brimming with colorful blossoms, you expect to see Miss Silver, Miss Marple, and their contemporaries there, and you do. Tea is served in a lounge furnished in what the decorating magazines would term "dignified English country." While we were there, a group of television actors ensconced in one corner were discussing their trade, and a rather threadbare-looking American clergyman led his wife and five children to a cozy corner, explaining as he walked by that, yes, it would be costly to have tea here, but it was an experience the children must have. In *The Dirty Duck* by Martha Grimes, Brown's made an appropriate, expensive place for Valentine Honeycut to take his exclusive Honeysuckle Tours.

Leaving Brown's, turn left and walk downhill on Hay Hill into Berkeley Street. Hay Hill gets its name from the old Hay Hill Farm, which stood on the Aye (or Eye) Brook. The brook still runs underground at the foot of the hill into Berkeley Street. While George IV was still Prince of Wales, he and two friends were accosted here by some footpads and robbed of two shillings and sixpence. In Berkeley Street was the Thomas Cook office where Katherine Grey, the companion of an old lady from St. Mary Mead, went to get a ticket for Nice on the Blue Train. There she met Derek Kettering, the dissolute husband of the rich American, Ruth Kettering, in Agatha Christie's *The Mystery of the Blue Train*.

From Berkeley Street, go into Berkeley Square. The square was named for Berkeley House, which stood on the south side from 1664 to 1733, when it was replaced by Devonshire House. The gigantic plane trees planted in 1790 are probably the oldest things around the square today. The garden in the center of Berkeley Square is said to be haunted by the ghost of Lord Clive, who committed suicide in his home at No. 45 in 1744. It was also the scene of the murder of another member of the Honeysuckle Tours in Martha Grimes's *The Dirty Duck*. In Patricia Moyes's *Who Is Simon Warwick?* the opulent office of Sir Percy Crumble, director of the Charlton business, was located here. The May Fair Inter-Continental Hotel, located off Berkeley Street, was probably the big, flossy hotel where Robert Parker's private eye, Spenser, was put up on his manhunt in London. There, he ambushed several members of the terrorist gang, Liberty, in *The Judas Goat*.

The Hungaria, a Mayfair nightclub, was once located in Berkeley Square. It was where Ngaio Marsh and the Lampreys went in the 1930s to hear Richard Tauber sing. They also saw the Prince of Wales, later Edward VIII, the writer Michael Arlen, and the fragile old Lord Alfred Douglas, once Oscar Wilde's lover, whose father, the Marquis of Queensbury, sued Wilde and sent him to Reading Gaol. Also in Berkeley Square was the Mirros Club, where Thalia Drummond, the daughter of Scotland Yard's Inspector Parr, was taken to dine by a cabinet minister, M.P. Raphael Willings, in Edgar Wallace's *The Crimson Circle*.

At 44 Berkeley Square is Annabel's, the very fashionable, exclusive, and best-known night spot in London today. It could have been the model for Julian Symons's Over and Under Club, where M.P. Sir Pountney took the actress who played Irene Adler in *A Three Pipe Problem*. Annabel's is not open to anyone who is not a member, and even temporary club memberships are very difficult to obtain.

In a small house on the east side of Berkeley Square, Horace Walpole, the father of the Gothic romance and the author of *The Castle of Otranto,* from which our detective stories are descended, lived during the last years of his life. In Sax Rohmer's *The Trail of Fu Manchu,* the Secretary for Home Affairs had a gloomy, stone-porched mansion a few paces from Berkeley Square. That was where Scotland Yard's Sir Denis Nayland Smith got permission to open the mausoleum of the Demurases in a London cemetery while chasing Fu Manchu. In Sherlock Holmes's "The Adventure of the Illustrious Client," General DeMerville lived on the east side of Berkeley Square, as did Admiral Sinclair in "The Adventure of the Bruce-Partington Plans." (Dr. Watson spelled Berkeley B-a-r-k-e-l-e-y, the way it is pronounced.) Leave Berkeley Square at the east side by way of Bruton Street, where, in 1926 at No. 17, Queen Elizabeth II was born.

Follow Bruton Street to Bond Street, where Judith Tavener drove to purchase a ravishing hat in Georgette Heyer's *Regency Buck*. Bond Street is really two streets, Old Bond and New Bond. They connect, but, confusingly, they have separate numbering systems. At best, the numbering system all over London is confusing to North Americans, who are used to even numbers on one side of the street and odd numbers on the other. Both Bond streets are known for luxurious shops. In Josephine Tey's *The Daughter of Time,* the hospitalized Alan Grant, talking about Mary, Queen of Scots, who was six feet tall and, so he claimed, frigid, explained to actress Marta Hallard that you can pick out the normal run of oversexed women any day on a walk down Bond Street between five and six o'clock.

Roger Sheringham, president of the Crimes Circle, went to a Bond Street hat shop after leaving Scotland Yard in Anthony Berkeley's *The Poisoned Chocolates Case.* The Ambassador Club, a fictional club located at Bond and Grafton streets, was the place where Fah Lo Sue, Fu Manchu's daughter, met the Governor of the Bank of England, Sir Bertram Morgan, and vamped him into going to meet her father, in Sax Rohmer's *The Trail of Fu Manchu.*

Across Grafton Street at No. 166, you will see the elaborate black, white, and gold corner facade of Asprey's, one of the most luxurious shops in London. In addition to being a goldsmith, a silversmith, a bookbinder, and a manufacturer of leather goods, Asprey's has a particularly important antique clock department featuring some items that are of museum quality. Founded in 1781 and moved to this location in 1847, Asprey's possesses the Royal Warrant. Asprey's is often mentioned in Georgette Heyer's Regency mysteries. Agatha Christie's Mrs. Packington got her young man, Claude, a gold cigarette case there in "The Case of the Middle-aged Wife."

Julian Symons's George Mortimer in *The Blackheath Poisonings* bought himself some gorgeous women's underclothes at Baker's in Bond Street.

Across Bond Street, at 34-35 Old Bond Street, is Sotheby's, the world's best-known auction house. Established in 1744 as a rare book dealer, it moved to this location in 1917. Above the kiosk to the right of the entrance is an Egyptian statue of the god Sekmet dating from about 1320 B.C.

John Dickson Carr probably had Sotheby's in mind as the

chief model for his Willaby's in Bond Street, where Martin
Drake saw the auction of a grandfather clock with a skeleton
inside in *The Skeleton in the Clock*.

Walking along Bond Street, you pass No. 147, which is
now an art gallery but where at one time Admiral Lord Nelson
lived. At No. 43, Agnew's is a gallery specializing in Old
Masters. It might well be Quinns, the Mayfair art sales room of
John Creasey's Baron John Mannering in *The Baron and the
Missing Old Masters*. At No. 39 is Marlborough Fine Art, Ltd.,
the main dealer in such contemporary artists as Henry Moore.

Cross Bond Street and turn left on Burlington Gardens.
Cork Street, which leads off Burlington Gardens, is the location of many of London's private art galleries. It was on a
street very much like this that the Wiltshire Gallery was located
in Ngaio Marsh's *Death in a White Tie*. "Troy hunched up her
shoulders, pulled her smart new cap over one eye and marched
into her one-woman show, feeling gruff with shyness." Mr.
Fitzjohn, a crony of young Peregrine Tavener, Lord Worth's
ward, had lodgings in Cork Street, an important Regency
street in Georgette Heyer's *Regency Buck*.

Turn right from Burlington Gardens and go into the Burlington Arcade. Just beyond the entrance is the Museum of
Mankind, in a building that once housed the University of
London. Walk through to Piccadilly, admiring the double row
of tiny, elegant shops. Thalia Drummond, who was accosted
on Regent Street by her swain, Jack Beardmore, Jr., escaped
through the Burlington Arcade in Edgar Wallace's *The Crimson Circle*. Harriet Vane ordered two dozen silk shirts from a
Burlington Arcade shop in Dorothy Sayers's *Busman's Honeymoon*.

Nina Crowther, abandoned by her husband for another
woman, wandered Mayfair in the rain until she found herself at
the bottom of Bond Street, where she paused outside Burlington House in Margaret Yorke's *Find Me a Villain*.

Burlington House, the home of the Royal Academy of the
Arts, is located on the north side of Piccadilly, next to the
Burlington Arcade. The Royal Academy, founded in 1768 on
the Strand, moved here from Somerset House in 1868. It is

the last of the great Piccadilly palaces, with a Renaissance facade where flags fly when there is an exhibition. In the courtyard, there is a statue of the Academy's first president, Sir Joshua Reynolds. In *Grave Goods* by Jessica Mann, Tamara Hoyland's friend and mentor Thea decided that they should have coffee at the Ritz (see St. James Walk), although Tamara thought the basement of the Royal Academy would do. Lathom, Dorothy L. Sayers's painter who lodged in Bayswater with John Munting over the heads of the unhappy Harrison couple, gave the Harrisons tickets for the private viewing of the annual show. Lathom's portrait of Mrs. Harrison (actually Lathom's mistress) was being exhibited there, in *The Documents in the Case*.

Come out of Burlington House courtyard and walk east along Piccadilly. Off to the left is Albany Court Yard, which leads to London's most exclusive address, known only as "Albany," where super crook Raffles had his chambers, as did Berkeley's Roger Sheringham. One of the apartments was occupied by Prime Minister Edward Heath, and Georgette Heyer realized a longstanding ambition in 1942 by moving into chambers there—No. F3, to be exact. Albany has an illustrious history. It was originally the home of the first Lord Melbourne and then of the Duke of York. Among other distinguished residents were Lord Byron, Thomas Babington Macaulay, Prime Minister Gladstone, Lord Beaverbrook, Graham Greene, and J.B. Priestley.

Just beyond Albany, walking east along Piccadilly, you will pass Swallow Street on your left. Turn and walk up it to Vine Street, where on your right you will see a police station. This appears to be the most likely choice for the "Bottle Street" Police Station where Margery Allingham's Albert Campion had a flat. Campion lived in a flat over the police station, marked by a brass sign which read "Albert Campion, Merchant Goods Department," with his unusual man, Mr. Lugg, a Rembrandt etching, and some mementos of his cases like the Black Dudley dagger.

Before you reach Piccadilly Circus Underground Station, there are just two more observations to be made. Benson, who was posing as Simon Warwick in Patricia Moyes's novel *Who Is Simon Warwick?* received a death threat in the middle of Piccadilly, just as he and the crowd were about to surge across the street. Dolly Godolphin, in Allingham's *Black Plumes,* dashed into traffic there and was hit; seconds later, he was dead.

But enough. Head for the tube station, watching your step as you conclude your walk.

7

ST. JAMES WALK

BACKGROUND

This walk takes place in the area known as St. James, one of the many small villages that make up London. It is a cluster of squares and lanes, narrow streets, cul-de-sacs, and courts in the area between Piccadilly and the Mall, bordered by Green Park and St. James's Park. It is an area long associated with royalty. When Whitehall Palace burned in 1698, St. James's Palace became the official residence of the monarch until it was succeeded by Buckingham Palace. Today, although nearly two centuries have passed since it was a royal residence, ambassadors are still accredited to the Court of St. James.

From the early seventeenth century onward, many fine houses were built in the area of St. James; it later became known for the bachelor apartments of young men about town like Beau Brummell. The most exclusive of the gentlemen's clubs are in St. James, as are antique and art dealers, as well as custom shops dealing in everything expensive, from wines, cheese, and tobacco to shirts, shoes, and guns. The neighborhood is also famous for its hotels, among them Dukes Hotel, which has been called the quintessential small London hotel.

Length of Walk: 3-plus miles

See map on page 127 for the boundaries of this walk and page 254 for a list of the books and detectives covered.

Places of Interest

St. James's Palace, Cleveland Row. Official seat of royalty, built by Henry VIII. Chapel Royal: Sun. service, Oct.–Palm Sunday, 8:30 A.M., 11:15 A.M.

Marlborough House, Pall Mall. Once the residence of Queen Mary, now Commonwealth Conference Centre. Queen's Chapel: Adjoins Marlborough House, Sun. service, Easter–July, 8:30 A.M., 11:15 A.M.

Buckingham Palace, London residence of H.M. Queen Elizabeth II. When the queen is in residence, the Royal Standard is flown. Changing of the Guard: Daily, April–Aug., 11:30 A.M. Every other day, Sept. to Mar., 11:30 A.M.

  Queen's Gallery, Buckingham Gate. Tues.–Sat., 11:00–5:00. Sun., 2:00–5:00 P.M. Admission charge.
  The Royal Mews: Buckingham Palace Road. Open Wed. and Thur., 2:00–4:00 P.M. Admission charge.

Lancaster House, Stable Yard. Open Sat.–Sun., 2:00–6:00 P.M.

Christie's International Auction House, 8 King Street. Mon.–Fri., 9:00–4:30 P.M. Closed Aug.

Places to Eat

Fortnum & Mason, 181 Piccadilly. The Soda Fountain, store hours; the Patio 9:00–11:00 P.M. 01-734-8040.

The Red Lion, Crown Passage, S.W.1. Pub food.

Overton's, 5 St. James's Street. Gentleman's club atmosphere. Known for fish and oyster bar. Book ahead. Open to 10:30 P.M. 01-839-3774.

Ritz Hotel, Piccadilly and Green Park. Expensive, excellent spot for tea. 01-493-8181. Open Mon.–Sat., noon to 2:30 P.M. and 6:30 to 11:00 P.M.; Sun., to 10:30 P.M.

——————— ST. JAMES WALK ———————

Begin this walk at the Green Park Underground Station. When you leave the tube, turn left and walk west along the south side of Piccadilly. This street, laid out in the seventeenth century, runs for almost a mile from Hyde Park Corner to Piccadilly Circus. The name comes from a sixteenth-century mansion known as Pickadill Hall because its owner, Robert Baker, manufactured pickadills—lace frills such as those favored by Elizabeth I.

As you walk, you will be skirting Green Park, the idea of Charles II, who loved to picnic there. It held one of the earliest refrigerators—a snowhouse and an icehouse to cool wines and drinks during the summer. The park is remarkable because, except for the daffodil fringes in the spring, it features no flowers, only grass and trees.

In *A Wreath for Rivera* by Ngaio Marsh, Inspector Roderick Alleyn was caught in one of Piccadilly's many traffic jams opposite Green Park.

As you walk along Piccadilly for several blocks, you will be looking for a proxy for the luxurious flat of Dorothy Sayers's Lord Peter Wimsey. Technically speaking, Lord Peter lived in Mayfair—in *Gaudy Night,* Dean Martin described him to Harriet Vane as "Fair and Mayfair," but it is easier to do our sleuthing from the south side of the street, which is in St. James. Our first stop is across from the Park Lane Hotel at No. 109. Its name is displayed in large, bright blue letters over the entrance, which has two-storey, black marble columns. The Park Lane, one of London's famous luxury hotels, is just one of several possibilities for Lord Peter's residence at the fictional 110A Piccadilly, across from Green Park. (Sayers deliberately cut Sherlock Holmes's address of 221B Baker Street in half.) Admire the facade of the Park Lane; then turn right and walk back along Piccadilly, observing other possible locations for Lord Peter's flat.

Any of this miscellany of white buildings, some of them bearing only remnants of their past grandeur, could have been used as sites for the various flats and rooms located "across

ST. JAMES

from the Park" by Agatha Christie, Dorothy L. Sayers, and the
like. Derrick Yale, the private advisor to Scotland Yard in Edgar Wallace's *The Crimson Circle* also had a tiny flat overlooking the Park.

Next, look across at 100 Piccadilly, located just past the
Brick Street leadoff. It is a lovely old building, certainly a
possibility for Lord Peter's luxury flat.

In *Whose Body?* Sayers gives a detailed description of the
flat. It had "black and primrose walls lined with rare editions
(occasionally attracting burglars), deep chairs and a Chesterfield sofa suggesting the embraces of the houris, a black baby
grand, a wood fire in an old-fashioned hearth and Sevres vases
filled with flowers of the season . . . a place not only rare and
unattainable, but friendly and familiar, like a colourful and
gilded paradise in a medieval painting."

Farther along, at 49 Piccadilly, is the Naval and Military
Club, known as "The In and Out" because of its driveway
signs. It was the site of the Bellona Club, where, in Sayers's
The Unpleasantness at the Bellona Club, old General Fentiman
was found dead in his chair on November 11. Adjacent to the
Naval and Military Club, note the blue historical marker that
identifies it as a onetime residence of Lord Palmerston. It was
his statue in Parliament Square on which a drunk Lord Peter
Wimsey climbed, after the Duke of Denver, Wimsey's brother,
was acquitted by the House of Lords in Dorothy L. Sayers's
Clouds of Witness.

You are back at the Green Park tube station, and just ahead
on your right is the Ritz Hotel. The Ritz is one of London's
old luxury hotels, although from the outside it resembles nothing more elegant than a train station. Recently restored to all
its Louis XVI-style grandeur, the lobby is resplendent in gold,
marble, and crystal. Absolutely nothing has been overlooked
to assure the comfort of the guests in its 142 rooms.

The restaurant is good, expensive, and French, and the tea
served in the Palm Court is both hearty and elegant, as well as
absolutely English. Tea at the Ritz has become so popular that
it is often necessary to book a table several days in advance.

Almost without exception, if Agatha Christie characters

were in London, they popped in and out of, stayed in, or ate at
the Ritz. In *The Secret Adversary,* for instance, the rich American, Julius Hersheimer, was staying at the Ritz while looking
for his missing cousin, Jane Finn. Tommy and Tuppence also
stayed there as soon as they had the wherewithal.

The Ritz became the Blitz in Christie's *The Golden Ball.*
Jane Cleveland was sent there to impersonate an American
journalist. She was also ready to take the place of the "Grand
Duchess Pauline of Ostrova."

Agatha Christie was not the only author to make use of the
Ritz in her work. In *Whose Body?* Dorothy Sayers had Sir
Reuben Levy dine there with friends before keeping an ap-
pointment with Sir Julian Freke in Battersea. In *Fog of Doubt*
by Christianna Brand, Raoul Vernet, who was later murdered
during a thick "London Particular" (fog) in a house in Maida
Vale, came to London from France and stayed at the Ritzhotel.
Edgar Wallace created the Ritz-Carlton, then sent Thalia
Drummond there to dine with a member of the Crimson
Circle.

Walk through the lobby and look around; then return to
Piccadilly and walk east to St. James's Street, where you will
turn right and walk along the west side of the street.

In the eighteenth century, no respectable woman would set
foot on St. James's Street because it was, as it is today, the
home of a number of elegant gentlemen's clubs. These clubs
evolved from the coffee and chocolate houses that became
fashionable for gossip and gambling in mid-seventeenth-cen-
tury London. By Regency times, the street was the hangout of
the dandies and the beaus, who would mercilessly ogle any
female who came into view. The street was laid out in the
seventeenth century, but was not built up until St. James's
Square was completed in 1675. In *Regency Buck,* one of Georgette Heyer's Regency mysteries, Sir Geoffrey Fairford stayed
in the Reddish Hotel in St. James's Street.

Stop to look across the street at No. 37, with its elegant
iron railings and entrance lamps. This is White's, founded in
1693 as a chocolate house. It is the oldest London club and the
most famous. White's is considered to be the model for every

other gentleman's club in London. The bow window, which was added in 1811, was a cause of wonder in many Regency novels. White's reputation was and is for Conservative arrogance and hard drinking. It was appropriate in *Whose Body?* for Dorothy Sayers to have her surgeon, Sir Julian Freke, belong to White's.

Boodles is just down the street from White's, at No. 26. It was founded as a coffee house in 1762. It, too, has a bay window, which was added in 1824. Boodles originally was a betting club where the Regency fashion arbiter, Beau Brummell, liked to gamble. (He played a cameo role in Heyer's *Regency Buck.*) According to Janet Morgan in *Agatha Christie,* Boodles was a favored spot at which Christie and her husband liked to entertain friends. Christie was especially fond of the veal dishes and of Boodles's Orange Fool.

Since Randall Mathews, too, was a gentleman of leisure who liked to bet and go to the races, it was entirely correct for Georgette Heyer to have his flat located "in a road off St. James's Street." You will pass several tiny cul-de-sacs like the one in which he lived, as you continue along the west side of St. James's Street.

Now take a look to your right into Park Place for a view of an almost unspoiled, eighteenth-century cul-de-sac; then continue your walk past John Walker and Sons, Ltd., which may interest you because whiskey drinking and mystery reading sometimes go well together. Lord Peter's eccentric Egotists' Club is somewhere around here. Lord Peter once arrived there disguised as a policeman from Scotland Yard in *Murder Must Advertise;* in *Gaudy Night,* he took Harriet Vane to dinner there, and she mislaid a postcard from the Shrewsbury College poison pen. You will have to use your imagination to find it, for Sayers gave no address, but the Eccentric Club is at 9 Ryder Street.

Continue south along St. James, but pause outside No. 69 (on the west side of the street). This is the site of the Carlton Club, originally known as Arthur's because it was founded in 1832 by Arthur Wellesley, Duke of Wellington.

In Sayers's *Murder Must Advertise,* Major Milligan, a drug

runner, belonged to the Carlton Club, but at its pre-World War II Pall Mall address.

Keep walking past Blue Ball Yard; then turn right at St. James's Place and have a look at Spencer House. Built in the Palladian style, it is the London residence of the earls of Spencer. Lady Diana Spencer became Princess of Wales in 1981. The Polish composer, Chopin, also had rooms in St. James's Place. Dukes Hotel, at the end of the gaslit cul-de-sac, is reminiscent of the Sherlock Holmes era. The roadway is just wide enough for a horse-drawn hansom cab. The cul-de-sac once led to the home of George II's mistress.

Return to St. James's Street, where you will see Berry Brothers and Rudd, Wine Merchants, on the east side of the street. Although the firm was established in 1680, these premises date only from 1730. An excellent selection of port and single-malt whiskies, plus superb wines, are stocked here. Through the archway to the north of Berry Brothers is Pickering Place, built in 1731. To get a closer look, wait until you reach the bottom of St. James's Street, cross, and then walk back. Walk through the archway into the courtyard. You have to keep your eyes peeled to spot the entrance, and if the gate is closed, you will only know that you are at Pickering Place by the number 3. The alleyway retains its eighteenth-century timber wainscotting, on which a plaque notes that the diplomatic office of "The Republic of Texas Legation 1842" was located here.

It was in this small square that the last duel in England was fought. Graham Greene lived in a flat here and placed Colonel Daintry, who was investigating security in *The Human Factor*, in the same location. Daintry had a two-room flat looking out over the tiny, ancient courtyard with its sundial. There is a back entrance into Overton's at 5 St. James's Street, well known for its oyster bar and club-like atmosphere. Colonel Daintry usually ate there.

Across the street from Overton's, on the west side of St. James's Street at the corner of Little St. James's Street, is a Japanese restaurant that was the site of Rumplemeyer's, the fancy ice cream parlor to which the Dowager Duchess took

Harriet Vane after a session with Murbles over the will in Dorothy Sayers's *Busman's Honeymoon.* Now walk to the end of St. James's Street and cross Cleveland Row to St. James's Palace, known as the Court of St. James. This red and blue brick mini-palace was commissioned by Henry VIII as a manor house for Anne Boleyn. St. James's Leper Hospital for Women had previously occupied the site. Only the clock tower, the Chapel Royal, and the sentry station remain from Tudor times. From the balcony of the Palace, each new monarch is proclaimed. St. James's Palace is also the official headquarters of the Yeomen of the Guard. Tourists gather at the gateway to photograph the sentry. Because of the increase in terrorism, you can no longer go inside the Palace, except to attend Sunday services at the Chapel Royal. Off the stable yard are offices of the Royal Household, including that of the Lord Chamberlain, who used to censor all plays in England; in 1941, he removed several witty lines from the play *Love All* by Dorothy L. Sayers.

After taking a long look at and a few pictures of St. James's Palace and its Yeomen Guards, recross Cleveland Row and turn to your right across the bottom of St. James's Street at Pall Mall. You can walk back up St. James's Street to Pickering Place or head down Pall Mall for a few yards and turn left into Crown Passage, which will take you through to King Street. The Red Lion Pub, located in Crown Passage, is a good place to stop for refreshments. Superb homemade pies and sandwiches, along with assorted brews, are served in its two tiny rooms. Graham Greene's Castle undoubtedly ate here.

Continue along Crown Passage, with its minute shops, wine bars, and its strong sense of the seventeenth century, until you reach King Street. Turn right and enjoy its varied art and antique shops until you sight Christie's International Auction House at 8 King Street (on the corner of King and Bury streets). Christie's, which was founded in 1766, traditionally flies a blue and white standard. Visitors are welcome, but Christie's is closed in August. In *Whose Body?* Lord Peter Wimsey, Dorothy L. Sayers's intrepid sleuth, made his first fictional appearance in a taxi on his way to Christie's. Having forgotten his catalogue, he drove back to his flat, took a call from his mother, and became involved with the body found in the Thipps's bathtub in Battersea.

Christie's is probably the site of the auction at which Martin Drake met Sir Henry Merrivale and his long-lost sweetheart, Jenny, in John Dickson Carr's *The Skeleton in the Clock.* (However, it might also be Sotheby's. See Mayfair Walk.) But this site seems better because the Savage Club, to which, in *The Skeleton in the Clock,* John Dickson Carr's Martin Drake belonged, is on King Street, too.

The St. James Theatre, which has been torn down, stood in King Street. There, the Mortimer family in Julian Symons's *The Blackheath Poisonings* went to see a performance of Oscar Wilde's *Lady Windermere's Fan,* which was first presented at the St. James in 1892.

Walk along King Street to Duke Street St. James's , where at 26-28 King Street you will find Almack House. It is on the site of the famous Almack's Assembly Rooms, which figure prominently in eighteenth-century Regency novels, like those of Georgette Heyer.

Turn left and walk north on Duke Street to Jermyn Street. Duke Street was another well-known residential street in the eighteenth century. It is now a combination of elegant shops, small restaurants, and flats.

Jermyn Street, laid out in the late seventeenth century, is a quietly charming street that recalls a London of more elegant days. There are many fashionable shops along Jermyn Street, but those that are gentlemen's shirtmakers, like Endicott's in Sayers's *Have His Carcase,* predominate.

At 97 Jermyn Street is Harvie & Hudson, London's largest and best-known shirtmaker. The shop has one of London's finest examples of mid-Victorian shop fronts. In Margaret Truman's *Murder on Embassy Row,* the British ambassador to Iran, Geoffrey James, had his club certification on file at Harvie & Hudson so that he could purchase his club ties there. Paxton and Whitfield, Cheesemonger to the Queen, is at 93

Jermyn Street. There, Graham Greene's Secret Service officer, Castle, bought cheese while on his lunch hour in *The Human Factor*.

In Agatha Christie's *The Seven Dials Mystery,* Bundle went to Jimmy Thesiger's flat at No. 103. The door was opened by an expressionless gentleman's gentleman, who let her into a "comfortable sitting room containing leather armchairs of immense dimensions" (and to another girl in the case). Christie also placed the ne'er-do-well playboy husband of the rich American, Ruth Van Aldin, in a flat in Jermyn Street in *The Mystery of the Blue Train*.

In *Duplicate Death,* Georgette Heyer located the flat of Mr. Seaton-Carew in Jermyn Street. Seaton-Carew was selling drugs and had blackmailed Beulah Birtley into working for slave wages for Mrs. Haddington. In *The Thirty-Nine Steps,* John Buchan's Richard Hannay, fresh from South Africa and bored by civilized London, had dinner at a Jermyn Street restaurant, where he ate little, but drank the best part of a bottle of burgundy. He then walked down to the corner of Duke Street, where he passed a group of young men in evening dress who attacked him. He finally broke free and dashed through Pall Mall, into St. James's Park, and south into Birdcage Walk.

Walk up Duke Street to the south side of Piccadilly. You are now in front of Fortnum & Mason, with its green-trimmed, small-paned display windows. Fortnum & Mason is the grocery store of the Royal Family. It is world famous for its unusual wares, morning-coated assistants, restaurants, and the great clock above the front door, where, on the hour, the figures of Mr. Fortnum and Mr. Mason come out to the tune of the Eton Boating Song. The store was established in 1707 by Mason, an experienced grocer, and Fortnum, one of Queen Anne's footmen. Fortnum & Mason is an excellent spot for afternoon tea.

Fortnum & Mason often figures in mystery stories. The murdered Arnold Vereker in Georgette Heyer's *Death in the Stocks* was in the habit of arriving at his weekend cottage with a hamper from Fortnum & Mason, so that he and his lady friend would not be obliged to shop. In *Unnatural Death,* Sayers's Lord Peter Wimsey was able to detect that the ham in a sandwich left beside a dead girl in Epping Forest had come from a Fortnum & Mason pig.

In *The Judas Goat,* Robert Parker's Spenser eyed the gorgeous packaged foods in Fortnum & Mason's windows and thought what fun it would be to stroll there with Susan and buy some quail's eggs or a jellied game hen or something imported from the Khyber Pass. His thoughts remind you of the feasts enjoyed by the decadent Oxford youth in Evelyn Waugh's *Brideshead Revisited,* which was based on a quotation from G.K. Chesterton's Father Brown in the story "The Queer Feet."

In *Find Me a Villain,* as Margaret Yorke's wretched Nina Crowther went into the muted, fragrant bustle of the grocery department, the Fortnum & Mason clock began to strike. She went upstairs to the mezzanine restaurant, where she met Priscilla Blunt and got a job house-sitting. Yorke took poetic license with Fortnum & Mason, however, because the restaurant she described resembles the Soda Fountain on the ground floor. Archie Roylance, a comrade in arms of John Buchan's Richard Hannay, went to Fortnum & Mason to stock up on delicatessen food and liqueurs before leaving on a secret mission to Norway in *The Three Hostages.*

Just east of Fortnum & Mason, at No. 187, is the black and white facade of Hatchard's, with its three bow windows brimming with tempting books. Hatchard's, established in 1797, and Fortnum & Mason are the sole remaining representatives of a thriving eighteenth-century shopping area that once lined Piccadilly. In Georgette Heyer's *Regency Buck,* Judith Tavener marveled at the bookshop, with its bow windows filled with all the latest publications, and almost fancied that she saw the great Sir Walter Scott, poet and author of the Waverley novels, there. Today Hatchard's is about the best bookstore in London. You will find a wide selection of your favorite mystery stories and every other book under the sun, just as you would expect of the bookseller to the queen, the Duke of Edinburgh, the queen mother, and the Prince of Wales.

Continue along Piccadilly until you come to St. James's Church, one of the loveliest and, to Christopher Wren, the most practical of the churches he designed. It was horribly bombed during World War II, but the carvings by Grinling Gibbons were saved. St. James's is a popular spot for weddings and memorial services.

Leave St. James's Church and take Church Place to your right, around the church. Turn right again on Jermyn Street and walk the short distance to Duke of York Street. Turn right into Duke of York Street and make your way to St. James's Square. In Duke of York Street, you will pass another pub called the Red Lion (remember the one in Crown Passage). This is a small Victorian "gin palace" with some exceptional cut glass, as well as glossy mahogany.

Dating from 1673, St. James's was the West End's first square. It was built by Henry Jermyn on land presented to him by Charles II, but most of the buildings there now are of eighteenth-century or later vintage. The equestrian statue in the center of the square is of William III. A rather macabre touch is the inclusion in the monument of the molehill over which the king's horse stumbled at Hampton Court in 1702. Complications from the fall led to William's death.

As you turn right into the square, you pass Chatham House at No. 9-10; three prime ministers have lived there: William Pitt the Elder, Lord Derby, and William Ewart Gladstone, G.K. Chesterton's boyhood hero.

In the northwest corner of the square at No. 14 is the London Library, a venerable subscription library, which is open to members only. In *Funeral Sites,* Jessica Mann's fugitive, Rosamund Sholto, had been given a life membership when she was 21. She hid in the newspaper room, only to bump into her cousin, Harriet, who obligingly drove her away down the Mall in a Rolls Royce. Georgette Heyer was a member of the London Library and used its facilities extensively in her research. In *Regency Buck,* she placed the home of Peregrine Tavener's crony, Fitzjohn, in St. James's Square. The fictional 38 St. James's Square was the mansion of John Dickson Carr's wealthy Caroline Ross, who married Dick Derwent in Newgate Prison at the time of Waterloo in *The Bride of Newgate*. She and her "wedding" guests saw Napoleon's captured eagles brought to Lord Castlereagh's home at No. 8 after the battle. Bill Eversleigh, Lady Bundle's intended, parked his car in St. James's Square in Agatha Christie's *The Secret of Chimneys*. Sallet Square in Margery Allingham's *Black Plumes* may have been St. James's Square, too. (See Soho Walk.)

The most violent episode in St. James's Square occurred in 1984, when a policewoman was shot to death from No. 5, then occupied by the Libyan Peoples Bureau.

After you have circled the square and looked at the various houses, come back to the southwest corner, turn left, and walk to Pall Mall. Pall Mall is named for the seventeenth-century French version of croquet, *paille maille,* which was first played along a tree-lined avenue on the north side of Pall Mall.

Like St. James's Street, Pall Mall has a number of clubs. Cross Pall Mall, turn left, and walk toward Waterloo Place. At No. 71 is the Oxford and Cambridge Club, to which Sayers's surgeon, Sir Julian Freke, belonged in *Whose Body?* The Reform Club, home of Liberalism, and the Travellers, originally for those who had taken the Grand Tour, stand side by side in identical Italian palaces. Next door, at No. 107 at the corner of Waterloo Place, is the prestigious Athenaeum Club.

Built on the site of the Prince Regent's Carlton House (where Georgette Heyer's Judith Tavener was propositioned by the Regent himself and fainted dead away), the Athenaeum is a pale stucco building with a neoclassical look. Above its portico, there is a gilded statue of Pallas Athena. Inside, its first-floor drawing room is considered one of the grandest in London.

The Athenaeum has always been known for its distinguished members. It is favored by the hierarchy of the Anglican Church, as well as prominent men from the arts, literature, and science. Among these was Sir Humphrey Davy, about whom E.C. Bentley wrote his first schoolboy clerihew. Bentley's boyhood chum, G.K. Chesterton, was made a member in 1936. In Michael Innes's *From London Far,* the absentminded, quotation-loving scholar Meredith left the British Museum bound for the Athenaeum with a valuable manuscript under his arm. His intention was to spend a couple of hours doing some light reading in recent numbers of the *Journal of Classical Archaeology,* but he never reached his destination. Another absentminded fellow, Canon Pennyfather, had had an early dinner at the Athenaeum before he, too, disappeared in Agatha Christie's *At Bertram's Hotel.*

Turn right on Waterloo Place and walk over to take a look at the statue of the Duke of York, high up on a pink granite column. Frederick, the second son of George III, was the subject of the nursery song "The Grand Old Duke of York." (He "marched them up to the top of the hill and he marched them down again.") Nearby is the Crimean War Memorial and a statue of Florence Nightingale with her lamp. To the south and east is lovely Carlton House Terrace built on the site of Carlton House, the mansion of the Prince Regent. It was demolished in 1829, and its columns are now part of the facade of the National Gallery. In Agatha Christie's *The Secret Adversary,* Carlton House Terrace was the home of Sir James Peel Edgerton, whom Tuppence Cowley bravely bearded about the disappearance of Jane Finn and Tommy. It is also the site of London's only Nazi monument. At the corner, you can see the tombstone of the little dog, Giro, who belonged to Leopold von Hoesch, Hitler's ambassador before World War II. Giro was buried here in 1934.

Leave Carlton House Terrace, return to Waterloo Place, and turn right into the wide, pink-surfaced Mall, the royal processional road that leads to Buckingham Palace. The Mall was remodeled in 1910 as part of the monument to Queen Victoria.

As you walk along the Mall, St. James's Park is on your left. It is the oldest of London's royal parks. Like all of the city's royal parks, it was created by Henry VIII from land he had seized from Westminster Abbey. The views toward both Whitehall and Buckingham Palace from the center of the lake's modern bridge are quite romantic. Indeed, St. James's is famous for both its wonderful views and its bird sanctuary. (See

Westminster Walk.) In Jessica Mann's *Funeral Sites,* Rosamund Sholto was driven along the Mall by her eccentric cousin Harriet, only to jump out and quickly make tracks for Cambridge. Just before you get to the Queen Victoria Memorial, you will pass, on the right, three royal residences that are really part of the Palace of St. James.

The first is the Wren-designed Marlborough House, once the residence of the termagant Duchess of Marlborough and, later, of Queen Mary, widow of George V. It was for Queen Mary's birthday that Agatha Christie wrote a play for the BBC called *The Mousetrap,* which was then made into a West End drama. It has played there for the past thirty years and is still going strong. Marlborough House is now a Commonwealth Center. You can attend Sunday services in the Queen's Chapel, designed by Inigo Jones.

Beyond Marlborough House is Clarence House, where Queen Elizabeth lived when she was first married and where the queen mother lives today. If you go by on August 4, you may hear the bagpipes celebrating the birthday of the Scottish queen mother, who was born in Macbeth's Glamis Castle.

Lancaster House, the third royal residence, is beyond Clarence House and adjoins the Queen's Walk through Green Park. Built for the Grand Old Duke of York, it now is the scene of official banquets and meetings.

Buckingham Palace, at the end of the Mall, is the principal residence of the British Sovereign. Most of the building is early nineteenth century. The Royal Family's private apartments are in the north wing overlooking Green Park, while the State Apartments are on the first floor in the west wing. After the Opening of Parliament, the Trooping of the Colour, a Royal Wedding, or some other suitable occasion, the Royal Family comes out on the balcony over the main entrance to wave to the crowds in the Mall. The Palace itself is not open to the public, but the Queen's Gallery and the Royal Mews, which are within the grounds, may be visited. When the queen is in residence, the Royal Standard is flown. In *The Judas Goat,* Robert Parker's private eye, Spenser, went to Buckingham Palace to see the Changing of the Guard. "He stood outside and stared at the wide, bare, hard-paved courtyard. 'How you doing, Queen,' he murmured."

Daily, weather permitting, at 11:30 A.M., April through August, the Changing of the Guard is held in the forecourt of the Palace. (From September to March, the ceremony is held on alternate days.) There are five Guards regiments who take turns guarding the queen: the Grenadier, the Scots, the Welsh, the Irish, and the Coldstream Guards, all with distinctive uniform details. A.A. Milne described the ceremony in his poem "Buckingham Palace," which is about a nursery maid who was marrying one of the guards. Many people who can recite his poem are unaware that Milne also wrote a classic detective story, *The Red House Mystery,* which Julian Symons in *Mortal Consequences* called the most entertaining book of its kind written in the 1920s.

Patrick Grant drove his friend, visiting Greek police officer Manolakis, past Buckingham Palace in Margaret Yorke's *Cast for Death.*

In *A Splash of Red,* Antonia Fraser's Jemima Shore and her friend, Detective Chief Inspector "Pompey" Portsmouth, agree that "Buck House is the best alibi in the world." The current ruler of Ng'ombwana, the Boomer, a prep school friend of Roderick Alleyn, dined royally at Buckingham Palace, while Alleyn and the CID sweated out an assassination attempt in Ngaio Marsh's *Black as He's Painted.*

Now follow Spenser, who took the Broad Walk from the Queen Victoria Monument, across Green Park, toward Piccadilly. This will bring you once again to the Green Park Underground Station and the end of this walk.

8

MARYLEBONE/ REGENT'S PARK WALK

BACKGROUND

This walk takes you through Marylebone, where Sherlock Holmes once lived (at 221B Baker Street, as everyone knows, for the Post Office still gets letters asking for Holmes's help) and Regent's Park, which covers 475 acres. The first part of the walk explores Regency town-planning at its best and the remnants of the medieval village of Marylebone. The village was on the Tye Bourne, or Tyburn, River, which ran into the Thames.

When Holmes lived there, Marylebone had already been developed as a suburban garden in the city by the Adam brothers. Then John Nash made it part of his Royal Mile, which began at the Prince Regent's Palace at St. James's. The area, much of it laid out in handsome squares, has remained fashionable. It contains the best-known art collection in London, as well as "medical" Harley and Wimpole streets, which still are full of the doctors' brass plates that figure so often in detective fiction.

The other half of the walk introduces you to Regent's Park, originally known as Marylebone Park, the northernmost part of Henry VIII's great belt of hunting forest. The part Nash developed can be seen today in the magnificent circles and terraces, which share the park with the Gardens of the Zoological Society of London, affectionately known as the Zoo.

LENGTH OF WALK: 4.5 miles (not including walking in or through Regent's Park or the zoological gardens)

See maps on pages 144 and 158 for boundaries of the walk and page 257 for a list of the detectives and their stories covered.

PLACES OF INTEREST

221B Baker Street (or thereabouts).

Broadcasting House (BBC), Portland Place.

London Planetarium, Marylebone Road. Open daily, April–Sept., 11:00–6:00. Oct.–March, 11:00–4:30 P.M. Admission charge.

London Telecom Tower (Post Office Tower), Maple Street. No admission.

Madame Tussaud's, Marylebone Road. Open daily, 10:00–5:30 P.M. Admission charge.

Regent's Park:

> *London Zoo.* Open daily, summer, 9:00–6:00; winter, 10:00–6:00 P.M. Admission charge.
> *Queen Mary's Gardens.*
> *Open Air Theatre.* Open July–Aug. Shakespeare and others.

Wallace Collection, Manchester Square. Open Mon.–Sat., 10:00–5:00; Sun., 2:00–5:00 P.M.

PLACES TO EAT

Prince Regent, 71 Marylebone High Street. Pub with mementos, cartoons of "Prinny," the Prince Regent. Cheese dishes, English grill steaks and chops. 01-935-2018. Closed Sat. and Sun.

Bertorelli Bros, 19 Charlotte Street. Italian restaurant dating from the 1920s. Open to 10:00 P.M. 01-636-4174. Closed Sun.

Madame Tussaud's, Marylebone Road. Cafeteria.

Regent's Park:

> *The Rose Garden Buffet,* Queen Mary's Gardens. Self-service English food outdoors when the weather is good. Open to 4:00 P.M. in winter, 11:00 P.M. in summer.
>
> *The Zoo,* Regent Restaurant on first floor; Regent Cafeteria on ground level. Both restaurants are licensed and serve lunch and tea. In addition, in the Zoo grounds there are the Pavilion Bar, Mappin Café, and Garden Café, all serving nonalcoholic light refreshments.

——MARYLEBONE/REGENT'S PARK—— WALK

MARYLEBONE

Begin this walk by taking the Oxford Street exit from the Marble Arch Underground Station. This is the tube station at which H.R.F. Keating's Inspector Ghote of Bombay, in London for the first time in his life, happily observed typical British behavior. In *Inspector Ghote Hunts the Peacock,* Ghote was in London to attend a conference on drugs and took the underground to his meeting in the City. The tube was crowded, but the people were very orderly, ignoring each other with magnificent calm. (Ghote eventually discovered that the British were not really supermen and that all London sights were not perfect.)

There are many detective story locales in the hinterland of Marylebone/Regent's Park. They are too far away to cover in this walk, but worth remembering now. To your right and northwest is the Edgware Road, the old Roman Watling Street. In G.K. Chesterton's *The Man Who Was Thursday,* the gigantic anarchist leader Sunday abandoned his taxi on the Edgware Road when traffic was stopped by a fire engine. He sprang at the fire engine, threw himself onto it, and rode off, talking to the astonished firemen.

REGENT'S PARK

MARYLEBONE

Farther north, Edgware Road becomes Maida Vale (not shown on map). Baroness Orczy's Lady Molly of Scotland Yard and her friend Mary Granard lived in a little flat in Maida Vale while Lady Molly tried to clear the name of her imprisoned husband. Christianna Brand originally set the scene of *Fog of Doubt* at Kensington Gore, south of Hyde Park. Then, because another author had used the same title, she moved her locale to Maida Vale and called her mystery *London Particular* (the Dickensian name for a real pea-souper). In America the book was entitled *Fog of Doubt*.

West of the Edgware Road is Paddington Station, and north of the station is a boat stop on the Grand Union Canal called Little Venice. In P.D. James's *Innocent Blood,* young Philippa Palfrey helped her ex-con mother toss all her prison belongings into the Grand Union Canal. Janet Reed (a.k.a. Edith Daybrook), Dorothy L. Sayers's playwright alter ego in the play *Love All,* has a London flat on the Grand Union Canal, aping the apartment on Venice's Grand Canal occupied by Reed's runaway husband, Godfrey Daybrook, and his mistress. In *Death of a Ghost,* Margery Allingham's artist, John Sebastian Lafcadio, R.A., had his home-cum-studio at Little Venice. After his death, his widow held a yearly private showing of a new painting of his until a murder was committed.

Just east of the Edgware Road is the area where Simon Brett located his WET (West End Television). Its studios were on fictitious Lisson Street, off Marylebone Street, not too far from the supposed Paddington Jewish Boys Club. There, middle-aged actor Charles Paris rehearsed for his role as bartender in a sitcom called "The Strutters." According to Paris in Brett's *Not Dead, Only Resting,* the trendiest unemployment office for actors is in Chadwick Street near Westminster Abbey, but he went to the one in Lisson Grove, which was a brisk half-hour walk from his bed-sitter farther west in Bayswater.

The TV studios where Charles Paris worked may have been near the Regent Studios "somewhere in Marylebone," where Keating's Inspector Ghote reluctantly interviewed the pop singer Johnny Bull. The fictitious Tagore House on Hyde Park Terrace, where Inspector Ghote stayed, must have been just past the Edgware Road, near Hyde Park Square and Hyde Park Crescent. This was also the neighborhood of the fictitious 12 Delaney Street, a cul-de-sac off Lisson Grove, where P.D. James's Philippa Palfrey and her mother rented a cheap flat over a greengrocer's.

Now turn left and walk along the north side of Oxford Street. This is a major London shopping street, always crowded with people, especially during the Christmas season, when it reminds you of the unpleasant murderer who hated being shoved, in Marian Babson's *The Twelve Deaths of Christmas*. It is a favorite shopping location in H.R.F. Keating's mysteries, too. Writing as Evelyn Hervey in *The Man of Gold,* Keating's redoubtable governess, Miss Unwin, took a cab to the largest bookstore on Oxford Street to purchase *Potherton on Poisons*. Somewhere here, too, was the seconds china shop to which Inspector Ghote was sent by a snooty clerk when he could not afford a genuine English teapot for his wife.

Cross Old Quebec Street, staying on Oxford Street, and walk to Portman Street; then continue one more block to Orchard Street. Selfridges, the largest London department store, occupies the block on Oxford Street between Orchard and Duke streets. Selfridges was founded by Chicagoan Gordon Selfridge in 1908. It is famous for its lavish decorations at Christmas, as well as other national holidays. In Dorothy Sayers's *The Unpleasantness at the Bellona Club,* artist Marjorie Phelps gave Lord Peter Wimsey a small statue of himself in Sherlockian dressing gown with book on knee. Thanking her, Lord Peter inquired if he would find copies of it on sale at Selfridges.

Turn left on Orchard Street and walk north three short blocks to Portman Square. Laid out in the late 1800s, it has a number of elegant hotels, a green garden forbidden to all but tiny dogs, and a few of its original, elegant town residences. It seems to be a likely spot for the townhouse of the Dowager Duchess of Denver, where Lord Peter Wimsey and Harriet Vane's wedding reception was held in *Busman's Honeymoon*. (They escaped the reporters by taking a cab to meet Bunter, parked on the far side of Regent's Park.) In Sayers's *Whose*

Body? the uncle of murdered Sir Reuben Levy lived in Portman Square, as did old Lady Dormer, with her companion, Ann Dorland, in *The Unpleasantness at the Bellona Club.* Lady Dormer's elderly brother, General Fentiman, came here to call on her for the first time in years. Septimus Crottle, who was kidnapped in A.E.W. Mason's *The House in Lordship Lane,* lived at 41A Portman Square.

No. 20, on the northwest corner, is a house built by Robert Adam, with handsome marble fireplaces, inlaid floors, and a circular staircase covered by a domed skylight. It was built for the rich ancestress of Prime Minister Sir Alec Douglas-Home (Lord Home) and restored by Samuel Courtauld, a notable art collector. Courtauld left the house and his collection of fabulous Impressionist and Post-Impressionist paintings, including the collection of Bloomsbury's Roger Fry, to the University of London. The collection is housed in the Courtauld Institute Gallery in Woburn Square. (See Bloomsbury Walk.)

North of Portman Square is narrow Montagu Square. Antonia Fraser's Jemima Shore was offered a spare flat there by developer Sir Richard Lionnel when the police moved her out of his Adelaide Square flat in *A Splash of Red.* In Wilkie Collins's *The Moonstone,* Lady Verinder's townhouse was in Montagu Square.

Walk along Portman Square's east side to the northeast corner and turn right on Fitzharding Street. Keep walking east to Manchester Square. On the north side of the square, you will see Hertford House, a large, reddish mansion, which is the home of the world-famous Wallace Collection. In *The Secret of Chimneys,* in fact, Agatha Christie allowed her gentleman adventurer, Anthony Cade, to joke about it. Cade was talking with a friend who had rescued the old prime minister of Herzoslovakia from muggers in Paris. Cade asked his friend if the prime minister had told him any state secrets. The friend replied that the prime minister said he knew where the Koh-i-noor—one of the British Crown jewels—was kept. Cade replied, "We all know that, they keep it in the tower. . . . Did Stylptitch say . . . he knew which city the Wallace Collection was in?" (See City Walk.)

Hertford House's owners have long been known as art lovers. Thackeray used one Marquis of Hertford, who liked Dutch paintings, as a model for his libertine Marquis of Steyne in *Vanity Fair*. The real marquis's son liked French art, while his illegitimate grandson, Sir Richard Wallace, collected medieval and Renaissance armor and art. Their entire accumulation and house were given to the nation by Sir Richard's widow. This is a "frozen collection," never added to, whose most famous painting is Frans Hals's *Laughing Cavalier*. There are also several paintings by Sherlock Holmes's great-uncle, Emile Vernet. The Greuze painting called *Innocence* may be the original of a Professor Moriarty forgery from the case of "The Valley of Fear."

Go left past Hertford House to the northeast corner of Manchester Square; then turn right to reach Hinde Street. You will be going past a number of other eighteenth-century houses, most of which are offices today. Turn left and walk along Hinde Street to Thayer Street. At this point, Hinde Street becomes Bentinck Street. Continue walking along Bentinck Street. At No. 7, Edward Gibbon completed the first part of his monumental *Decline and Fall of the Roman Empire,* in which he solved the mystery of why the Roman Empire became Christian. (The British-born Emperor Constantine ordered all his troops to be baptized at one fell swoop. Dorothy L. Sayers wrote a lengthy, pageant-like play, *The Emperor Constantine,* about him for a festival at Colchester.)

Next, cross the southern end of Marylebone High Street, here called Marylebone Lane. Once a winding village lane, it is now a shopping area with good restaurants, pubs, and smart shops. The area around the high street is still full of tiny streets and alleys. There once was a pleasure garden here, like Vauxhall or Ranelagh, which became a haunt of vice and later was swamped by the city's northern development. This must have been the site of the Fields of Eden mentioned in the mysterious kidnap note in John Buchan's *The Three Hostages*. With this faint clue, Richard Hannay and Archie Roylance investigated a Marylebone mews behind an old furniture storage building.

They went into a little bakery that proved to be the back of a swinging 1920s nightclub, where they found and freed one hostage.

Keep walking east on Bentinck Street to Welbeck Street. This is the intersection in which Sherlock Holmes was nearly killed by a runaway van in "The Final Problem." Somewhere on Welbeck was the doctor's office in *Forfeit* to which Dick Francis's reporter, James Tyrone, managed to drive his polio-stricken wife in her special van, even though he had been heavily drugged.

Turn left and walk north up Welbeck Street, where Anthony Trollope died at No. 33 in 1882, to Queen Anne Street; then turn right and walk along until you reach Wimpole Street. In the case of "The Adventure of the Illustrious Client," Dr. Watson had his surgery offices at 9 Queen Anne Street, and James Boswell worked on his *Life of Samuel Johnson* here in 1791. H.C. Bailey's Reggie Fortune, the police department doctor, lived on New Cavendish Street, which crosses Wimpole Street.

You are now in the heartland of the medical profession. Wimpole Street, of course, is also famous because the invalid poet Elizabeth Barrett lived at No. 50 with her tyrannical father. She eloped from here with the poet Robert Browning. G.K. Chesterton was a great admirer of both Brownings, and his first biography, written in the British Museum's famous Reading Room, was *Robert Browning*.

Wilkie Collins spent the last months of his life at 82 Wimpole Street, dying there in 1889. Wimpole Street was also where, in Buchan's *The Three Hostages*, the disguised German Dr. Newhover, who was working hand in glove with the master criminal, Medina, had his office. Richard Hannay found Newhover's office in "one of those solid, dreary erections which have the names of half a dozen doctors on their front doors . . . with a drab waiting room furnished with Royal Academy engravings, fumed oak, and an assortment of belated picture-papers."

Continue walking along Queen Anne Street to the next

street, which is Harley Street, certainly the high street of the medical profession. In Agatha Christie's *At Bertram's Hotel,* Lady Selina Hazy, one of the old ladies who gave the hotel lobby that true "olde English" atmosphere, had gone "to Harley Street to see that man about my arthritis." He had wrung her neck for her, and it was much improved.

Harley Street originally was a very fashionable street. Henry James's young governess in *The Turn of the Screw* came up from the country to answer an ad at a Harley Street address. There, in his big house filled with the "spoils of travel and the trophies of the chase," she met her employer, a handsome bachelor in the prime of life, who bewitched her into taking charge of his weird wards, Miles and Flora.

In Dorothy L. Sayers's *The Unpleasantness at the Bellona Club,* young Dr. Penberthy had his office in Harley Street. This made it easy for old General Fentiman to come and see him when he was taken ill at his sister's house in Portman Square. Ngaio Marsh's society doctor, Sir Daniel Davidson, had his offices at 50 St. Luke's Chambers, Harley Street. Here, in *Death in a White Tie,* Inspector Alleyn found a very luxurious office with an Adam fireplace and handsome gifts from grateful patients.

In Sayers's *Whose Body?* neurologist Sir Julian Freke, who treated Lord Peter Wimsey about his nerves, had an office at 282 Harley Street. Agatha Christie's diffident peer, Lord Caterham, was told by his high-priced Harley Street doctor to avoid all worry, but he found that impossible when Foreign Office official George Lomax had diplomatic schemes afoot. P.D. James also described an old-fashioned but very shrewd Harley Street practitioner, Dr. Crantley-Mathers, in *The Skull Beneath the Skin.* He did not allow Ivo Whittingham to force him to pronounce an unpleasant diagnosis. Agatha Christie herself went to a psychiatrist on Harley Street after her sensational disappearance and memory loss in 1926, when her marriage to Archie Christie was breaking up.

After gazing at the many brass plates with doctors' names, turn right on Harley Street and walk south into Cavendish Square. Dating from the early eighteenth century, this square began the suburban development of the old village of Marylebone. On the north side, there are two Palladian buildings with columned facades, which were part of a great mansion begun by the Duke of Chandos. An archway connecting these two has an Epstein Madonna. To the south, Lord Byron lived at No. 21, now a department store. In *The Unpleasantness at the Bellona Club,* Lady Dormer's elderly brother, General Fentiman, hailed his war-scarred grandson, George, in Cavendish Square and took him for a taxi ride through Regent's Park, lecturing him on being kinder to his working wife.

In the Regency whodunit, *Regency Buck,* Georgette Heyer's Corinthian buck, Lord Worth, had his townhouse in Cavendish Square. It was a great, stucco-fronted house with an imposing portico, at which the young Taveners arrived uninvited. The most likely-looking mansion is the cream-colored house at the northeast corner of Cavendish Place and Chandos Street. In that mystery, the Four-Horse Club, a select gathering of all the best whips, met the first and third Thursdays in May and June in Cavendish Square and drove in yellow-bodied barouches to Salt Hill at a strict trot. In *The Man in the Queue* Josephine Tey's Miss Dinmont, the nice Scottish girl who befriended a fugitive and then came to London to help him, stayed at her club in Cavendish Square.

Now take Chandos Street north, passing by Chandos House, a beautiful example of Robert Adam's best work, and walk to Portland Place. Turn right on Portland Place and walk east to Langham Place. At the corner of Portland Place and Queen Anne Mews, you will pass by the Langham Hotel. It was once a very exclusive Victorian hotel, where the King of Bohemia stayed in the Sherlock Holmes case, "A Scandal in Bohemia." It now has offices of the BBC and the BBC Club Bar, where Simon Brett's Charles Paris found actor Martin Sabine in *Not Dead, Only Resting.*

Langham Place runs into Portland Place, the widest roadway in London. John Buchan lived at 76 Portland Place when he wrote *The Thirty-Nine Steps* in 1914, as did the novel's protagonist, Richard Hannay. The roadway was designed by the Adam brothers to be a kind of parkway surrounded by the mansions of the wealthy, but it was changed by Nash's sweeping drive north with Regent Street, which he ended at Langham Place with the famous All Souls Church. It has a circular, columned porch and a conical church spire; inside, it is all gold and cream. Today both the church and Langham Place are dominated by their taller, heavier neighbors, especially the 1930s skyscraper Broadcasting House, where BBC radio shows are still produced. (The TV studios are out west, in Shepherd's Bush.) The BBC's massive front has a sculpture of Prospero and Ariel by Eric Gill, the Distributist friend of G.K. Chesterton.

Chesterton was one of the BBC's first successes. He debated G.B. Shaw in an early broadcast and then had his own weekly show reviewing books. During the 1930s, Detection Club members Agatha Christie, Dorothy L. Sayers, Hugh Walpole, E.C. Bentley, Anthony Berkeley, Clemence Dane, Ronald Knox, and Freeman Wills Crofts collaborated on two radio serials for the BBC, "Behind the Screen" and "The Scoop." Like their collaborative mysteries, *The Floating Admiral* and *Crime on the Coast*, these stories were recently reissued by long-time mystery publisher Victor Gollancz. Sayers was in charge of "The Scoop" and wrote to Agatha Christie that the BBC producer didn't seem to want a detective story but a "simple love-tale or something." Christie did her part of this broadcast from Devon.

It was the BBC that George Orwell was caricaturing in his grim *1984,* a futuristic date used by G.K. Chesterton in *The Napoleon of Notting Hill,* written in 1904. The BBC is probably also the model for Megalithic House, where Antonia Fraser's Jemima Shore did her TV show in *Quiet as a Nun.* A number of other mystery writers, like Simon Brett, have worked at the BBC.

Walk up Portland Place to Cavendish Street, cross Portland Place, and go east on Cavendish Street to Great Portland Street. This area is known for car dealers, so it was logical that Sayers's George Fentiman in *The Unpleasantness at the Bellona Club* was taken on as a car salesman in Great Portland Street. As her mysteries show, Sayers herself was "into" motorcycles and cars. She had a love affair with a car mechanic, and later she married war veteran Atherton Fleming, who wrote advertising copy for Daimler.

As you walk up Great Portland Street, pause at Clipstone Street and look to your right, where you will see the towering presence of the London Telecom Tower, usually called the Post Office Tower. At 620 feet, this is the tallest structure in London, built to make it easier to send telecommunications without interference from other high buildings. Its entrance is east on Maple Street, and it had a revolving restaurant at its top, which is now closed indefinitely because of terrorists' threats. This fact makes it the more ironic that in *The Judas Goat* Robert B. Parker's American private eye, Spenser, in London to chase a terrorist group called Liberty, was very fond of the Post Office restaurant and described it in great detail.

East of Great Portland Street is the western edge of Bloomsbury, around the Tottenham Court Road. So, in addition to the small cafés and pubs about Great Portland Street that cater to the BBC, there are many restaurants to be found in this vicinity. One of these is Bertorelli Bros Italian restaurant, at 19 Charlotte Street, which dates from the 1920s.

The next street you come to on your right is Carburton Street, down which Spenser trailed his female "judas goat." The girl's apartment was farther east on Tottenham Court Road, diagonally across from University College Hospital, where Agatha Christie dispensed drugs as a volunteer during World War II. (See Bloomsbury Walk.)

Keep walking north on Great Portland Street to Devonshire Street. Turn left on Devonshire and walk back to Portland Place; then turn right, taking Portland Place north into Park Crescent. Park Crescent is a perfect semicircle of gleaming buildings with Ionic colonnades, designed by the Regent's architect Nash to provide a formal approach to the Regent's Park. It was restored after being badly bombed in World War II. Most of the buildings now are used as offices.

Directly north is Park Square, with Holy Trinity Church, which was built by Sir John Soane. Penguin Books began in 1935 in Holy Trinity's crypt. In 1985, Penguin Books celebrated its 50th birthday anniversary. All mystery readers owe Allen Lane a great vote of thanks for making available in green and white paperbacks the detective stories by our favorite authors. You are now at the Regent's Park Underground Station, where you can use the facilities, end the walk, or decide to continue walking to Baker Street and into Regent's Park.

If you want to continue this walk, go halfway around Park Crescent to your left until you reach Marylebone Road. This street was built in the mid-1800s to connect Paddington and Islington with the north of London. Walk westward along Marylebone Road. At this corner, there is a 1965 bust of President John F. Kennedy in front of the International Students' House. Continue walking, passing Park Crescent Mews, Harley Street, and Devonshire Place, until you reach Marylebone High Street, the beginning of the old medieval village.

On the far corner across Marylebone High Street, there used to be a house in which Charles Dickens lived while he wrote *The Old Curiosity Shop, Martin Chuzzlewit, David Copperfield, A Christmas Carol,* and *Dombey and Son;* and on the wall of Ferguson House there is a carved sculpture of characters from these Dickens novels. Young Dr. Arthur Conan Doyle used to walk from Montague Place in Bloomsbury, to his oculist's consulting room in Devonshire Place, where he waited from 10 until 4 o'clock for patients. If none came, he used the time to write. (See Bloomsbury Walk.)

Somewhere in this vicinity was the Marylebone Police Court, where Edgar Wallace's heroine, Thalia Drummond, was sentenced for stealing in *The Crimson Circle.* Thalia also "appeared" to live on Marylebone Road in a luxurious flat with a lady's maid to wait upon her.

In *Jemima Shore Investigates,* the Prideaux brothers also had a flat in a large Edwardian mansion block near Marylebone Road. When Jemima Shore visited them to find out why they had tried to murder the Duchess of Montford, she decided that these mansions were on their way up in the world again but that the Prideaux brothers were probably going down. (Like her creator, Antonia Fraser, Jemima Shore is very sensitive to London's architecture.)

On Marylebone Road, just opposite the formal entrance into Regent's Park at York Gate, is St. Marylebone Parish Church, where Elizabeth Barrett and Robert Browning were secretly married in 1846. There is a stained-glass window dedicated to the Brownings in the north aisle. Charles Dickens also had Paul Dombey christened here in *Dombey and Son*. Somewhere near here, in Julian Symons's *A Three Pipe Problem*, Sheridan Haynes, who acted the role of Sherlock Holmes on TV, met with his Baker Street Irregulars (a group of traffic wardens) at a fictional pub called the Bear and Staff. To substitute the Prince Regent pub at 71 Marylebone High Street, turn to your left at York Terrace.

Keep walking along Marylebone Road past Oldbury Place, Nottingham Place, and Bingham Place to Luxborough Street. These are all short blocks, filled with modern buildings mixed with occasional Georgian houses. Cross Luxborough Street and then Marylebone Street to reach the London Planetarium. It has a huge dome on which it projects the heavens above.

The Planetarium is next door to the world-famous Madame Tussaud's Exhibition of Waxworks, bedecked with flags and, typically, a long line waiting to get in. This is one museum you must see as a detective story reader, for it has a number of exhibits related to murder and mystery.

Madame Tussaud was a real person. She was employed at the Court of Louis XVI to make wax figures, but was imprisoned during the French Revolution, when she made wax models of the heads of guillotine victims. In her little bonnet and steel-rimmed spectacles (see her waxwork figure), Madame Tussaud finally escaped to London in 1802, bringing her wax heads with her. She opened her shop in the Strand, but moved to Baker Street in 1835. After a fire in 1884, the waxworks was moved to its present site on Marylebone Road, just east of Baker Street.

The life-size figures of famous persons, living and dead, are made of wax but wear real clothes. There is a real guillotine, a Chamber of Horrors, which the guidebooks recommend *not taking children* to see, and an East End Victorian street on which Jack the Ripper can be stalked. (The best-known detective story account of his murders is Marie Belloc-Lowndes's *The Lodger.* Mme. Belloc-Lowndes was the sister of G.K. Chesterton's friend Hilaire Belloc. (See Inns of Court/Fleet Street Walk.)

At one time, the wax figure of Sherlock Holmes's creator, Sir Arthur Conan Doyle, was on display, but now the only mystery writer so honored is the late Dame Agatha Christie. She knew Madame Tussaud's well, for in *At Bertram's Hotel,* Christie's Miss Marple rather shamefacedly chose to revisit Madame Tussaud's on her nostalgic visit to London. There is a wax model of Conan Doyle's Sherlock Holmes, but most viewers find it somewhat inferior to the one in the case of "The Mazarin Stone." Madame Tussaud's museum also may remind you of the smaller, private museum at Tether's End, whose wax figurines are used to commit a crime in Margery Allingham's story. There are restrooms and a cafeteria in Madame Tussaud's, if you want to stop for lunch or a cup of tea.

Walk past Madame Tussaud's, turn to your right, and cross Chiltern Street to reach the real hub of this neighborhood: Baker Street, where Sherlock Holmes lived at No. 221B. You will pass the Baker Street Underground Station, the original terminus of the Bakerloo Railway, which opened in 1906. The station itself has been grandly redecorated with large ceramic tile pictures from seven of Sherlock Holmes's most famous cases. On one level of the station, there is a Moriarty's Pub for Baker Street Irregulars. (Several Baker Street pubs and hotels have Sherlockian names, but most of them do not even date from his time.)

Sexton Blake once lived in Baker Street with his housekeeper, Mrs. Bardell; dog, Pedro; and assistant, Tinker. Somewhere near Baker Street in fictional Montague Mansions lived Patricia Wentworth's intrepid old tabby, Miss Silver. Also nearby was the boardinghouse run by Maude Daneson in Babson's *The Twelve Deaths of Christmas,* where the killer rented a room.

Today Baker Street is a major traffic route from the north, with only a few of the shops and buildings of Holmes's day left. Nostalgia for the good old days is one reason why modern traffic and its wardens are a vital clue in Julian Symons's *A Three Pipe Problem.* TV actor Sheridan Haynes lived in a flat on Baker Street that was furnished with the museum room created for the 1951 Festival of Britain (at Sherlock Holmes, 10 Northumberland Street. See Westminster Walk.)

Haynes, an ardent Holmes buff who played at detecting, preferred the foggy London of Holmes without the noisy motor traffic. When a rare fog hit London (the Clean Air Acts have cut down on the pea-soupers), Haynes found it a pleasure to have Baker Street transformed into soft yellow gaslight, with people crowding the pavements even though the fog made the traffic jam worse than ever.

Turn right at Baker Street and walk north. The present day building with the number 221 is a building society that has to hire a regular staff person to act as Sherlock Holmes's secretary, answering the many requests for his help or his autograph. In the late nineteenth century, you would have had to turn left at Baker Street and walk south past Porter Street to Paddington Street, for Baker Street did not go north of Paddington Street then. The probable "real" address of 221B Baker Street would be between Paddington Street and Blandford Street, at No. 34. But that building is not from the Holmesian period, so it is better to imagine No. 221B on Baker Street, seeing in your mind's eye his sitting room with the violin, the syringe, and Holmes and Watson, waiting for adventure to knock at their door.

You have now finished the Marylebone part of this walk and can return to the Baker Street Underground Station.

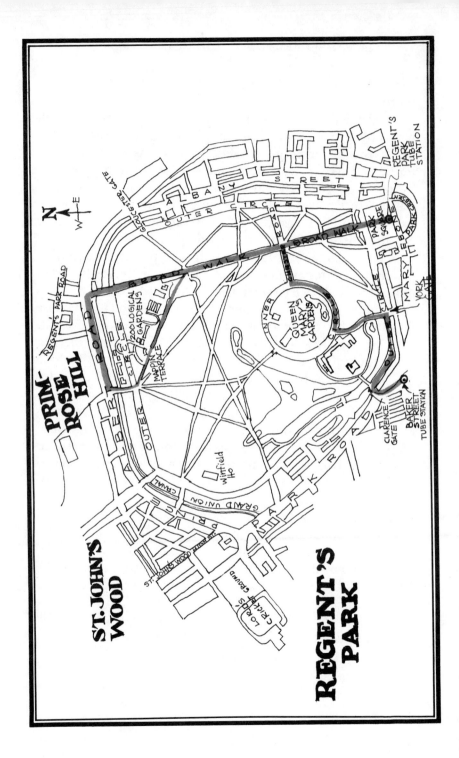

REGENT'S PARK

This walk is related to and adjoins the Marylebone Walk. You may begin it by continuing on after the Marylebone Walk or by arriving at the Baker Street Underground Station. Come out on Baker Street. Turn to your right and take Baker Street north to Park Road. To your left, northwest of Regent's Park, lies St. John's Wood, a wooded and hilly part of "suburban" London, where artists and writers have lived since the time of E.C. Bentley's *Trent's Last Case*.

Lord's Cricket Ground is on St. John's Wood Road. Dorothy L. Sayers's Harriet Vane went to see the Eton-Harrow Match with Lord Peter Wimsey and met his old friend Freddy Arbuthnot, as she remembered later in *Gaudy Night*. St. John's Wood was familiar territory to Sayers, for her Somerville College friends, Muriel St. Clare Byrne and Marjorie Barber, lived at 28 St. John's Wood Terrace. A portrait of Barber painted by Sayers's husband, Atherton Fleming, hung in their dining room. Byrne and Sayers wrote the play *Busman's Honeymoon* together, and it is possible that Marjorie Barber helped Sayers write the play *Love All*.

Agatha and Archie Christie had their first flat at 5 Northwick Terrace, St. John's Wood, and 5 Albany Street was the home of Michael Gilbert's arrogant Superintendent Charles Knott, who was in charge of the investigation into the murder in *The Killing of Katie Steelstock*. In *The Root of All Evil*, E.X. Ferrars's amateur sleuth, the widowed and retired professor, Andrew Basnett, also lived there. Like Ferrars's real-life husband, Basnett seldom bothered to wear shoes. Bertram Hamstone, who was involved with the claimants, lived in St. John's Wood in Patricia Moyes's *Who Is Simon Warwick?*

Cross Park Road to your right to reach Clarence Gate and go into the Park itself. Turn right on the Outer Circle, built as a carriage drive and lined with a spectacular row of Georgian houses, many of which are government offices. The Outer Circle goes around Regent's Park to the other Nash terraces to the east.

It was at 35 Outer Circle that Nicholas Blake's Nigel Strangeways came to interview Alice Lake, the wife of Ministry of Morale Director Jimmy Lake in *Minute for Murder*. These houses have been beautifully restored, but in Blake's story, which took place just after World War II, Strangeways found the house on the curve of the "noble crescent. . . . Stucco discoloured and peeling, the magnificent row of houses was gapped in two places, where bombs had fallen, but its grandeur had not departed from the place." It was probably on the Outer Circle that Dorothy Sayers's old General Fentiman, later found dead in his armchair at the Bellona Club, was driven with his nephew, George Fentiman, around Regent's Park, for George Fentiman got out at Gloucester Gate to go home to Finsbury.

When you reach York Gate, turn left and walk north to the Inner Circle, just to the east of the lake filled by the Tyburn, which surrounds Queen Mary's Gardens, with its outdoor restaurant and Open Air Theatre. In P.D. James's *Innocent Blood*, Philippa Palfrey and her mother came to spend a quiet Sunday afternoon among the roses, only to meet the man who was tracking them face to face. The killer in Marian Babson's *The Twelve Deaths of Christmas* found a young punk lying drunk in the Rose Garden and cut his throat because "blood makes an excellent fertilizer for roses." Circle to your right to reach Chester Road and then go left to take the Broad Walk north to the "Zoo."

The Gardens of the Zoological Society were begun in 1828 by the Zoological Society of London. One of the founders was Sir Humphrey Davy, about whom E.C. Bentley wrote his first schoolboy clerihew. Today the zoo has the finest and most representative collection of animals in the world. Its newest feature is the Lion Terraces, completed in 1976. They were not finished in 1968, when Dick Francis's sportswriter, James Tyrone, in *Forfeit* was picked up by some racecourse crooks and driven to Regent's Park Zoo to meet the boss at the lions' cages. Tyrone later was driven back into Regent's Park by the same crooks but managed to make them crash their limousine in the Regent's Canal.

The zoo's Mappin Terraces are a reinforced concrete amphitheater in which bears and other animals wander freely without bars. In *A Splash of Red,* Antonia Fraser's Jemima Shore commented unfavorably on the Lionnel building in Adelaide Square, Bloomsbury, saying that it resembled the Mappin Terraces at the zoo.

Robert B. Parker's Spenser followed his potential "judas goat" to Regent's Park. He then checked out the entire zoo to be certain he could not be jumped unexpectedly. He went past the cranes, geese, and owls at the north gate entrance and, using the tunnel by the insect house, came out by the restaurant and a cafeteria with flamingos in a grass park. The next day, Spenser returned by the south gate near Wolf Wood and sat in the zoo cafeteria, watching a gang member try to locate him. Finally, he followed a girl gang member around the northern edge of the Park on Prince Albert Road, along Albany Street, and across Marylebone Road to her flat on Carburton Street.

It was this route that was taken in reverse by G.K. Chesterton's Sunday. In *The Man Who Was Thursday,* Sunday jumped off the fire engine and climbed a high railing to vanish into the zoo. He then reappeared riding an elephant down Albany Street on his way to Hyde Park and the Albert Memorial. (See Brompton/Hyde Park Walk.)

To the north of Regent's Park lies Primrose Hill, which is over 200 feet high. On a clear day, Primrose Hill gives you a view south across London, into Kent and Surrey. In "The Woman in the Big Hat," Baroness Orczy's female sleuth, Lady Molly, was told that Elizabeth Lowenthal was out taking a brisk walk on Primrose Hill when Mark Culledon was murdered, which gave her an alibi of sorts.

To end the walk, you have to walk back south through Regent's Park on the Broad Walk to the Regent's Park Underground Station in Park Square.

9

WESTMINSTER
WALK

BACKGROUND

This walk takes place in the city of Westminster, originally a village west of London on the Thames River. Since the eleventh century, kings have been crowned and buried in Westminster Abbey and have governed from Westminster's royal palaces. For the mystery lover, however, Westminster's chief interest is that it is the home of Scotland Yard, the nerve center of crime, where most detective stories begin or end. On this walk, we pass Old Scotland Yard, then New Scotland Yard, and finally the "newest" New Scotland Yard, located on 10 Broadway since 1967. The walk covers three distinct localities: Whitehall, the seat of the Crown, or executive government; Westminster, the home of Parliamentary, or legislative, power; and Victoria, the neighborhood behind Victoria Station, which includes St. James's Park.

LENGTH OF WALK: **3.3 miles**

See map on page 164 for the boundaries of this walk and page 262 for a list of the detectives and their stories covered.

PLACES OF INTEREST

Trafalgar Square.

Whitehall Banqueting House. Tues.–Sat., 10:00–5:00; Sun., 2:00–5:00 P.M. Admission charge.

Changing of the Guard, Horse Guards. Weekdays, 11:00 A.M.; Sun., 10:00 A.M.

No. 10 Downing Street.

The Cenotaph.

New Scotland Yard, Norman Shaw Building.

New Scotland Yard, 10 Broadway.

St. James's Park.

Big Ben, the Clock Tower.

Westminster Bridge.

Westminster Abbey. Open daily, 8:00–6:00; Wed., 8:00–8:00 P.M. Admission charge for Royal Chapels, Poets' Corner.

Westminster Cathedral, Ashley Place. Open daily, 10:30 to dusk. Admission charge for lift in campanile.

St. Margaret's Church, Westminster.

Houses of Parliament. Queue at St. Stephen's Porch or contact an M.P.

Jewel Tower. Weekdays, Mar. 15–Oct. 15, 9:30–6:30 P.M.

PLACES TO EAT

Sherlock Holmes, 10 Northumberland St. Pub food. Reservations needed for restaurant. 01-930-2644. Open Mon.–Sat., to 9:15 P.M.

St. Stephen's Tavern, 10 Bridge Street. Victorian restaurant with a view of the Thames. Traditional English food. Reservations needed. 01-930-2541. Open to 9:00 P.M., closed Sundays.

The Albert, 52 Victoria Street. Victorian pub with carvery restaurant upstairs.

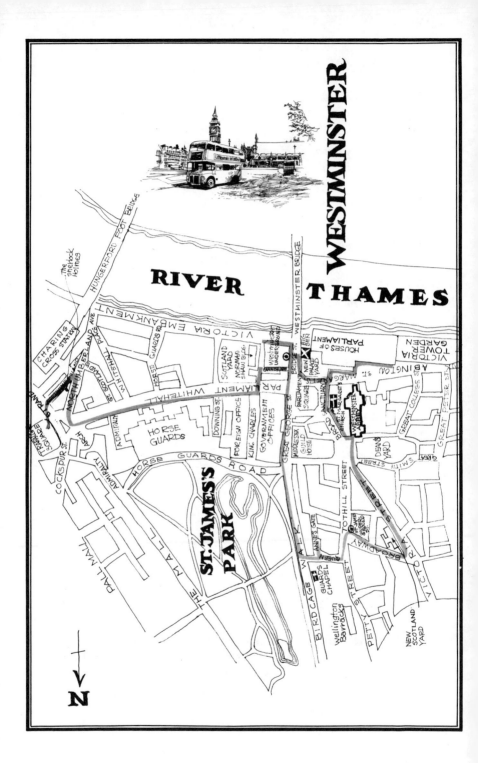

RIVER THAMES

WESTMINSTER

ST. JAMES'S PARK

N

—————————— WESTMINSTER WALK ——————————

Take the Trafalgar Square exit from the Charing Cross Underground Station. This will bring you out into Trafalgar Square, London's most dramatic open place, whose north side is the columned National Gallery. To the west lies Canada House; to the east, South Africa House; and to the south, Whitehall, with the equestrian statue of Charles I, from which all distances in London are measured. Designed by Nash and created by Charles Barry to celebrate the great naval victory of Lord Nelson in 1805, Trafalgar Square replaced a jumble of buildings and stables with a handsome open space, dominated by the 170-foot Nelson Monument, guarded by four huge Landseer lions, with a Luytens fountain nearby. No wonder that in *The Judas Goat,* Robert B. Parker's American private eye, Spenser, in London to track down the terrorist group called Liberty, walked there like any tourist to see "Nelson and the lions and the National Gallery and the goddamned pigeons."

John Dickson Carr's publicity-seeking Mad Hatter plants the homburg of a well-known Jewish war profiteer on a lion in Trafalgar Square, while Dorothy Sayers's Lord Peter Wimsey, playing the role of Death Bredon, the supposedly shady copywriter in *Murder Must Advertise,* led Scotland Yard a merry chase up Whitehall, doubling back around the Cenotaph, before his sensational capture in the middle of Trafalgar Square. (Never mind that this was a marathon of a race; we know Lord Peter is in tiptop shape!) Sir Arthur Conan Doyle also had Stapleton catch a cab here to tail Henry Baskerville in the Sherlock Holmes case, *The Hound of the Baskervilles.*

Trafalgar Square is the scene of many of London's open-air meetings: revivals, rock concerts, and demonstrations; so, it was natural for Antonia Fraser's Jemima Shore to see a photograph in the *Times* of her M.P. lover, Tom Amyas, taking part in a rally there for Welfare Now. In Agatha Christie's *The Secret Adversary,* the Labour Day meeting that was meant to begin a general strike was thwarted by the sudden death of Sir James Peel Edgerton. There were only speeches in Trafalgar Square and a straggling procession singing the "Red Flag."

Now cross the street to South Africa House, then turn right and cross the Strand, and turn right again to Northumberland Street. Walk down Northumberland Street to Craven Passage, where you will find the pub, Sherlock Holmes. It has mementos of Holmes's cases and a replica of the sitting room at 221B Baker Street. The sitting room can be seen through a window at the head of the stairs before you go into the dining room. You need reservations for the restaurant, but during pub hours you can always drop by and see the museum, too.

In Julian Symons's *A Three Pipe Problem,* this replica, built for the Festival of Britain, is placed in the flat of amateur detective Sheridan Haynes, who played Sherlock Holmes in a TV series. (According to H.R.F. Keating, the name for Symons's mystery was suggested to him by Ngaio Marsh while all three writers were on a promotion tour. It is a quote from Sherlock Holmes's story, "The Red-Headed League.") The pub building used to be the Northumberland Arms, where Sir Henry Baskerville stayed when he came to London. And across Craven Passage is the Midland Bank Building, which once housed Nevill's Turkish Bath, patronized by Holmes and Watson. Gladys Mitchell also recalled that, at the Northumberland Hotel, opposite, she was made a member of the Detection Club by the first Ruler, G.K. Chesterton himself.

When you leave the pub, turn left and walk toward the river. At the point where Northumberland Avenue runs into Whitehall Place is the building that houses the Ministry of Defense. It once was the exclusive Hotel Metropole in Sherlock Holmes's case of "The Noble Bachelor" and was also visited by Agatha Christie's Hercule Poirot. Then turn right and walk back along the south side of Northumberland Avenue to Trafalgar Square and the statue of King Charles I, which faces down Whitehall, toward the site of the royal palace of Whitehall. Its Banqueting House was the scene of Charles I's execution on January 30, 1649.

The wide street known as Whitehall, down which royal processions parade to Westminster Abbey and the Houses of Parliament, follows an earlier roadway called King Street. Since a "white hall" at one time meant a grand hall built for public occasions, the entire area became known as Whitehall. After the fire of 1698, royalty moved from Whitehall, but the name remained synonymous with government, and characters in detective stories often report to mysterious officials "at Whitehall." In *Cast for Death,* intent on showing him the famous sights, Margaret Yorke's amateur sleuth, Patrick Grant, drove his visiting Greek policeman, Manolakis, down Whitehall; in *All Hallows Eve,* Charles Williams's Lester Furnival, unaware that she herself had died in a plane crash, walked up Whitehall from Westminster Bridge, finding the offices and shops full and furnished with everything—but people.

As you go south on Whitehall, you will walk on the west side of the street until you cross Whitehall at Derby Gate, but several important sights on the other side are worth mentioning. The first object of interest you pass on your right is Admiralty Arch, which leads to The Mall and Buckingham Palace. Beyond it, past the Whitehall Theatre, is the Old Admiralty, where Lord Nelson got his orders. Next door is the red-brick Admiralty House, entered from the internal courtyard, where, in John Buchan's thriller, *The Thirty-Nine Steps,* Foreign Office Permanent Under-Secretary Sir Walter Bullivant took Richard Hannay to determine where to look for those mysterious "39 steps." In "The Priory School," Sherlock Holmes knew the Duke of Holdernesse, who was First Lord of the Admiralty, and it was here that the British naval codes were changed in "His Last Bow."

Across Whitehall to your left is the entrance to Great Scotland Yard, originally the palace of the Kings of Scotland and later, until 1890, the first home of the Metropolitan Police. Between Whitehall Place and Horse Guards Road, on the river side of Whitehall, stands the ponderous Victorian War Office, where, in Nicholas Blake's *Minute for Murder,* war hero Charles Kennington reported for duty after a secret mission in which he captured a top Nazi.

Next, on the west side of Whitehall is the Horse Guards, a low, Portland stone building with a courtyard and an archway with a clock tower. Two mounted sentries are stationed there daily, from 10 to 4 o'clock, in twin sentry boxes. At 11:00 A.M.

(noon on Sundays), you can see the Mounting of the Guard carried out by the two regiments of the Household Cavalry: the Life Guards in red tunics and white plumes or the Royal Horse Guards in blue tunics and red plumes. Every June, on the Official Birthday of the Queen, there is a Trooping of the Colour on Horse Guards Parade westward through the arch. If there aren't too many tourists, walk close and see for yourself what Robert Parker's Spenser meant when he said that the two mounted sentries had "young and ordinary faces."

Directly across Whitehall, you can see the Portland stone Banqueting House, all that remains of the Palace of Whitehall. Designed by Inigo Jones in 1619, it has a glorious ceiling painted by Peter Paul Rubens. Through one of its windows, Charles I walked out to his execution (a judicial murder?) in 1649. Beyond the Banqueting House is Welsh Gwydyr House, then the Ministry of Defense, in front of which stands a statue of Sir Walter Raleigh. On your side of Whitehall, south of Horse Guards, are the Scottish Office, the Treasury, and, finally, tiny Downing Street, the official residence of the prime minister. For security reasons, Downing Street is now closed to all visitors.

Many fictional detectives have been summoned to No. 10 Downing Street in times of great national crisis. In *The Crimson Circle,* Edgar Wallace's "commonplace" Inspector Parr, whose daughter Thalia Drummond had infiltrated the nefarious Crimson Circle, went to No. 10 to talk to the prime minister about the murder of Cabinet Minister Raphael Willings. Agatha Christie's mysterious Foreign Office official known as "Mr. Carter" also talked to the prime minister about the sinister plot of Sir James Peel Edgerton in *The Secret Adversary.* In Antonia Fraser's *A Splash of Red,* Sir Richard Lionnel's watertight alibi for the murder of his mistress was that he was attending a meeting at No. 10 Downing Street, while John Dickson Carr's Mad Hatter planned to pin the top hat of old-fashioned patriot Sir William Bitten to the door of No. 10 with a crossbow bolt.

Directly across Whitehall from Downing Street is Richmond Terrace. It has an apartment building that has been identified as the Whitehall Terrace in which the Secretary for European Affairs lived in Sherlock Holmes's case "The Second Stain." It is probably the site of "Westminster Court or Mansions, next door to Scotland Yard," where Sax Rohmer's Sir Denis Nayland Smith, former Assistant Commissioner of Scotland Yard, lived. This location made it easy for Sir Denis and Scotland Yard's Chief-Inspector Gallaho to confer secretly over the disappearance of Dr. Petrie's daughter, Fleur, smuggled into England by Fu Manchu as a statue called the "living Venus."

South of Downing Street, along Whitehall's west side and occupying the entire block to King Charles Street, is the elaborate Italianate front of the Foreign Office. It, too, is the haunt of several detective-story characters. In Charles Williams's *All Hallows Eve*, Richard Furnival served there during World War II. In *Gaudy Night*, Dorothy L. Sayers's Harriet Vane found out from Freddy Arbuthnot that Lord Peter Wimsey was abroad doing what he called "plumbing" for the FO, and in *Black as He's Painted*, Ngaio Marsh's delightful Mr. Whipplestone, having retired from the FO with two solid Georgian gravy-boats, impulsively adopted the stray cat Lucy Lockett. She, in turn, led him to buy No. 1 Capricorn Walk in time to be party to a murder at the Ng'ombwana Embassy. Agatha Christie's pompous George Lomax was Permanent Under-Secretary of State for Foreign Affairs and employed Bundle's Bill Eversleigh, who calls him Codders behind his back. Of course, Sherlock Holmes was often called to the Foreign Office. In "His Last Bow," the Foreign Minister himself persuaded Holmes to take on the mission against Von Bork.

Somewhere near here is hidden the wartime Ministry of Morale, where in *Minute for Murder* Nicholas Blake's Nigel Strangeways looked out on discolored plane trees and the rubble of bombed houses near the park, just before the Director's secretary was poisoned. Dorothy Sayers's tartar, Helen, Duchess of Denver, was probably employed by the same department during World War II, but the actual Ministry of Information turned Sayers herself down because she was "too difficult and loquacious." Carter Dickson (a.k.a. John Dickson

Carr) had Sir Henry Merrivale, known as the "Old Man," nap "in a rabbit warren behind Whitehall," but Sir Henry was such an obvious look-alike for [Sir] Winston Churchill that he may really have been working below ground in the Cabinet War Rooms, which you will pass a little later.

In front of the Foreign Office, in what is now called Parliament Street, stands the Cenotaph, decorated with many flags, which is Britain's chief monument to her war dead. Men used to raise their hats when they still wore hats, and official ceremonies were held here annually on November 11, the anniversary of Armistice Day, 1918. Now the observance is held on the Sunday nearest November 11. Both the original date and the ceremony are important clues in the mysterious death of old General Fentiman at Dorothy Sayers's Bellona Club.

Now cross Parliament Street at King Charles Street to Derby Gate. You will find yourself at the back of New Scotland Yard, home of the Metropolitan Police for most of a century. In 1967, the CID moved to 10 Broadway, which is also called New Scotland Yard; so "old" New Scotland Yard is now called the Norman Shaw Building after its architect. Take time out to look at that massive, red- and white-striped hulk, crouching between the Italianate Whitehall buildings to its north and the Gothic towers of Westminster: It is a tiger among the bureaucratic lions here in C.P. Snow's "corridors of power."

To reach the front of Scotland Yard, where it faces the Thames River, walk toward the river on Derby Gate. Then turn right and go along Cannon Row past the Cannon Row Police Station (confusingly, there is one in the City, too). Go left on Bridge Street past St. Stephen's Tavern, the Westminster Underground Station, and a group of souvenir shops and snack bars.

Stop and take a good look at the view across Bridge Street of the fairy tale Gothic-style Houses of Parliament, with their impressive Clock Tower, which houses the famous bell, Big Ben. The distinctive sound of Big Ben, made famous around the world by the BBC, is probably a result of a crack made in the bell when it fell off the cart taking it to the Clock Tower. At night, when Parliament is sitting, a light shines in its tower.

In *The Trail of Fu Manchu,* Sax Rohmer wrote that Big Ben was clearly visible in the night as Sir Denis chased off to Limehouse after Fu Manchu. In Marsh's *A Surfeit of Lampreys,* New Zealander Roberta Grey heard a clock strike a single great note and asked Henry Lamprey what it was. "I suspect it was Big Ben, you hear him all over the place at nighttime." "I've only heard him on the air before." "You're in London now," he told her. In Sayers's *Clouds of Witness,* Big Ben also solemnly struck 11 deep ones as the trial of the Duke of Denver opened in the House of Lords.

Now turn left again and walk north along the Embankment to the ornate, impressive iron gates at the entrance to "old" New Scotland Yard. The small sign on the building simply tells you this is the "Norman Shaw Building." In spite of the fact it is no longer the headquarters of the Metropolitan Police, there is still tight security, and it is impossible for the ordinary tourist to get inside. A police sentry at either end will stop you at once, politely demanding your business. All London policemen seem to be both young and polite, cheerfully stopping to pull out their little black guides to help you find the most unlikely places or strolling along, hands behind their backs, no gun in sight.

In support of the authenticity of detective stories, remember that in *Mortal Consequences* Julian Symons stated that before Scotland Yard was founded in 1829 there may have been over 10,000 murders in Britain every year and parts of London were "immune" to the police. Symons credits Charles Dickens with creating the popular idea of Scotland Yard as the protector of society and G.K. Chesterton with calling the policeman on the beat the modern "knight-errant." John Creasey wrote a history of the formation of the London police in *The Masters of Bow Street,* while, as recently as 1980, in *The Murders of the Black Museum,* Gordon Honeycombe reported that murder is a very rare event in modern Britain, with only 564 cases reported, 70 percent of these murders were women and children, most of them domestic in origin. The fictional hierarchy of the Metropolitan Police, founded in 1829 by Sir Robert Peel to replace the Bow Street Runners, can be found in Dilys Winn's

Murder Ink. Its origins are also described in John Dickson Carr's *Fire Burn!* set in 1829.

So take a photograph of the man on duty and then settle down in a nearby café or snack bar while we remind you of the times your favorite detectives were found in this building, either as working police or as helpful amateurs. The following are a "jury's worth" of those characters who reported to Scotland Yard in the books we used. They range in rank from Police Constable to the Commissioner himself, but the incomparable Sherlock Holmes (a Nietzschean Superman, according to Julian Symons) usually received Scotland Yard's Mr. Lestrade of an evening in Baker Street, where his visits were welcome because they allowed Holmes to keep up with what was going on at the Yard.

All lesser sleuths, however, had to come to Scotland Yard themselves. In *Tether's End (Hide My Eyes),* Margery Allingham's Albert Campion closed the door of Chief Superintendent Yeo's room and walked up two flights of stairs to tap on the door of the room that belonged to the newest superintendent, Charles Luke. Campion and Oates had been "hunting companions" since Oates was an inspector. Now Oates wanted him to "drop a hint" to Luke, whom Campion felt to be the most interesting personality the CID had produced in a decade. But Campion soon discovered that Charlie Luke wanted him to do the same with Oates.

By the time of his "last" case, E.C. Bentley's Philip Trent was so well acquainted with Inspector Murch that he visited him at home, met his wife, and played with his children, while Dr. Gideon Fell, John Dickson Carr's G.K. Chesterton lookalike, lived nearby on the Embankment at 1 Adelphi Terrace so he could be called over by Chief Inspector Hadley. Sir Henry Merrivale, Carr's (or Carter Dickson's) "Old Man," worked across the way in Whitehall but was handy for consultation.

In his mystery about the Detection Club, *The Poisoned Chocolates Case,* Anthony Berkeley (a.k.a. Francis Iles) had President Roger Sheringham invite Inspector Moresby to their monthly dinner, then persuaded him to let the club try to solve a murder for him. G.K. Chesterton's French detective,

Valentin, upon his arrival in London came at once to "regularize" his position with Scotland Yard and then began his search for the crook Flambeau and his companion, Father Brown.

Agatha Christie has several detectives who work out of the Yard. Superintendent Battle, with a wooden face, was a man of the utmost discretion, according to nervous Foreign Office dignitary George Lomax, but Battle also created the secret Seven Dials Society, to which Bill Eversleigh and Lady Bundle belonged. Julius Hersheimer, the rich, young American seeking his kidnapped cousin, Jane Finn, also felt free to call upon the services of Scotland Yard, while Inspector Japp, a friend and colleague of Hercule Poirot, worked with him on cases like *The Big Four*. John Creasey's the Honorable Richard Rolliston, a.k.a. "the Toff," was actually "pulled in" by Scotland Yard because officials were suspicious of his motives for snooping about in the East End.

Edmund Crispin's Oxford don, Gervase Fen, met his friend Inspector Humbleby in London while Fen was acting as consultant for a film on Alexander Pope. Back at the Yard, Humbleby shared his wrath with Fen when a private letter by a film star involved in the case suddenly appeared in the press. Michael Gilbert's young Nap Rumbold of Markby, Wragg and Rumbold came to pump Chief Inspector Hazelrigg about Victoria Lamartine. He found Hazelrigg in an office with waxed linoleum, green filing cabinets, and a neat, unused-looking desk, where the only thing missing was the camp bed Hazelrigg had there during the war. Georgette Heyer's Chief Inspector Hemmingway was told that the Mayfair murder of Mrs. Haddington, "in a very classy joint," was just the kind of case he liked, but Hemmingway was more pleased to discover that the case involved young lawyer "Terrible Timothy" Harte.

Ngaio Marsh often showed Roderick Alleyn at the Yard, usually late at night, sometimes with reporter Nigel Bathgate in tow, always with his team of Fox, Curtis, Bailey and Thompson. He sat there the night of the Carrados debutante ball, as "out there in the cold Big Ben struck one. The row of lamps hung like a necklace of misty globes." And Alleyn thought, "Fog in June, this England," just as a frightened taxi driver delivered the corpse of Lord Robert (Bunchy) Gospell to the Yard. Gladys Mitchell's Chief Detective Inspector Robert Gavin was not only the fiancé of Dame Beatrice Bradley's large secretary, Laura Menzies, but in *Watson's Choice* he escorted them to Sir Bohun's Sherlock Holmes masquerade party on the Heath where a murder had been committed.

In *Whose Body?* Dorothy L. Sayers deliberately made Sir Andrew Mackenzie, the head of Scotland Yard, a Wimsey family friend. Then she gave Lord Peter Detective-Inspector Charles Parker as a close friend and, later, a brother-in-law. In Parker's last appearance in Sayers's unpublished *Thrones, Dominations,* when Lord Peter came calling, Parker was sitting in his office sorting through reports on possible assassins likely to attend the funeral of George V.

Like Marsh's Alleyn, Josephine Tey's detective Alan Grant is in love with London. One night, putting away the gilt dagger that stabbed the man in the theater queue, he came out on the Embankment to find it was a fine night, "with a light, frosty mist in the air," and decided to walk home through the city he found even more beautiful by night than by day.

Enough of Scotland Yard for now. Cross the street to the Embankment that runs along the Thames River, near the great bronze statue of Iceni Queen Boadicea, who sacked Londinium around 60 A.D. to drive the Romans away. You are at the point where, between May and September, you can pick up the river tour boats that go east to the Tower and past the Port of London to Greenwich, or west to Kew, Richmond, and Hampton Court. In Tey's *The Daughter of Time,* Grant promised a trip by river to Greenwich to his young American researcher, who asked him, "What's at Greenwich?" "Some very fine architecture and a fine stretch of muddy water," replied Grant.

Looking north, you can see the City skyline, with the great dome of St. Paul's Cathedral and the many Wren church spires. Since it was built as London's second bridge in 1748, Westminster Bridge has been the haunt of poets like Wordsworth and painters of the London scene like Turner, Constable, and Monet. Westminster Bridge brings out the artist or philosopher in detective-story writers, too. Parker's private eye, Spenser, also stood musing on Westminster Bridge. Below him, he saw the platform where excursion boats loaded, and he was struck by the realization that Shakespeare himself must have crossed the river here (there would have been ferry boats in Elizabethan times) to reach the Globe Theatre on the other side. At the end of Margery Allingham's *Black Plumes,* when David Field and Frances Ivory went for a walk down White-hall, they reached the bridge and paused to look over the parapet. "Big Ben blinked down on them and the coloured advertisement signs from upriver stained the water below." The lovers remained there until they had agreed to marry after all.

In *A Surfeit of Lampreys,* Marsh's Chief Inspector Alleyn crossed the Embankment, and leaning on the parapet looked down into "the black shadows of Westminster Pier where the river slapped against the wet stones." He was challenged by a police constable on the beat. They talked about an Old Vic production of *Macbeth* in the famous theater on the South Bank, not far from the site of Shakespeare's Globe, giving Alleyn a clue to the murder.

Charles Williams, too, clearly was thinking about Words-worth's famous poem about London as a sleeping animal when he had dead Lester Furnival stand on the bridge and see the huge body of the airplane that had killed her lying half in the river and on the Embankment. In *Cast for Death,* as soon as he heard about the corpse found in the river, Margaret Yorke's Patrick Grant rang up Detective-Inspector Colin Smithers at Scotland Yard, only to learn that the body was his actor friend Sam's. The suicide of Gloria Scott, a promising film ingénue, from Westminster Bridge started a chain of murders in Ed-mund Crispin's *Frequent Hearses.*

Most mysterious of all, in *The Man Who Was Thursday,* G.K. Chesterton's poet, Gabriel Syme, having joined Sun-day's anarchists, came downriver in a tug from an under-ground meeting in an old pub at Chiswick. He was landed at Cleopatra's Needle, where he was met by another anarchist, who walked with him to Sunday's breakfast on a balcony overlooking Leicester Square. From Westminster Bridge, you can see Cleopatra's Needle downriver on the Embankment. It is the oldest monument in London, one of a pair, which records the deeds not of Cleopatra, but of Thothmes and Ramses II and was given to London in 1819 by the Viceroy of India but not set up here until 1878. Its companion is now in New York City.

Turn right and walk back along Bridge Street west, across the top of Parliament Square, which becomes Great George Street, where the spy Adolph Meyer lived in the Sherlock Holmes case "The Adventure of the Bruce-Partington Plans." Great George Street, in turn, becomes Birdcage Walk. On his first day in London, Robert Parker's Spenser walked along the south side of St. James's Park on Birdcage Walk all the way to Buckingham Palace.

To your right as you come to St. James's Park, you will see the sign pointing to the Cabinet War Rooms exhibit in Horse Guards Road. In this underground bunker, Winston Churchill and his Cabinet met during air raids in World War II. Among the rooms that can be seen are the Cabinet Room, Map Room, and Churchill's office and bedroom.

St. James's Park was once a marsh, which was drained by Henry VIII and made into a royal deer park. Charles II let the Londoners in to see him feeding the birds; then it became a public park and bird sanctuary, famous for its pelicans. Today it is a favorite lunchtime haunt of the Whitehall civil servants, and you, too, on a good day, can lunch in the park by buying a sandwich at one of the stands and finding a deck chair to sit in. An attendant will collect a small fee for the chair, and during the summer a military band plays there between 1:00 and 2:00 P.M.

Across the lake in the center of St. James's, there is a bridge (a new one) that gives you the famous fairy tower view of Whitehall. G.K. Chesterton proposed to his future wife, Frances, there when they met in the park on their lunch hour. In Christie's *The Secret Adversary,* Tuppence, leaving Tommy Beresford after they had tea at a Lyons Corner House, walked home across St. James's Park, followed by "Mr. Whittington."

He made an appointment to see her the next day in the City, starting their first "paid" adventure. Somewhere near here, too, was the intelligence headquarters of Brigadier James White, who is spy Davina Graham's boss in Evelyn Anthony's *The Defector.*

At the first stoplight on Birdcage Walk, turn left and cross to Queen Anne's Gate, which is hard to locate because there are no street signs, only a faded gatepost set into the black railings. The street that first goes east and then turns south to your left has a row of attractive red-brick houses that are among the best examples of early eighteenth-century domestic architecture in London. The National Trust is at Nos. 40-44, and before No. 15 is a stone statue of Queen Anne, England's fattest queen and the last Stuart to sit on the throne.

In Anthony Berkeley's *The Piccadilly Murder,* Major Lynn Sinclair of the Guards, whose barracks are just beyond the Guards' Military Chapel, had his flat here. (The Chapel was shattered by a bomb in June 1944 but was rebuilt in 1961–63.) Major Sinclair was accused of poisoning his aunt in the lounge of the Piccadilly Palace Hotel. Even more impressive—for this is a very posh area to live or work—in *The Thirty-Nine Steps,* Buchan's Richard Hannay came here to the home of Sir Walter Bullivant. His house was in the narrow part of Queen Anne's Gate, with a wide hall and rooms on both sides. Hannay waited in an alcove with a telephone and a couple of chairs and saw the First Sea Lord come in, but realized he was really an impostor. In John Buchan's day, Lord Haldane, head of the Foreign Office before he became Lord Chancellor, lived at No. 28, and at No. 16 lived Admiral Lord Fisher, who really *was* the First Sea Lord, from 1905 to 1910, and again in 1914–15.

No. 50 Queen Anne's Gate is the new Home Office building, but when most of our detectives consulted its pathologists, the Home Office was in a building on Whitehall. In Christie's *The Big Four,* for example, Hercule Poirot and Hastings visit the Secretary of State for Home Affairs, the Right Honorable Sydney Crowther. In Sayers's *The Documents in the Case,* after the Reverend Mr. Parry's dinner party, writer John Munting and a professor friend hunted up Sir James Lubbock at his Bedford Square home. Then they went with him to his Home Office laboratory late at night, where he tested their mushroom samples. Sir James ghoulishly told them the lab was "his Bluebeard's Chamber with plenty of plots for novels."

Continue south on Queen Anne's Gate until you reach Broadway, a curving street that runs into Victoria Street past Tothill Street and the St. James's Park Underground Station, above which is the London Transport headquarters, with statues by Epstein, Eric Gill, and Henry Moore. To your right, as you follow Broadway, you will see Caxton Hall, named for printer William Caxton, who set up his business here during the reign of Richard III, chiefly famous in modern times as the scene of many fashionable out-of-church weddings. It is the probable site of Carr's Westminster Registry Office, where artist Martin Drake and his long-lost love, Lady Jennifer, were going to be married by Special License in *The Skeleton in the Clock*.

Somewhere here in a cul-de-sac "off Victoria Street" must be the flat of Marsh's Honorable Edward Manx, theater critic and nephew of eccentric Lord Pastern, where he took his cousin Carlisle in *A Wreath for Rivera* after she was grilled by Alleyn. Bentley's Trent and Mrs. Manderson's Uncle Burton Cupples walk together along Victoria Street after leaving the St. James's Park flat of Manderson's former secretary, Marlowe, in *Trent's Last Case*. And, in "The Eye of Apollo," Bentley's friend G.K. Chesterton had Father Brown and private detective Flambeau walk along Victoria Street to see Flambeau's new office in a modern "skyscraper." They were just in time to hear Big Ben strike noon and watch a fellow tenant worship the sun on the rooftop.

You have come past the rear of the new, 20-storey-high headquarters of the Metropolitan CID, home of New Scotland Yard since 1967, which P.D. James describes as "a bastion of concrete and glass." Here, in *An Unsuitable Job for a Woman*, Cordelia Gray was called in for questioning by Adam Dalgleish in connection with the suicide of her partner, Bernie Pryde, and the murder of Cambridge student Mark Callender. Dalgleish's office has regulation bookcases and furniture, and the only personal touches are a large watercolor of the old Norman Shaw Building on the Embankment and a bowl of real garden roses on his desk. You may stand and gaze at the front of the Yard as long as you like, but no visitor who is not an international police official can get inside. The same restriction is true of the famous Black Museum, with its grisly exhibits from real cases.

Westward along Victoria Street, you would come to the Army and Navy Stores, where Agatha Christie shopped with her grandmother and where Miss Marple came from Bertram's Hotel. Still farther west on Ashley Place, off Victoria, is the Roman Catholic Westminster Cathedral. It was in this red- and white-striped Byzantine basilica in 1936 that Monsignor Ronald Knox gave the panegyric at the Requiem Mass for G.K. Chesterton. The Stations of the Cross were carved by Chesterton's friend Eric Gill, who did G.K.C.'s tombstone in Beaconsfield. Mr. Scase, who was pursuing his child's murderer in P.D. James's *Innocent Blood,* wandered into Westminster Cathedral. He was unprepared for its interior, with the rough brick and great pillars of smooth marble rising to the immensity of its huge domed roof.

Before going back to Parliament Square, this is a good chance to rest your feet by going to the Albert, where you can have a pint and a snack or a full English meal upstairs in the Victorian carvery. Then walk directly east on Victoria Street, following the lure of the tall twin towers of Westminster Abbey. When Victoria Street becomes Broad Sanctuary, cross Storey's Gate to the open driveway called the Sanctuary and go into Westminster Abbey at the west porch.

The Abbey is a minster, or mission church, built to the "west" of London. It is not a cathedral. The original church was built on Thorney Island in the Thames, but its principal founder was the saintly Anglo-Saxon king, Edward the Confessor, who rebuilt it about 1050. The present church—with the exception of the twin towers, added in the early eighteenth century—is the work of King Henry III, who rebuilt it in 1245 as a shrine to Edward the Confessor, his patron saint.

Officially known as the Collegiate Church of St. Peter's at

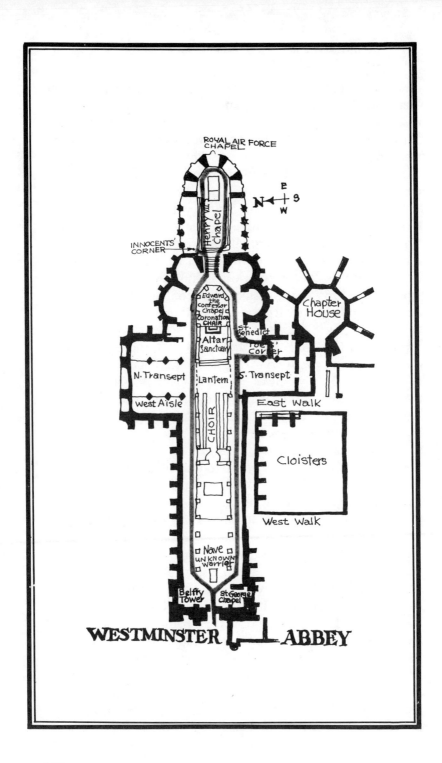

WESTMINSTER ABBEY

Westminster, whose Dean is answerable only to God and the Queen, Westminster is the place where English kings since William the Conqueror have been crowned and buried. It survived the Cromwellian Reformation, despite having its monastery dissolved, because it was already associated in the public mind with government. Today the Abbey is both a large and handsome thirteenth-century church and a vast and cluttered memorial to British kings and heroes. It was for the latter reason that Yorke's Patrick Grant took his visiting Greek policeman to see Westminster Abbey in *Cast for Death*.

One of the best ways to introduce yourself to the Abbey is to attend a church service there, but at those times the rest of the church is closed to sightseers. At the same time, sadly, the increasing number of tourists who make the Abbey one of their "must" stops has meant that to go into the eastern end you must pay an admission charge and often stand in line and move with the crowd.

From our detective-story point of view, there are certain parts of the Abbey that you must see. As you enter, pass by the Tomb of the Unknown Warrior to the north aisle and go down the nave to the choir and the sanctuary, where the kings and queens are crowned. Pay your admission fee here, keeping in mind that the Abbey has close associations with the boy-king Edward V, whose supposed murder by his uncle Richard III exercised the wits of Josephine Tey's hospitalized Inspector Grant in *The Daughter of Time*. Not only was Edward V born here while his father, Edward IV, was in exile, but his mother, Elizabeth Woodville, again bolted into sanctuary here with his younger brother Richard, Duke of York, at his father's death.

Go by the High Altar and the Chapel of Edward the Confessor, where you can see the scarred, old, wooden Coronation Chair, with its special shelf for the Royal Scottish Stone of Scone, and continue past the Plantagenet tombs into the northern aisle of Tudor Henry VII's beautiful chapel. There, just beyond the tomb of Elizabeth I, you will find Innocents' Corner, with the tombs of two infant daughters of James I. Above them is a casket designed by Sir Christopher Wren in which were solemnly reburied the bones of two boys found at the White Tower in the reign of Charles II. These bones are commonly accepted as those of Edward V and his brother, the princes in the Tower. But as Catherine Aird commented in *Murderess Ink,* just by writing *The Daughter of Time,* Josephine Tey has kept alive our doubts about that murder and the authenticity of the Shakespearean portrait of Richard III. (See City Walk.)

Walk across Henry VII's Chapel, admiring the starkly modern blue window dedicated to the flyers of the Battle of Britain, and go into the south transept, which is affectionately known as the Poets' Corner. It is filled with memorials to British artists, musicians, and writers, beginning with Geoffrey Chaucer. But you should be especially interested in locating the tablet to Henry James, the American-born author of *The Turn of the Screw,* who died in London in 1916, and the burial place of one of mystery's Grand Masters, Charles Dickens.

Come out of Westminster Abbey and turn to your right to cross the parkway to the small church at the northeast corner. This is St. Margaret's, Westminster, the parish church of the House of Commons, built in 1500. Since then it has been the scene of many fashionable weddings, like John Milton's in 1655 and Sir Winston Churchill's in 1908. Inside, it has a 1501 window celebrating the betrothal of Catherine of Aragon to Prince Arthur. The headless body of Sir Walter Raleigh, executed across the street in Old Palace Yard, is supposed to be buried beneath the altar.

Detective fiction has also had a number of famous weddings and funerals here. In Jessica Mann's *Funeral Sites,* Phoebe Sholto was married here in a society wedding to secret Communist Aidan Britton. Dorothy Sayers's cub reporter, Hector Puncheon of the *Morning Star,* had to get down to St. Margaret's by 10:30 to report the wedding of a fashionable beauty who was being married in the strictest secrecy at that early hour. On April 22, 1904, Captain Huber de Mazaren and Baroness Orczy's Lady Molly of Scotland Yard were married there by Special License. Since the other St. Margarets's are far away in the City, it is tempting to identify this one with the church in Anne Perry's *Resurrection Row,* where the disinterred corpse of Lord Augustus Fitzroy-Hammond was found kneeling in the family pew.

Finally, on January 15, 1958, a memorial service was held at St. Margaret's for Dorothy L. Sayers. It was attended by a representative of the Archbishop of Canterbury, as well as the Red Dean and five other bishops of the Church of England. Bishop Bell of Chichester, who had persuaded Sayers to write a play for Canterbury (leading her, as a schoolboy wrote, "from a life of crime to the Church of England"), read the panegyric written by C.S. Lewis. The first lesson was read by her old BBC producer, Val Gielgud (brother of Sir John), and the second lesson was read by His Honour Judge Gordon Clark (a.k.a. detective writer Cyril Hare).

Leave St. Margaret's and cross Broad Sanctuary to Parliament Square, where the first traffic roundabout system was started in 1926. Around its sides there are statues of many famous men, among them prime ministers Sir Winston Churchill, Canning, Derby, Disraeli, Peel, and Palmerston, as well as one of Abraham Lincoln, copied from the Saint Gaudens' statue in Chicago's Grant Park.

Cross Parliament Street east to New Palace Yard and Westminster Hall, the oldest remaining part of the Palace of Westminster, where the Royal Courts sat until the nineteenth century. It was built by William Rufus, with a glorious hammerbeam roof added by Richard II. Outside stands a massive statue of Oliver Cromwell, booted and spurred, guarding Parliament and reminding us that mystery writer Antonia Fraser wrote his biography. Westminster Hall was the site of many famous trials, including those of Edward II, Richard II, Guy Fawkes, and Sir Thomas More, but terrorists' threats have now closed the Hall, like the Houses of Parliament, to tours.

Beyond Westminster Hall, continue south along St. Margaret's Street to St. Stephen's Porch, the public entrance to the Houses of Parliament, where you can join the queue for the Public Gallery of the House of Commons or the Strangers' Gallery of the House of Lords. Inside to the north lies the rebuilt House of Commons, destroyed by bombing in World War II, and to the south lies the House of Lords. Beyond it are the Royal Gallery, the Sovereign's Robing Room, and the Royal Entrance under Victoria Tower—at 336 feet, the world's highest square stone tower. The entire group of buildings making up the Houses of Parliament were rebuilt after a fire in the Victorian era and represent the neo-Gothic imaginations of Sir Charles Barry and Augustus Pugin.

As an M.P. (Member of Parliament), Fraser's Tom Amyas spent his evenings at the House of Commons, where Jemima Shore sent him unsigned notes congratulating him on a telling speech or met him first at their favorite little trattoria "behind Victoria." The Wimseys came there to meet with handsome Sir Impey Biggs, who had defended Harriet Vane, to engage him for Crutchley's defense in Sayers's *Busman's Honeymoon*. In Christie's *The Secret of Chimneys*, the Hon. George Lomax declared that "St. Stephen's is ruined, absolutely ruined . . . by women in politics." There is also a Members' Terrace on the river, which is mentioned in *Murder Must Advertise*. Dorothy Sayers's office boy, Ginger Joe, checking alibis for Lord Peter Wimsey, discovered that Mr. Vibart's alibi was that he was "at Westminster making a sketch of the Terrace of the House of Commons for Farley's Footwear."

The House of Lords' most impressive appearance in detective fiction undoubtedly occurs in Sayers's *Clouds of Witness*. Here, the Duke of Denver, as a peer of the realm, was tried for the murder of Denis Cathcart. (Sometime earlier, Lord Peter had discovered the missing Attenbury emeralds in the woolsack on which the Lord Chancellor sits to preside over the Lords.) Sayers told us that the Royal Gallery was packed, while the witnesses were held in the Royal (Sovereign's) Robing Room, and the Garter-King-of-Arms tried to make three hundred or so sheepish peers stay in line in order of rank. As usual, the Lord Chancellor held the temporary appointment as Lord High Steward, and above the Bar there were red-covered benches for the peers, each in his own right a judge of the highest court in the land. As the ceremony began, the Dowager Duchess said irrepressibly, "So picturesque . . . quite High Church."

Outside the Houses of Parliament, if you have time, cross

to the Jewel Tower, a small stone tower set in a tiny moat. It is part of the old Palace of Westminster, built by Edward III to hold his royal plate and jewelry.

Then turn right to retrace your steps toward Parliament Square, where, after the Duke of Denver was acquitted, the crowd began to stir. As he appeared, a bullet crashed through the window of the Denver limousine. A big, bearded man (Grimethorpe) was then chased by the crowd to Westminster Bridge, where a taxi hit and killed him. Following this excitement, in the early hours of the morning Inspector Sugg came upon a cabbie arguing with the statue of Lord Palmerston, who was sharing his pedestal with a gentleman in evening dress. It was Lord Peter Wimsey, who, with Charles Parker and Freddy Arbuthnot, had celebrated the acquittal of the Duke by getting plastered. Inspector Sugg saw them all safely stowed away in cabs, just as the House of Commons came out from a late-night sitting. You have now completed the walk and can cross Bridge Street to the Westminster Underground Station.

10

BROMPTON/ HYDE PARK WALK

BACKGROUND

Brompton, which is also called Knightsbridge, lies directly south of Hyde Park. It was first mentioned in history as the Knights Bridge over the Westbourne, another London stream that runs into the Thames. The knights who owed service to the Bishop of London rode across the bridge to his palace at Fulham for a blessing before going off to war. Later, Queen Caroline used the Westbourne's waters to create the Serpentine. Today Brompton is known for two things: its shops, especially Harrods, and its museums. The museums were built on land purchased with the proceeds of the Great Exhibition of 1851, which was organized by Queen Victoria's husband, Prince Albert. Its main building was the Crystal Palace, a glass and iron exhibition hall designed by Sir Joseph Paxton, later moved to Sydenham and finally, in 1936, destroyed by fire.

Hyde Park is the largest park in London. Together with adjoining Kensington Gardens, it covers over 630 acres. At the end of Kensington Gardens is the Royal Palace of Kensington, where Queen Victoria was born and where the Prince and Princess of Wales now live. Like St. James's Park and the Green Park to the east and Regent's Park to the north, Hyde Park was part of the monastery land seized by Henry VIII for his own use. Its name came from the Saxon word "hide," a unit of land measurement.

Elizabeth I reviewed her troops in Hyde Park; then, in 1637, Charles I opened it to the public. During the Civil Wars, Parliament fortified it. Then, under the later Stuarts, Hyde Park became society's favorite riding place, as well as a haunt of highwaymen, and a site for duels. Queen Caroline, wife of George II, created the Serpentine (called the Long Water, in Kensington Gardens). Hyde Park is London's beach in summer and its skating rink in winter, but, above all else, Hyde Park is the place Londoners go to walk.

LENGTH OF WALK: 3 miles

Not counting the museums you tour or a walk across Hyde Park.

See maps on pages 190 and 197 for boundaries of this walk and page 267 for a list of the detectives and stories covered.

PLACES OF INTEREST

Albert Memorial, Kensington Gardens (near the site of the Crystal Palace).

Geological Museum, Exhibition Road. Huge rock collection, including moon rock. Open Mon.–Sat., 10:00–6:00; Sun., 2:30–6:00 P.M. Free.

Harrods, Knightsbridge and Brompton roads. Best-known London department store, famous for its Harrods lady shoppers, a place where you can buy anything, from fresh meat to a riding horse.

Hyde Park/Kensington Gardens:

 Marble Arch (Tyburn Hill).
 Hyde Park Corner:

Royal Artillery Memorial.

Wellington Monument.

Wellington Museum (Apsley House). Open Tue.–Thurs., Sat., 10:00–6:00; Sun., 12:30–6:00 P.M. Admission charge.

Kensington Palace, State Apartments. Open Mon.–Sat., 9:00–5:00; Sun., 1:00–5:00 P.M. Formal Gardens open year-round, but gates close at dusk.

The Round Pond, The Broad Walk, Kensington Gardens.

Statues:

Peter Pan.

Physical Energy.

Natural History Museum, Cromwell Road. One of world's finest natural history collections. Open Mon.–Sat., 10:00–6:00; Sun., 2:30–6:00 P.M. Free.

The Oratory, Brompton Road. Italian Baroque, known for musical services. Cardinal Newman served here after joining the Roman Catholic Church. Open 7:00 A.M.–8:00 P.M. daily.

Royal Albert Hall, Kensington Gore. Largest concert hall in London. Oval design. Concerts, recitals.

Science Museum, Exhibition Road. Collection of scientific, engineering, and industrial exhibits. Open Mon.–Sat., 10:00–6:00; Sun., 2:30–6:00 P.M. Free.

Victoria and Albert Museum, Cromwell Road. One of world's greatest museums of fine and applied arts. Open Mon.–Thurs., Sat., 10:00–5:00; Sun., 2:30–5:00 P.M. Donations requested.

PLACES TO EAT

Harrods, Brompton Road. A variety of restaurants ranging from inexpensive to luxurious, all licensed:

Georgian Restaurant, fourth floor. Carvery with buffet. Attractive and expensive.

Way in Circle, fourth floor. Self-service.

Dress Circle, first floor. Inexpensive self-service.

West Side Express, ground floor. Open from 7:45 A.M. American-style food.

Paxton's Head, 153 Knightsbridge Road. Pub opposite the Knightsbridge Gate to Hyde Park. Commemorates Sir Joseph Paxton.

Rembrandt Hotel, Thurloe Place and Brompton Road. A carvery restaurant. Open to 9:30 P.M. 01-589-8100.

Hyde Park, The Dell, open daily in summer.
  The Serpentine, open all year.

Victoria and Albert Museum, Cromwell Road. Licensed restaurant and self-service café. Open to 5:30 P.M.

——— BROMPTON/HYDE PARK WALK ———

Begin your walk by coming out of the Brompton Road exit of the Knightsbridge Underground Station and walking southwest along Brompton Road. You will soon find yourself at Harrods, a block-long, Edwardian terra-cotta department store with elegant green awnings over its display windows, outlined by lights at night. The queen does her Christmas shopping here, and you may purchase virtually anything from school uniforms to an estate in the country to brightly colored tea towels decorated with a red Harrods bus. The first-floor Meat Hall rivals Fortnum & Mason (see St. James Walk), and, as our detective writers make plain, there is still an unmistakable "Harrods shopper," definitely "U," indomitable, wearing tweeds and pearls, precisely the kind of lady who is murdered in English country houses. Harrods is well worth a visit, if not a shopping trip, but be warned that, like London herself, Harrods is an international mecca for tourists and jammed year round, particularly when it has sales, for which people fly across the Atlantic.

In Antonia Fraser's *A Splash of Red,* artist Kevin John Athlone did a funny, but biting, imitation of a Harrods lady shopper for Jemima Shore. In *Funeral Sites,* Jessica Mann's fugitive, Rosamund Sholto, tried to escape pursuit by using her credit cards at Harrods to buy a disguise. She dashed about in a variety of Harrods' departments until she realized that her trail had already been picked up by her pursuers who used her credit cards against her. During the chase, Rosamund kept remembering with nostalgia the good old days when Harrods

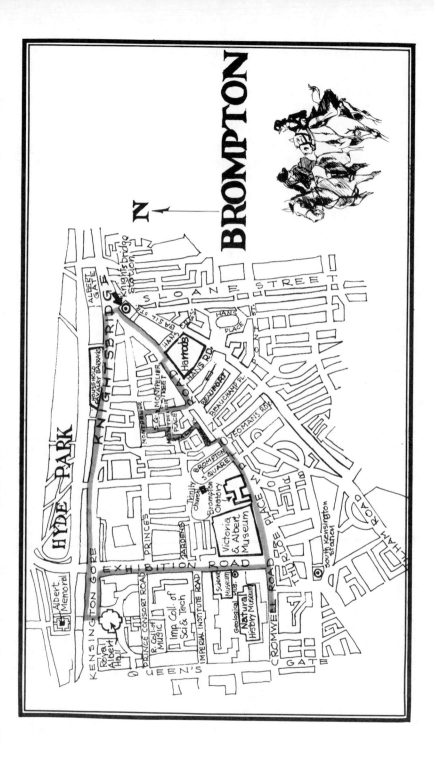

had been her family store, where she and her sister bought their school uniforms and had their hair cut. Harrods was a guarantee of unblemished excellence when Julian Symons's Paul Mortimer bought the box of chocolates there with which he then poisoned his Uncle George in *The Blackheath Poisonings*.

Just outside Harrods, at the beginning of Brompton Road, there used to be a famous horse market called Tattersall's, where all the young Regency bucks bought their horseflesh. In Georgette Heyer's Regency mystery, *Regency Buck*, Lord Worth took his spirited ward, Judith Tavener, there to buy a matched pair, with which she then raced her brother to Brighton, incurring Worth's wrath.

Leave Harrods by the Brompton Road exit on the north side of the store. Cross Brompton Road, turn left, and walk along the north side of Brompton Road. Despite its heavy traffic, Brompton Road is wide and tree-lined, with a fascinating number of specialty shops. No. 70 Brompton Road is the headquarters of the ITA, the Independent Television Authority, whose studios you can tour. More interesting to mystery buffs, however, you are now in Ngaio Marsh's heartland, where Marsh herself lived in a number of places and where many of her characters also lived.

After crossing Knightsbridge Gate and Lancelot Place, you will come to Montpelier Street. Turn right, and it will lead you past Montpelier Place into Montpelier Square. To the west is Montpelier Terrace, which runs into Montpelier Walk.

Walk around Montpelier Square. During one of her periodic stays in England (when she could bear to be away from New Zealand and her dramatic work, for which she was made a dame of the British Empire), Ngaio Marsh lived in Montpelier Walk. She described it as "a little house . . . on the sunny side of the street, looking towards the dome of the [Brompton] Oratory." She furnished the flat with secondhand goods from Fulham Road and enjoyed Montpelier Square's "decorous pub," the Prince of Wales. The Montpeliers, as we might call them, contain nicely kept small terrace houses with tiny balconies and delicate ironwork railings, all built about 1830. There are also antique shops filled with Victoriana, and in Montpelier Street you will find Bonham's auction rooms, with good buys in pictures and furniture.

This little enclave must have been the model for the delightful, fictitious group of streets, mews, and squares that Marsh named "the Capricorns" in *Black as He's Painted*. In that mystery, a tiny terrace house at 1 Capricorn Walk was impulsively purchased by Mr. Whipplestone, a retired Foreign Office official. One bright morning, he had left his dark and boring flat, and, after a 10-minute walk across Hyde Park, he came through "Baronsgate" into Brompton. (Whipplestone probably took Rutland Gate, where Miss McKay ran the Ecole de Dance, at which Frobisher and Mrs. Temple were taking dance lessons. Those lessons kept Frobisher from drinking Chateau Fleet Street at Pommeroy's Wine Bar with John Mortimer's Rumpole of the Bailey.)

Once in Brompton, Mr. Whipplestone followed a small cat named Lucy Lockett into a pleasing street that Marsh described as "narrow, orderly, sunny, with a view, to the left, of tree-tops and the dome of the Baronsgate Basilica [Brompton Oratory]." The houses were small, well-kept Georgian and Victorian houses with iron railings and at one corner was a pub, the Sun in Splendour.

Marsh's mythical Capricorn Place led into Capricorn Square, where there was a tiny grocery store, the Napoli, and the sinister Piggy Potterie, where two fat African emigrés manufactured pottery pigs and ceramic fish. Lucy liked to steal the fish and bring them home. The Capricorns were just "around the corner" from the African Ng'ombwana Embassy in fictitious Palace Park Gardens, probably the Princes' Gardens on Exhibition Road, north of the Victoria and Albert Museum, which can be reached from Montpelier Square by a series of mews and lanes. "The Boomer," Superintendent Alleyn's black prep school pal, who was the Ng'ombwana head of state, was staying at the Embassy when a murder was committed.

After walking around Montpelier Square, take Montpelier Walk south to Cheval Place. Turn right on Cheval Place and follow it as it turns south again to Brompton Road. Yeoman's

Row is just west of Beauchamp Place, on the south side of Brompton Road. It has some nice, red-brick, late Georgian houses. Marsh's Jenny Jenkins had a flat here at No. 99 in *Death in Ecstasy*. Jenny was the girlfriend of drug user Maurice Pringle, and both were initiates of the House of the Sacred Flame and suspected of murder.

Ngaio Marsh and her friend "Charlot Lamprey" opened a gift shop in the 1930s on Brompton Road, which proved to be wildly successful. But when they moved to a larger shop on Beauchamp Place, on the south side of Brompton Road, it unfortunately failed. In *A Surfeit of Lampreys*, Marsh's fictional Lampreys also moved to a duplex flat in Beauchamp Place to "economize" on their return from New Zealand. Marsh herself and a student secretary lived there during another 1950s' visit "home."

Walk past Cheval Place on the north side of Brompton Road to Brompton Square. It is a long, narrow, half-circle with elegantly kept houses and the Brompton Oratory looming up next door. Officially, it is called the London Oratory of St. Philip Neri, an order brought to England and moved to Brompton by Cardinal Newman in 1854. Its landmark dome is 200 feet high, and the Oratory, built in ornately Italian Baroque, is famous for its choral music.

In Georgette Heyer's *Behold, Here's Poison,* the widowed Mrs. Mathews reported to her bereaved family that, finding herself in Knightsbridge (shopping), she slipped into the Oratory for a few moments. "There was something in the whole atmosphere of the place which I can hardly describe," she gushed. Her matter-of-fact sister-in-law replied doubtfully that it must have been the incense. Across the Brompton Road from the Oratory stands the large, white Hotel Rembrandt, with a carvery restaurant serving English fare. Ngaio Marsh lived here one winter while getting ready to help run the gift shop with Charlot Lamprey.

At this point, just in front of the Victoria and Albert Museum, to the west of the Oratory, Brompton Road becomes Cromwell Road. (Cromwell Road goes on west toward Earl's Court and Hammersmith. Near Earl's Court, off Cromwell Road, Georgette Heyer and her barrister husband had their first flat. Heyer used the same location for her ex-con heroine Beulah Birtley, who worked for Mrs. Haddington in *Duplicate Death*.)

In *Odd Man Out,* Dick Francis put Hunt-Radnor Associates, the private detective agency where ex-jockey Sid Halley worked, off Cromwell Road in a graceful, six-storeyed Victorian house that was blown up with a bomb. Nearby was the Western Air Terminal, where Halley took Dolly, the office manager, for a drink and a sandwich in the snack bar. At the Air Terminal, they were not far from the Gloucester Road Underground Station, used by Mortimer's Rumpole of the Bailey when he headed for home and Hilda (She Who Must Be Obeyed).

You are now in front of the world-renowned Victoria and Albert Museum, built in the most impressive Victorian Gothic, which extends along Cromwell Road to Exhibition Road. This enormous museum houses the world's greatest collection of English furniture and much else. At any one time, only a part of its collections is on view, and as you walk into its lofty, cream and black marble lobby, with its great dome, you feel the Victorian Age had its moments. Even its gift shop is large and filled with interesting things to buy, and there is a restaurant, as well.

It was from a cubbyhole at the Victoria and Albert that Josephine Tey's actress, Marta Hallard, dug out James (doubtless a very important curator). She dragged James off to a print shop to find some portraits of famous historical criminals to amuse Inspector Grant in hospital. This creative idea of Hallard's paved the way for Grant to take up his bedside investigation of Richard III, described by Tey in *The Daughter of Time*.

When you emerge from the Victoria and Albert Museum, you have two choices. You can walk to the corner, cross Exhibition Road, and, turning to your right, walk the half block to the Geological Museum. Or you may cross Exhibition Road and continue walking along Cromwell Road to the Natural History Museum. Just beyond the Natural History Museum is the Royal College of Art.

In Dick Francis's *Odd Man Out,* Sid Halley's father-in-law borrowed a special rock collection from the Geological Museum to entrap a racecourse criminal (who stole a specimen). In Dorothy L. Sayers's *Murder Must Advertise,* the police found reporter Hector Puncheon knocked out on the second floor of the Natural History Museum. The police had been following Puncheon, who, in turn, had been following the man in evening dress who had given him dope in a Covent Garden pub. Unfortunately for Puncheon, the police had waited too long on the first floor, looking at the stuffed birds (still found in the gallery to the left of the main entrance).

Behind the Geological Museum on Exhibition Road is the Science Museum, with industrial and technological exhibits. (Here, you can go into the entrance to the Underground just north of the Science Museum by the Post Office, ending the walk.) If you want to continue the walk, cross Imperial Institute Road. Next, you will pass the Imperial College of Science and Technology and the Royal College of Music. Across Exhibition Road on the east side, you will see a large Mormon Church, a memorial tablet to those killed in the 1956 Hungarian Uprising, and a Polish Club. The next cross street is Prince's Gardens, which would take you back to the Montpeliers in a roundabout way.

Continuing on Exhibition Road, you come to Prince Consort Road. After crossing Prince Consort Road, you come upon the rear of the massive Royal Albert Hall, a great oval auditorium built facing Hyde Park and the Albert Memorial. In G.K. Chesterton's *The Man Who Was Thursday,* on his wild ride from Leicester Square, Sunday flew past the Royal Albert Hall, riding the elephant he had stolen from the Zoo. Mass meetings are often held there, too, but it is rare for a speaker to be assassinated, as an internationally known pacifist was in Evelyn Anthony's *Avenue of the Dead.* In *Death in the Stocks,* Georgette Heyer's young artist, Kenneth Vereker, went to a charity ball at Albert Hall the night his seedy brother, Roger, was murdered in his flat, just around the corner on Kensington Gore. Most of all, Albert Hall is famous for concerts and recitals. In *Lady Molly of Scotland Yard,* Baroness Orczy's

Elizabeth Lowenthal, accused of murdering Mark Culledon, was proud of singing there.

Albert Hall replaced Gore House, the home of Lady Blessington, who entertained writers like Dickens and Thackeray. In honor of the house, this part of the road is called Kensington Gore. According to Heyer, Roger Vereker's flat was in a new block of buildings erected between Queen's Gate and Exhibition Road, which placed it on Kensington Gore, while Kensington Gore was the original site and title of Christianna Brand's *Fog of Doubt*. Upon discovering that there was another book by that name, Brand moved her story—lock, stock, and Georgian house—north to Maida Vale.

Walk left a short way along Kensington Gore to the front of Albert Hall. You are right across from the Albert Memorial, which stands at the border between Hyde Park and Kensington Gardens at the spot where the Crystal Palace once stood. As a tiny child, when his family lived on Campden Hill just west of Kensington Gardens, G.K. Chesterton remembered seeing the fairy glitter of the Crystal Palace in the distance.

Designed by Sir Gilbert Scott, the Albert Memorial is a large Victorian Gothic edifice with a seated statue of Prince Albert beneath an arched cathedral roof. The Prince Consort, holding a catalogue of the Exhibition, sits facing south, as if blessing the vast array of museums it spawned.

Kensington Gardens, to the left of the Memorial, has had its share of scenes from detective stories, too. In Agatha Christie's *The Secret Adversary*, Tommy Beresford had disappeared, so Tuppence Cowley bearded the arch traitor himself in his Carlton Terrace house, but got no information. She came out and walked all the way across Hyde Park and into Kensington Gardens. In *Black as He's Painted*, Ngaio Marsh had a top security man complain to Alleyn that the Boomer was like all visiting VIPs. They wanted to go look at Peter Pan in Kensington Gardens without considering how difficult that made life for Security.

South of Sir George Frampton's statue of Sir James Barrie's hero Peter Pan, near the Long Water, is *Physical Energy*, a rampaging bronze horse by G.F. Watts. Watts did the murals

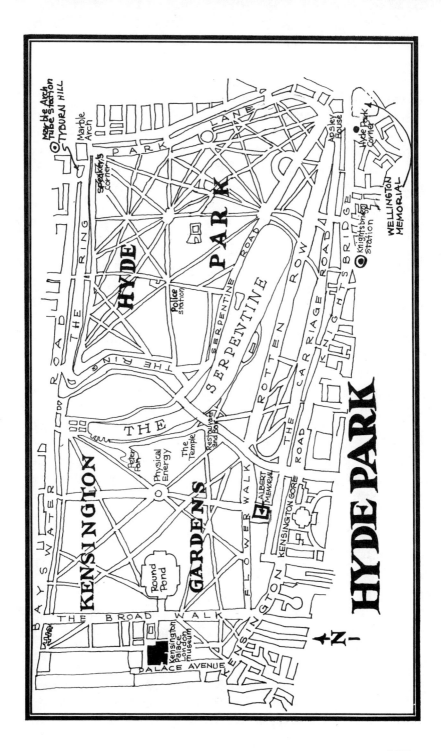

for the rebuilt Houses of Parliament, and G.K. Chesterton wrote his biography in the same series as his book on William Blake. The statue itself was used as a secret rendezvous by the members of the terrorist organization Magma in Geoffrey Household's *Hostage: London,* but Kensington Gardens is firmly associated in literature with nannies and children. In P.D. James's *Innocent Blood,* the malicious young aristocrat, Gabriel Lomas, told Philippa Palfrey that he became addicted to gossip during childhood afternoons spent about the Round Pond listening to the nannies chat.

Turn right at Kensington Gore and walk east along Kensington Road, which forms the southern boundary of Hyde Park. For centuries, Hyde Park has been associated with horseback riding, as well as highwaymen and duels. As you walk along, you may see riders on the famous Rotten Row, originally the Route du Roi, the way William III rode from Westminster to his palace of Kensington.

In Julian Symons's *A Three Pipe Problem,* Sherlock Holmes enthusiast Sheridan Haynes wondered if Sherlock Holmes and Watson ever walked in the park. He decided that they must have, and that idea made Haynes feel as if he, too, were back in the nineteenth century. He strolled towards the Serpentine, where he saw two borzois galloping and a boxer trotting beside a girl. He saw children on horses and felt that England was again the way it had been, gentler and more attractive. Later in the mystery, however, Haynes was lured into Hyde Park at night by some reporters, where he tripped over the supposedly murdered body of Irene Adler.

In Agatha Christie's *The Big Four,* Hastings, who was Dr. Watson for Hercule Poirot, was crossing Hyde Park when he was stopped by a limousine. Countess Vera Rossakoff, a minion of the Big Four, leaned out to tell Hastings not to mourn for Poirot (who was playing dead) but to go back to his wife in South America.

In *The Judas Goat,* Robert Parker's American private eye, Spenser, jogged daily through Hyde Park along the Serpentine; while, in Regency days, Georgette Heyer's heroine, Judith Tavener, was taught that ladies in polite society were to be seen promenading in Hyde Park between the hours of 5:00 and 6:00 P.M. Manolakis, the Greek policeman who was visiting don Patrick Grant in Margaret Yorke's *Cast for Death,* informed Grant that he greatly admired Hyde Park; and Ray Marcable, star of the musical comedy *Didn't You Know?* was photographed riding in Rotten Row in Josephine Tey's *The Man in the Queue.*

Keep walking east on Knightsbridge past the Hyde Park Barracks, the Knightsbridge Gate, and the Edinburgh Gate. You will reach the Knightsbridge Underground Station, which is the end of the walk. But if you walk straight on, you will come to Hyde Park Corner, the official entrance to the park itself. Then you can take the underpass to reach the Hyde Park Corner Underground Station.

Hyde Park Corner is the busiest traffic corner in Europe. Its official title is Duke of Wellington Place, in honor of the great Duke who defeated Napoleon. The monument to Wellington is the Wellington Arch, placed opposite Constitution Hill, which leads to Buckingham Palace. It is topped by a quadriga, or four-horse chariot, driven by the figure of Peace. In Ngaio Marsh's *A Surfeit of Lampreys,* Roberta Grey looked up in a taxi at night and saw "four heroic horses snorting soundlessly against a night sky," as she and Henry Lamprey went to stay at the Wutherwood mansion in Mayfair.

On the north side of Hyde Park Corner is No. 1, London, which was Apsley House, Wellington's home, which is now a museum to him. On an island across the roadway, you can see a bronze statue of Wellington, riding his favorite horse, Copenhagen, who was buried with full military honors. In Georgette Heyer's sequel to *Regency Buck, An Infamous Army,* Judith Tavener (now Lady Worth) flirted with the duke at the great Brussels ball before Waterloo.

Up Park Lane, north along Hyde Park, you come to Speaker's Corner, where you can climb a soap box to speak out on any subject you like. Then you come to the Marble Arch at the western end of Oxford Street. Marble Arch was designed by Nash to be the triumphal entrance to Buckingham Palace, but it turned out to be too narrow for the State Coach; so it was placed here instead. Traffic problems have caused Marble Arch to be isolated on a small concrete island that can be reached only at your peril.

Just to the west of Marble Arch stood Tyburn Tree, with its three gallows, built in the shape of a triangle. For 600 years, executions were held here in front of great crowds of sight-seers. At these executions, which took place every six weeks, as many as 15 men, women, and children were hanged. An estimated 20,000 spectators saw highwayman Jack Shepherd hanged in 1724.

Today a triangular memorial stone marks the spot where hundreds of prisoners, brought here from Newgate and the Tower, were hanged, drawn, and quartered and their bodies set up at the gates of London as a warning to others. Among the more famous victims was Perkin Warbeck, who pretended to be the younger of the princes in the Tower, written up in Josephine Tey's *The Daughter of Time*. John Creasey's *The Masters of Bow Street* opened with a hanging at Tyburn watched by a small boy. Dr. Samuel Johnson deplored the end of these public executions, however, because they helped rid the London public of the footpads and highwaymen and kept up the spirits of the hanged!

In *The Case of William Smith* by Patricia Wentworth, Katherine Eversley had her taxi drop her at the Marble Arch tube station so that no one could figure out where she lived. If you have walked all the way to Marble Arch, go through the underpass and take the Marble Arch Underground Station to end your walk.

11

BELGRAVIA/ PIMLICO WALK

BACKGROUND

This walk will cover the neighborhoods known as Belgravia and Pimlico. Laid out by the builder Thomas Cubitt in 1825, Belgravia became—and still is—the most fashionable neighborhood in the West End. Long a marshy swamp, it was first developed because of its closeness to Buckingham Palace and Westminster. Cubitt and his successors built simple, terraced houses and garden squares that have worn well, although it is the smaller houses and the mews that are most sought after today. The Victorians came to think that Belgravia looked monotonous, with its thousands of stucco or brick houses, nearly all shining cream or white, but it is still a very desirable area, with its quiet neighborhoods like deserted villages by day. Early in the morning or late in the long summer evenings, Belgravia makes a beautiful part of London to walk in.

Walking through this home of very important people, companies, and embassies, you can think about the ironic words of mystery writer C.P. Snow. In his last book, a detective story called *A Coat of Varnish*, Lord Snow insisted that Belgravia's civilization was only skin deep, "a coat of varnish." Snow's real subject was the end of the empire and civilization itself, for which he used Belgravia as the symbol.

Pimlico, Belgravia's neighbor to the south, named for a long-forgotten drink, is a cheaper, shabbier version of Belgravia. It was heavily bombed in World War II (the Germans were aiming at Victoria Station), but its Victorian atmosphere lingers in its rows of tall, identical houses with solid, columned porticos. Once cream or white like their neighbors to the north, many have been repainted in rainbow colors that range from dark chocolate to pink and bright yellow. Instead of specialty shops catering to the wealthy, Pimlico has odd shops offering bargains, small cafés, and a multitude of bed and breakfast hotels patronized by the hordes of backpacking tourists who descend on the neighborhood from Victoria Station. At its southern boundary along the Thames, once an area of docks and warehouses, there are modern blocks of high-rise housing quite alien to the essential character of Pimlico or Belgravia.

LENGTH OF WALK: 3 miles

See map on page 204 for the boundaries of this walk and page 270 for a list of the detectives and stories covered.

PLACES OF INTEREST

Belgrave Square:
> Foreign embassies. They include, counterclockwise from the northwest corner: Syria, Portugal, Ghana, Austria, Germany, Spain, Saudi Arabia, Trinidad, Turkey, Malaysia, and Mexico.

Eaton Square:
> *St. Peter's Church.*
> *Embassies:* Belgium, Bolivia.

Chester Square:
> *St. Michael's Church.*

Gerald Road Police Station.

Tate Gallery, Millbank. British painting since 1500, foreign painting and modern sculpture. Special collections of Constable, Blake, Turner, Pre-Raphaelites. Open Mon.–Sat., 10:00–6:00; Sun., 2:00–6:00 P.M. Admission charge for special exhibits.

PLACES TO EAT

Ebury Court Hotel, 26 Ebury Street. Alcoved restaurant in old-fashioned hotel. English atmosphere with English food— roasts, grills, steak and kidney pie, sherry trifle. Reservations needed. 01-730-8147.

Tate Gallery, Millbank. Two places to eat on lower ground floor. Restaurant (licensed) with murals by Rex Whistler, elegant and expensive. Open weekdays, 12:00–3:00 P.M. Reservations needed. 01-834-6754. Refreshment Room (cafeteria). Open Mon.–Sat., 10:30–5:30; Sun., 2:00–5:30 P.M.

Duke of Wellington, 63 Eaton Terrace. Cozy neighborhood pub with wood-paneled walls, decorated with brasses and military prints. Good curry, cottage pie, and quiche. Real ale.

———— BELGRAVIA/PIMLICO WALK ————

BELGRAVIA

This is a residential walk, especially pleasant on a sunny day. Begin by taking the Grosvenor Gardens exit from Victoria Underground Station and turning to the left to walk along Grosvenor Gardens. You will pass by a tiny, green, fenced park, with its backpacking tourists and bums and a mounted statue of Marshal Foch, who led the Allied armies in World War I. Cross Hobart Place to Grosvenor Place, which stretches all the way along the back wall of Buckingham Palace's extensive grounds. It was inside these grounds that Aidan Mackey set the beginning of his delightful story *Mr. Chesterton Comes to Tea,* based on G.K.C.'s drawings for the children of literary editor Archibald Marshall. In that adventure, the king, who

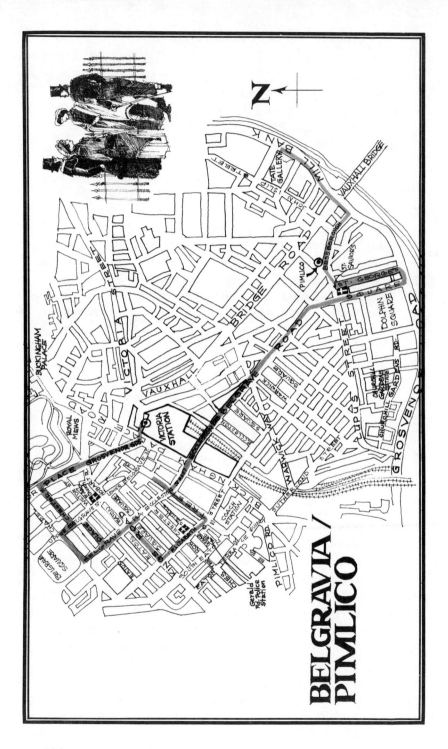

BELGRAVIA / PIMLICO

was tired of being good and opening public buildings, slipped out of the palace one night by a forgotten door near Constitution Hill and caught a hansom cab in search of adventure.

Cross Wilton Street and keep going until you reach Chester Street. Turn left and go down Chester Street to Upper Belgrave Street. You will begin to pass the typically elegant Belgravian terraces of townhouses. Turn right and walk straight into Belgrave Square, an enormous park covering ten acres. It is often called the most notable square in all London.

A century ago, this square, now home to a variety of foreign embassies, whose gaily colored flags will test your international savoir faire, was the home of three dukes, thirteen peers, including baronets, and as many M.P.s. The surrounding terraces now house institutions, societies, colleges, and professional associations, but there are still private homes there, too.

No. 21 Belgrave Terrace was the residence of Patricia Moyes's fabulously wealthy Lord Charlton in *Who Is Simon Warwick?* The mystery began on a rainy November night. Only a few scurrying pedestrians under black umbrellas and pale chiffon ladies who shivered under the neoclassical porticoes were visible when Lord Charlton summoned his solicitor, Ambrose Quince, to tell him to search for his missing nephew, Simon Warwick. Scotland Yard detective Henry Tibbett, who later handled the murders that resulted from this search, lived to the west, in Chelsea, in a shabby flat on the ground floor of a Victorian house.

Belgrave Square was the location of Marsden House, where, in Ngaio Marsh's *Death in a White Tie,* the fatal debutante ball for Lady Carrados's daughter Bridget was held. After the ball, Inspector Alleyn's friend, Lord "Bunchy" Gospell, was murdered in a taxi by another guest whom the unsuspecting cabbie dropped off at Lord Bunchy's home at 200 Cheyne Walk, Chelsea. When the frightened cabbie discovered the body, he drove it to Scotland Yard.

Turn to your left and walk across the southern side of Belgrave Square. Go past the statue of the South American liberator, Simon Bolivar, at the southwestern corner at Belgrave Place. Turn left and walk down Belgrave Place past Belgrave Mews to Eaton Place.

There are a number of fictional mystery addresses in Eaton Place, so turn to your left and walk along the square, choosing likely houses. In Ngaio Marsh's *A Wreath for Rivera,* the fictional 3 Duke's Gate, Eaton Place, was the townhouse of eccentric Lord Pastern, who insisted on playing the drums in Breezy Bellairs's band and secretly wrote a lovelorn advice column. In contrast to his eccentric manners, the front of his house, with a fanlight and beautifully designed doors, had "an air of reticence." His lordship's band practiced in the dining room beyond the drawing room on the first floor.

In *Cool Repentance,* Antonia Fraser's actress, Christabel Herrick, took her scandalous young lover, Barry Blagge, to her flat in Eaton Place. Blagge then used Christabel for publicity en route to stardom in the pop music world as the singer "Iron Boy." The murdered Arnold Vereker in Georgette Heyer's *Death in the Stocks* had a "consciously opulent" mansion in Eaton Place, which his bohemian brother and sister loathed.

Walk back to Belgrave Place and turn left to walk south toward Eaton Square, a parkway made up of two long, narrow green strips divided by the roaring traffic of King's Road. At the northeast corner stands the colonnaded front of St. Peter's Eaton Square, scene of many large, society weddings. Although mostly divided into flats, these houses remain fashionable today. In a fussy, feminine drawing room there in P.D. James's *The Skull Beneath the Skin,* Cordelia Gray returned a lost cat and met actress Clarissa Lyle.

In C.P. Snow's mystery, *A Coat of Varnish,* 36 Eaton Square was the home of a rich, upwardly mobile Labor M.P., Tom Thirkell. Rich Graham Bendix had his townhouse in Eaton Square in Anthony Berkeley's *The Poisoned Chocolates Case.* It was the murder of Bendix's wife that Roger Sheringham had the Crimes Circle undertake to solve for Scotland Yard. Eaton Square was also where Lady Nest and Geoffrey Poulton lived in Georgette Heyer's *Duplicate Death.* Lady Nest had been a 1920s "Bright Young Thing," the kind who used to go to Limehouse in the East End for a thrill. She now took dope and was implicated in the Mayfair murder of social climber Mrs. Haddington.

Turn right and walk through Eaton Square along King's Road. (Farther west, beyond Sloane Square, King's Road becomes the village "high street" of Chelsea, where you can see contemporary fashion—mod or punk—on display.) Ngaio Marsh's old Miss Wade, who belonged to the House of the Sacred Flame, lived here in *Death in Ecstasy*. John Le Carré's George Smiley and his unfaithful wife, Lady Ann, lived on Bywater Road off King's Road in Chelsea; while Agatha Christie herself rented a flat at 48 Swan's Court off King's Road during the 1950s.

Turn left when you reach Elizabeth Street and walk across the southwestern side of Eaton Square. In *A Coat of Varnish*, it was between Eaton Square and Chester Square that C.P. Snow placed his imaginary Aylesworth Square, which lay just east of Elizabeth Street. Lord Snow described Aylesworth Square as symbolic of all Belgravia, a part of the "most homogeneous residential district in any capital city in the world and in a quiet and seemly fashion, the most soothing to the eye." Snow wrote that "although the mansions now had basement flats and little domestic help, they were still big and gracious. Built around a fenced garden, they had tiny patio gardens in back, which opened into mews" (just as the houses do in Eaton Square).

Snow's mystery opened on a hot summer's night when Humphrey Leigh, a retired civil servant, set out to pay a visit to his neighbor in the square, old Lady Ashbrook. Leigh, a rather Jamesian detached observer of society, thought that it was ironic that Elizabeth Street, now a posh shopping quarter, was once Eliza Street, where prostitutes worked the river traffic. Snow's Aylesworth Square had its own parish church, in which Lady Ashbrook's funeral was later held. A real-life substitute would be St. Michael's Church at the corner of Elizabeth Street and Chester Row.

Later on, Leigh and a Jewish-American friend went to a pub between Eaton Square and Buckingham Palace Road. Because the two men were interested in the habits of the English natives, they met for a ritual Saturday drink there in the quiet, comfortable surroundings of stained glass and varnished wood. One summer Saturday, a bunch of rowdies stormed in from a cricket match and terrorized everyone until the police got there. They were called from the Gerald Road Police Station south off Elizabeth Street. (There are a number of pleasant neighborhood pubs that you might choose for Leigh's local drinking spot; one good one on Eaton Terrace is the Duke of Wellington, which is two blocks to your right along King's Road, running parallel to Elizabeth Street.)

Continue along Elizabeth Street past Eaton Mews to Chester Row. Charles Dickens lived at 1 Chester Row in 1846, the year that he founded and began to edit the *Daily News*. Chester Row leads to your left into Chester Square. It was in this vicinity that the House of the Sacred Flame was found in Ngaio Marsh's *Death in Ecstasy*. It stood at the end of one of her pet fictional cul-de-sacs called Knocklatcher's Row, off fictitious Chester Terrace.

One rainy Sunday, reporter Nigel Bathgate looked out his window and saw a small hanging sign made of red glass and shaped to represent a flame rising from a cup. Bathgate went to investigate and found that, inside, the House looked like nothing so much as an ultramodern art exhibit gone completely demented. There was a feathered serpent on the altar, and the walls were lined with Nordic gods and goddesses, all proving, as Dame Ngaio wrote, that there are "many strange places of worship in London and all sorts of little religions squeak, like mice in the wainscotting."

Continue to walk south along Elizabeth Street past Gerald Road, with its police station, St. Michael's Church, and Ebury Mews, until you come to Ebury Street. Turn left on Ebury Street and walk northeast until you have crossed Eccleston Street. The Ebury Court Hotel is in the middle of the next block on the north side of the street.

There are a number of cafés and restaurants around here, but the Ebury Court Hotel, 26 Ebury Street, is small and cozy in a very English way and has a good restaurant serving excellent English food. If you didn't know that she stayed at Bertram's Hotel in Mayfair, you would expect to see Agatha

Christie's Miss Marple sitting in the lounge. (See Mayfair/ Oxford Street Walk.)

The Ebury Court Hotel has both the atmosphere and geography of two Father Brown stories in G.K. Chesterton's *The Innocence of Father Brown*. It could be the place in "The Blue Cross" where Father Brown and the French master thief, Flambeau (disguised as another Roman Catholic priest), had breakfast, and Father Brown put salt in the sugar and threw coffee at the wall. The two then caught a bus that they took all the way north to Hampstead Heath, pursued by the French detective, Valentin.

The Ebury Court Hotel could also be Chesterton's Vernon Hotel, situated at the corner of a square in Belgravia, where the annual dinner of the exclusive men's club called the Twelve True Fishermen was held. In the story "The Queer Feet," Father Brown was called to administer extreme unction to a dying waiter and stopped Flambeau from stealing the club's silver fish service. He realized someone wearing evening clothes was pretending to be both a waiter and a gentleman. When Father Brown explained the trick to the club members, they hastily decided to wear *green* evening clothes to prevent such an embarrassing episode from happening again.

The band leader Breezy Bellairs, in Ngaio Marsh's *A Wreath for Rivera*, lived on Pikestaff Row near Ebury Street, while the two acolytes of the House of the Sacred Flame shared a flat at 17 Ebury Mews in *Death in Ecstasy*.

Turn right at the Ebury Court Hotel and walk back along Ebury Street to Eccleston Street. Then turn left again and follow Eccleston Street over Victoria Railroad Station on Eccleston Bridge. This street becomes Belgrave Road at Buckingham Palace Road, which is the boundary between Belgravia and Pimlico, which you are now entering.

PIMLICO

In the area just north of Victoria Station, Ann Radcliffe lived at 5 Stafford Row, which used to be located where Bressenden Place joined Buckingham Palace Road. Her Gothic novels combined horror, sensibility, and the picturesque in a manner that made her a forerunner of modern mystery writers like Ruth Rendell, whose macabre stories Antonia Fraser's Jemima Shore adores.

The fictional Amber Street in Pimlico, where Josephine Tey's Danny Miller lived, was also around here. He was a gangster in *The Man in the Queue* who was called to Scotland Yard to talk to Inspector Grant. To the west, Buckingham Palace Road runs into Pimlico Road. The drummer in Breezy Bellairs's band lived there in Marsh's *A Wreath for Rivera*. It was on fictional Parrot Street that Albert Campion nearly walked into thin air in Margery Allingham's *Flowers for the Judge*.

Keep walking down Belgrave Road, crossing Hugh Street, and the next street will bring you into Eccleston Square, which will be to the right. This is an attractive, large square containing a fenced garden with grass, flowers, and tall trees, surrounded by colonnaded townhouses. Winston Churchill lived for a time at No. 9. A number of the houses, like the cream-colored Elizabeth Hotel, are bed-and-breakfast places or have been broken up into flats. Both Eccleston Square's appearance and its geography make it a good substitute for P.D. James's fictional Caldecote Square.

In James's *Innocent Blood*, sociology professor Maurice Palfrey was first married to Lady Helena, an earl's daughter, who had been raised in a Palladian mansion in Wiltshire. Lady Helena had decided views on what kind of London residence was appropriate. According to her, "Hampstead was too trendy, Mayfair too expensive, Bayswater too vulgar, Belgravia too smart." Fortunately they found a house in fictional Caldecote Terrace, on the fringes of Pimlico, southeast of Victoria Station and Eccleston Bridge.

Like Antonia Fraser, P.D. James is fascinated by architecture; so, she described the perfectly decorated Palfrey house in great detail. Through the eyes of Palfrey's adopted daughter, Philippa, you see its restored elegance, with twin panels of Burne-Jones stained glass in the front door and a delicate stair banister in polished pale mahogany that curves up to the landing. The dining room had French doors that led by wrought-iron steps into a small, walled garden, with roses and white-painted tubs of geraniums, where the Palfreys had coffee on summer nights. Philippa Palfrey had her own long, low room on the top floor, sparsely furnished in pale, modern wood, with a view over the treetops.

Several of the houses in Eccleston Square could be converted into the Palfrey house with enough money and taste; choose one to suit yourself. Then walk around the square to choose one of the bed-and-breakfast places to be the shabby, stuccoed Hotel Casablanca, which catered to weekly groups of Spanish tourists. The avenging Mr. Scase, on the trail of Philippa Palfrey's real mother, rented a room at the Hotel Casablanca to sit with his binoculars and watch the Palfrey house at No. 68.

Then return to Belgrave Road at the southeast corner of Eccleston Square and, turning right, follow Belgrave Road. You will first cross Warwick Way; then, farther south and to your right, Warwick Square. As you walk south through Pimlico toward the river, you will cross the intersection of Gloucester Street and Denbigh Street, Charlwood Street, and, farther along, Moreton Street. You will pass by rows and rows and rows of old Victorian housing, some being gentrified, some falling to bits, and side streets with shops, stores, and cafés of all varieties, reflecting Pimlico's polyglot population.

Finally, you will reach Lupus Street, a major crossroads across Pimlico's southern end. To the west (or right), where Belgrave Road and Lupus Street meet, you will find yourself at St. George's Square.

Long and narrow, a square in name only, it leads to Grosvenor Road and the Thames. St. George's Square was laid out in the 1850s. No. 97A, St. George's Square (a fictitious address near the Thames end of the square on your left, as you face south on Lupus Street) was Miss Climpson's flat, rented for her by Lord Peter Wimsey. In Dorothy L. Sayers's *Unnatural Death,* Lord Peter mischievously took Charles Parker there, acting as if they were going to see his latest mistress. Sayers commented that the house, designed for a Victorian family with fatigue-proof servants, had been dissected by the late 1920s into half a dozen inconvenient bandboxes let out as flats.

After ringing the bell, Lord Peter and Parker mounted six flights of steep stairs to meet the head of the Cattery. Miss Alexandra Katherine Climpson, a thin, middle-aged woman with a sharp, sallow face and a very vivacious manner, wore a neat dark coat and skirt, a high-necked blouse, and a long gold neckchain with a variety of small ornaments. Miss Climpson was Dorothy Sayers's model for Agatha Christie's Miss Marple and Patricia Wentworth's Miss Silver. In a letter to Christie about their joint project for the BBC, Sayers described such female detectives as "Dear Old Tabbies," a compliment, of course, because Sayers adored cats. Given Miss Climpson's devoted high-churchmanship, it adds just the proper realistic Sayers touch to note that St. Savior's, the church at the head of St. George's Square on Lupus Street, follows only the most Anglo-Catholic of practices.

Off to the west along the Thames toward Chelsea, stretches the modern high-rise development called Churchill Gardens Estate. It might possibly be an appropriate model for the disputed Powers Estate owned by confused Sister Miriam in Antonia Fraser's *Quiet as a Nun*. It was also once the site of the kind of warehouses in which Fu Manchu, crated like furniture, once again escaped in Sax Rohmer's *The Trail of Fu Manchu*.

You now can do one of two things. Either walk back from No. 97A to Lupus Street and turn right to the Pimlico Underground Station on Bessborough Street to end the walk. Or walk past the Pimlico Underground Station, turn right on Bessborough Street, and follow it to Vauxhall Bridge Road. Cross Vauxhall Bridge Road to Millbank, which runs beside the Thames River. Cross Ponsonby Place and Atterbury Street. On your left, you have arrived at the Tate Gallery, with its famous collections of modern painting and sculpture.

The Tate was built in 1897 on the site of the 18-acre brick fortress of the Millbank Penitentiary, demolished in 1890. In *The Sign of Four,* Sherlock Holmes and Watson landed by the penitentiary after crossing the Thames River. This building was near the neighborhood that Anne Perry's Inspector Pitt knew as the dreadful, brothel-ridden slum called the Devil's Acre, "under the shadow of Westminster."

The Tate houses the national collection of British and foreign modern art. Its holdings include famous examples of the "Golden Age" of British painting, with Reynolds, Gainsborough, Romney, Lawrence, George Stubbs, and Constable, as well as many works by Turner and William Blake. (G.K. Chesterton wrote one of his small, insightful biographies about Blake.) There are also representative contemporary works displayed here.

On the lower level you can find refreshment at either the Refreshment Room cafeteria or the expensive Rex Whistler Restaurant, noted for its murals, wine list, and excellent food. In Jessica Mann's *Grave Goods,* Tamara Hoyland was taken to the Rex Whistler Room by an art dealer before going to look at an alleged Giotto in Pimlico. The two ended up in a mad chase after the Horn Treasure, which was the regalia of Emperor Charlemagne. (Dorothy Sayers had translated *The Song of Roland,* in which Charlemagne starred.)

In Antonia Fraser's *A Splash of Red,* the painter Kevin John Athlone had a painting hung at the Tate. He was one of the lovers of Jemima Shore's murdered friend, Chloe. Chloe owned his canvas called "A Splash of Red," and the similarity between the paintings was noticed by Jemima's pal "Pompey" from Scotland Yard.

After you are finished enjoying the Tate, exit to Millbank, where Charles Williams's Lester Furnival lived with her husband, Richard, in *All Hallows Eve.* Turn to your right and walk across Vauxhall Bridge Road. Turn right into Bessborough Street, which you will follow back to the Pimlico Underground Station.

SPECIAL HELPS

PLACES TO EAT BY WALK

In choosing from these listings, remember that currently pub hours are 11:30–3:00, 5:30–11:00 P.M., weekdays; 12:00–2:00 P.M., 7:00–10:30 P.M., Sundays.

CITY WALK

Most City restaurants and taverns are closed Saturdays and Sundays, so you may have to do the walk and then return to Covent Garden or Soho to eat.

Sweetings, 39 Queen Victoria Street. London's first fish restaurant, established 1830. Tiny and crowded. Open Mon.–Fri., 11:45–3:00 P.M. 01-248-3062.

Bow Wine Vault, 10 Bow Churchyard. High-ceilinged bar with good salads, cheeses. Open Mon.–Fri., 10:00–7:00 P.M. 01-248-1121.

Ye Olde Watling, 29 Watling Street. Archetypal City tavern with great beams and leaded windows. Intimate restaurant upstairs. Open Mon.–Fri., 12:00–2:15 P.M. 01-248-6235.

Barbican Waterside Café, Level 5, Barbican Centre. Self-service cafeteria by man-made lake. Open Mon.–Fri., to 5:30 P.M. in good weather. 01-638-4141.

INNS OF COURT/FLEET STREET WALK

Most pubs and restaurants are closed on weekends.

El Vino, 47 Fleet Street. Wine bar. Women not served at bar, ties required for men.

Ye Olde Cock Tavern, 22 Fleet Street. Elizabethan tavern. 01-353-8570.

Ye Olde Cheshire Cheese, 145 Fleet Street. Dr. Johnson's haunt. Reservations necessary. 01-353-6170.

The Devereux Pub, Devereux Court. G.K. Chesterton's Distributists met here to drink and sing. 01-583-4562.

Edgar Wallace Pub, 41 Essex Street. Mementos of the writer.

The Royal Courts of Justice, the Strand. Café for lunch or tea.

The Central Criminal Courts (Old Bailey), Old Bailey Street. Canteen.

COVENT GARDEN/THE STRAND WALK

Lyons Corner House, the Strand. New version of gold and white chain of restaurants popular with detective story characters. Garden Restaurant serves meals, brunch, and afternoon tea. Open daily to 8:00 P.M.

Tutton's, 11-12 Russell Street, Covent Garden. Inexpensive international restaurant, café, and pub in old Potato Market. Sidewalk tables. Open daily, 9:00–11:30 P.M. 01-836-1167.

Rule's, 35 Maiden Lane. Famous restaurant with Victorian decor and English fare. Haunt of VIPs from Charles Dickens to Dorothy Sayers. Expensive. Open Mon.–Fri., to 11:30 P.M. Closed in August. Cover charge and no credit cards. Reservations needed. 01-836-5314.

Simpson's-in-the-Strand, 100 Strand. An "English institution." Known for its carvery roasts served from carts. Open Mon.–Sat., to 10:00 P.M. Reservations needed. 01-836-9112.

The Salisbury, 90 St. Martin's Lane. Theatrical pub opposite the Coliseum. Handsome etched glass, paneling, and red velvet seats.

BLOOMSBURY WALK

Lamb's, 94 Lamb's Conduit Street. Charles Dickens's favorite, with Victorian decor and small garden. Rowlandson prints and photos of theatrical people. 01-405-0713.

Pizza Express, 30 Coptic Street. Good chain with wine by the glass. 01-636-2244. Open daily to midnight.

Museum Tavern, 49 Great Russell Street. Pub across from the British Museum, where Karl Marx, Bloomsbury Group drank. Stained glass and velvet drapes. 01-242-8987.

SOHO WALK

This area abounds in restaurants, both cheap and expensive. Its Chinatown places stay open Sundays and late.

Quality Inn, Coventry Street and Rupert Street. Good, inexpensive chain.

Manzi's, 1-2 Leicester Street. Famous fish and seafood restaurant on two floors. Reservations needed. Open Mon.–Sat. until 11:30 P.M. Closed Sundays. 01-734-0224.

Au Jardin des Gourmets, 5 Greek Street. French, famous for old claret. Open Mon.–Sat., to 11:30 P.M. Closed Sundays. Reservations needed. 01-437-1816.

National Gallery, Trafalgar Square. Restaurant. Open Mon.–Sat., 10:00–5:00; Sun., 2:30–5:00 P.M.

Tom Cribb, Panton Street (behind Haymarket). A Regency pub once called Union Arms. Prize-fighter mementos.

Red Lion, 14 Kingly Street.

La Terrazza, 19 Romilly Street. Expensive Italian restaurant near Moulin d'Or, favorite restaurant of Dorothy Sayers. Open daily, to 11:30 P.M. Reservations needed. 01-734-2504.

Regent Palace Hotel, Sherwood Street. Coffee shop, pub, and English carvery in main dining room, with 1920s Hollywood decor.

Pizzaland (the "green and white" chain), Leicester Square.

Loon Fung, 37 Gerrard Street. Popular with Chinese. 01-437-5429. Open to 1:00 A.M.

MAYFAIR/OXFORD STREET WALK

Most of the big department stores on Oxford Street have restaurants.

Café Royal, 68 Regent Street. Grill, Le Relais restaurant, with rococo decor from time of Oscar Wilde. Site of the Detection Club Initiations. Continental. Expensive, but very friendly service. Open daily to 11:00 P.M. Reservations needed. 01-439-6320, -6082.

The Connaught Hotel, Carlos Place. Grill and restaurant serving English and French fare. Jackets and ties required. Popular with mystery story TV personnel. Open daily, 12:30–10:30 P.M. Reservations needed. Grill closed, Sat., Sun. 01-492-0668.

Brown's Hotel, 21-24 Dover Street. Restaurant with genuine old English atmosphere in paneled dining room. Open Mon.–Sat., 12:30–10:00 P.M.; Sun., to 9:00 P.M. Afternoon tea served in the lounge. 01-499-6122.

Shepherd's Tavern, 50 Hertford Street, Shepherd Market. 300-year-old paneled pub. R.A.F. clientele. Real ale. 01-499-3017.

Claridge's Hotel, Brook Street. Elegant 1930s-style restaurant with orchestra. Huge menu card. Causerie with good cold buffet. Open to 11:00 P.M. Reservations needed. 01-629-8860.

ST. JAMES WALK

Fortnum & Mason, 181 Piccadilly. The Patio; The Soda Fountain. Open Mon.–Sat., 9:00–11:45 P.M. 01-734-8040.

The Red Lion, Crown Passage. Pub food in narrow alley. Crowded at noon.

Overton's, 5 St. James's Street. Gentleman's club atmosphere. Famous for fish and oyster bar. Reservations needed. Open to 10:30 P.M. 01-839-3774.

The Ritz Hotel, Piccadilly and Green Park. Louis XVI Restaurant, Edwardian Baroque; Palm Court for afternoon tea. Dress correctly. Reservations needed. Open Sun., 7:30 A.M. for brunch. Mon.–Sat., noon to 11:00 P.M. 01-493-8181.

MARYLEBONE/REGENT'S PARK WALK

Prince Regent, 71 Marylebone High Street. Regency decor with mementos of "Prinny." Open Mon.–Fri., to 10:30 P.M. 01-935-2018.

Bertorelli Bros, 19 Charlotte Street. Italian restaurant dating from the 1920s. Open Mon.–Sat., to 10:00 P.M. 01-636-4174.

Madame Tussaud's, Marylebone Road. Cafeteria.

REGENT'S PARK:

The Rose Garden Buffet, Queen Mary's Gardens. Self-service outdoors. Open to 4:00 P.M. in winter, 11:00 P.M. in summer.

The Zoo, Regent Restaurant on first floor; Regent Cafeteria on ground level. Both licensed and serve lunch and tea. Also in zoo grounds there are the Pavilion Bar, Mappin Café, and Garden Café for light refreshments.

WESTMINSTER WALK

Sherlock Holmes, 10 Northumberland Street. Sherlock Holmes Museum with replica of 221B Baker Street sitting room, across from first floor restaurant. Open Mon.–Sat., to 9:15 P.M. Reservations needed. 01-930-2644.

St. Stephen's Tavern, 10 Bridge Street. Victorian restaurant with view of Thames River and Members bell for House of Commons. Open Mon.–Sat., to 9:00 P.M. Reservations needed. 01-930-2541.

The Albert, 52 Victoria Street. Victorian pub with carvery restaurant upstairs. Real ale. 01-222-5577.

BROMPTON/HYDE PARK WALK

Harrods, Brompton Road. A variety of places to eat within the store.

4th floor: **Georgian Restaurant, Carvery and Cold Table, Way in Circle** (self-service).
1st floor: **Dress Circle** (self-service).
Ground floor: **West Side Express,** open from 7:45 A.M.

Paxton's Head, 153 Knightsbridge Road. Pub commemorating Sir Joseph Paxton, who built the Crystal Palace Exhibition Hall. Victorian bar. 01-589-6627.

Hyde Park restaurants:

The Dell, open daily in summer.

The Serpentine, open all year.

Victoria and Albert Museum, Cromwell Road. Licensed restaurant and self-service cafeteria. Open to 5:30 P.M.

BELGRAVIA/PIMLICO WALK

Ebury Court Hotel, 26 Ebury Street. Old-fashioned English atmosphere and food. Reservations needed. Open to 10:00 P.M. 01-730-8147.

Tate Gallery, Millbank. Two places to eat on lower ground floor:

Rex Whistler Room. Expensive and elegant restaurant with murals by Rex Whistler. Open Mon.–Fri., 12:00–3:00 P.M. Reservations needed. 01-834-6754.

Refreshment Room. Cafeteria. Open Mon.–Sat., 10:30–5:30; Sun., 2:00–5:30 P.M.

Duke of Wellington, 63 Eaton Terrace. Cozy neighborhood pub with wood paneling, brasses, military prints. Curry, cottage pie, and real ale. 01-730-3103.

PLACES OF INTEREST BY WALK

CITY WALK

St. Paul's Cathedral, Ludgate Hill. Open daily, April–Oct., 7:30–6:00 P.M.; Nov.–March, 7:30–5:00. Free except for special areas like the crypt, ambulary, and galleries, which are open only Easter to Sept., Mon.–Fri., 10:00–5:00; Sat., 11:00–4:45; Oct. to Easter, to 4:00 P.M.

Bank of England, Threadneedle Street. Open by appointment only. Free.

Mansion House, Mansion House Street. Open by appointment only on alternate Saturdays. Free.

The Guildhall, Gresham Street. Open May–Sept., Mon.–Sat., 10:00–5:00; Sun., 2:00–5:00 P.M. Free.

Tower of London, Tower Hill. Open Mar.–Oct., Mon.–Sat., 9:30–5:00; Sun., 2:00–5:00 P.M.; Nov.–Feb., 9:30–4:00 P.M. Admission charge, extra for the Jewel House.

Barbican Arts Centre, Aldersgate. London equivalent of New York City's Lincoln Center, Paris's Centre Pompidou. Home of London Symphony Orchestra and the Royal Shakespeare Company.

Museum of London, London Wall. Open Tues.–Sat., 10:00–6:00; Sun., 2:00–6:00 P.M. Free.

The Monument, Monument Street. Open May–Sept., Mon.–Sat., 9:00–6:00; Sun., 2:00–6:00 P.M.; Oct.–April, Mon.–Sat., 9:00–3:40 P.M. Admission charge.

All-Hallows-by-the-Tower, Byward Street. Open Mon.–Sat., 10:30–6:00; Sun., 10:30–5:30 P.M. Services at 11:00 A.M.

St.-Mary-le-Bow, Bow Street.

INNS OF COURT/FLEET STREET WALK

Inns of Court (closed weekends):
  Gray's Inn
  Lincoln's Inn
  Inner Temple
  Middle Temple

Royal Courts of Justice, The Strand. Open Mon.–Fri., 10:30–4:30 P.M.

Temple Bar, Fleet Street/The Strand.

Staple Inn, High Holborn. Closed Sun.

Public Record Office Museum, Chancery Lane. Open Mon.–Fri., 1:00–4:00 P.M.

St. Clement Dane's Church, The Strand.

The Old Bailey (Central Criminal Courts), Old Bailey Street. Open Mon.–Fri., 10:15 A.M. to the Rising of the Courts.

Dr. Johnson's House, 17 Gough Square. Oct.–April, Mon.–Sat., 11:00–5:30 P.M. Admission charge.

Sir John Soane's Museum, Lincoln's Inn Fields. Tues.–Sat., 10:00–5:00 P.M. (Closed in August.)

Somerset House, The Strand. Mon.–Fri., 8:30–4:30 P.M.

COVENT GARDEN/THE STRAND WALK

St. Martin's-in-the-Fields, St. Martin's Place.

Covent Garden:
> **St. Paul's Church.** Closed Sundays.
> **London Transport Museum.** Open daily, 10:00–6:00 P.M. Admission charge.
> **The Royal Opera House**

Bow Street Police Court, Bow Street.

Cleopatra's Needle, Victoria Embankment.

Queen's Chapel of the Savoy, Savoy Hill. Tues.–Fri., 11:30–3:30 P.M.; Sun. service, 11:15 A.M.

BLOOMSBURY WALK

University of London:
> **University College,** Gower Street. Open Mon.–Fri., 9:30–5:00 P.M. **The Petrie Museum.** Open Mon.–Fri., 10:00–5:00 P.M.

British Museum, Great Russell Street. Open Mon.–Sat., 10:00–5:00; Sun., 2:30–6:00 P.M. Free.
Reading Room, Tours on the hour, 11:00–4:00 P.M.
Admission by Reader Card only.

Dickens's House, 48 Doughty Street. Museum in home of Charles Dickens. Open Mon.–Sat., 10:00–5:00 P.M. Admission charge.

Percival David Foundation of Chinese Art, Gordon Square. Open Mon., 2:00–5:00 P.M.; Tues.–Fri., 10:30–5:00; Sat., 10:30–1:00 P.M. Free.

Courtauld Institute Galleries, Woburn Square. Open Mon.–Sat., 10:00–5:00; Sun., 2:00–5:00 P.M. Admission charge.

Jewish Museum, Woburn House, Tavistock Square. Open Mon.–Thurs., 12:30–3:00 P.M.; Sun., 10:30–12:45. Free.

Soho Walk

Statue of Eros, Piccadilly Circus.

Leicester Square: half-price ticket office.

National Gallery, Trafalgar Square. Mon.–Fri., 10:00–6:00; Sun., 2:00–6:00 P.M. Free.

National Portrait Gallery, St. Martin's Place. Mon.–Fri., 10:00–5:00; Sat., 10:00–6:00 P.M.; Sun., 2:00–6:00 P.M. Free.

Carnaby Street.

Foyles, Charing Cross Road.

Palladium Music Hall, 8 Argyll Street.

House of St. Barnabas, 1 Greek Street, Soho Square. Open by written appointment only.

Guinness World of Records, Trocadero Centre, Coventry Street. Open daily 10:00–9:30 P.M. Admission charge.

Mayfair/Oxford Street Walk

Sotheby's, 34-35 New Bond Street. World's oldest and largest auction house. Open Mon.–Fri., 9:00–4:30 P.M. Closed Aug. and Sept.

Marlborough Fine Art, Ltd., 6 Albemarle Street. Open Mon.–Fri., 10:00–5:30; Sat., 10:00–12:30 P.M. Free.

Museum of Mankind, 6 Burlington Gardens. Mon.–Fri., 10:00–5:00; Sun., 2:30–6:00 P.M. Free.

U.S. Embassy, Grosvenor Square.

The Royal Academy of Arts, Burlington House, Piccadilly. Open daily, 10:00–6:00 P.M. Free, but there is a charge for major exhibitions.

St. James Walk

St. James's Palace, Cleveland Row. Official Seat of Royalty.
   Chapel Royal, Sun. service, 8:30, 11:15 A.M., Oct.–Palm Sunday.

St. James's Church, Piccadilly.

Marlborough House, Pall Mall. Former residence of Queen Mary, now Commonwealth Conference Centre.

Queen's Chapel. Sun. service, 8:30, 11:15 A.M., Easter–July.

Buckingham Palace, London residence of Her Majesty Queen Elizabeth II. Royal Standard is flown when she is in residence.

Changing of the Guard. Daily, 11:30 A.M., April–Aug.; every other day, 11:30 A.M., Sept.–Mar.

Lancaster House, Stable Yard, St. James's Palace. Open Sat.–Sun., 2:00–6:00 P.M., Easter–mid-Sept. Admission charge.

Queen's Gallery, Buckingham Gate. Tues.–Sat., 11:00–5:00; Sun., 2:00–5:00 P.M. Admission charge.

Royal Mews, Buckingham Palace Road. Wed.–Thurs., 2:00–4:00 P.M. Admission charge.

Christie's Auction House, 8 King Street. Open Mon.–Fri., 9:00–4:00 P.M.; closed in August.

MARYLEBONE WALK/REGENT'S PARK WALK

221B Baker Street.

Broadcasting House (BBC), Portland Place.

London Planetarium, Marylebone Road. Open daily, April–Sept., 11:00–6:00 P.M.; Oct.–Mar., 11:00–4:30 P.M. Admission charge.

London Telecom Tower (Post Office Tower), Maple Street. No admission.

Madame Tussaud's, Marylebone Road. Open daily, 10:00–5:30 P.M. Admission charge.

Regent's Park:

London Zoo. Open daily, summer, 9:00–6:00 P.M.; winter, 10:00–6:00 P.M. Admission charge.

Queen Mary's Gardens.

Wallace Collection, Manchester Square. Open Mon.–Sat., 10:00–5:00; Sun., 2:00–5:00 P.M. Free.

WESTMINSTER WALK

Trafalgar Square.

Banqueting House, Whitehall. Open Tues.–Sat., 10:00–5:00; Sun., 2:00–5:00 P.M. Admission charge.

Horse Guards, Whitehall. Changing of the Guard: Weekdays, 11:00 A.M.; Sun., 10:00 A.M.

No. 10 Downing Street.

The Cenotaph.

New Scotland Yard, Norman Shaw Building.

New Scotland Yard, 10 Broadway.

St. James's Park.

Big Ben (Clock Tower), Bridge Street.

Westminster Bridge.

Westminster Abbey, Parliament Square. Open daily, 8:00–6:00; Wed., 8:00–8:00 P.M. Admission charge for Royal Chapels, Poets' Corner.

Westminster Cathedral, Ashley Place. Campanile open 10:30 to dusk. Admission charge.

St. Margaret's Church, Westminster.

Houses of Parliament, Parliament Square. Queue at St. Stephen's Porch or contact an M.P.

Jewel Tower, Old Palace Yard. Mon.–Fri., 9:30–6:30 P.M., Mar. 15–Oct. 15.

BROMPTON/HYDE PARK WALK

Hyde Park:

    Serpentine
    Marble Arch (Tyburn Hill)
    Hyde Park Corner: Wellington Arch, Apsley House.
    Speakers' Corner

Kensington Gardens:

    Kensington Palace. Daily, summer, 10:00–6:00; winter, 10:00–5:00 P.M.
    The Long Water
    Peter Pan

Physical Energy
Albert Memorial
The Round Pond

Geological Museum, Exhibition Road. Mon.–Sat., 10:00–6:00;
Sun., 2:30–6:00 P.M. Free.

Harrods, Brompton Road.

Natural History Museum, Cromwell Road. Open Mon.–Sat.,
10:00–6:00; Sun., 2:30–6:00 P.M. Free.

Oratory of St. Philip Neri, Brompton Road. Open daily, 7:00
A.M.–8:00 P.M.

Royal Albert Hall, Kensington Gore.

Science Museum, Exhibition Road. Mon.–Sat., 10:00–6:00; Sun.,
2:30–6:00 P.M. Free.

Victoria and Albert Museum, Cromwell Road. Open
Mon.–Thurs., Sat., 10:00–5:00; Sun., 2:30–5:00 P.M.
Donations requested.

Belgravia/Pimlico Walk

Belgrave Square, Foreign embassies.

Chester Square, St. Michael's Church.

Eaton Square: St. Peter's Church.

Gerald Road Police Station.

Tate Gallery, Millbank. Mon.–Sat., 10:00–6:00; Sun., 2:00–6:00
P.M. Admission charge for special exhibits.

St. Savior's Church, Lupus Street, Pimlico.

THEATERS AND CONCERT HALLS BY WALK

City Walk

Barbican, Barbican Arts Centre, Silk Street, Moorsgate.

Covent Garden/The Strand Walk

Adelphi, The Strand.
Savoy, The Strand.

The Theatre Royal, Drury Lane, Catherine Street.
National Theatre, South Bank.
Old Vic, Waterloo Road.
Player's, Villiers Street.
Royal Opera House, Covent Garden.
Coliseum, St. Martin's Lane.
Albery Theatre, St. Martin's Lane.
Arts Theatre Club, 6 Great Newport Street.
Ambassadors, West Street.
St. Martin's, West Street.
Phoenix Theatre, Charing Cross Road.
Royal Festival Hall, South Bank.
Vaudeville, The Strand.

SOHO WALK

Half-price same-day Ticket Office in Leicester Square.
Criterion, Piccadilly.
The Haymarket, Haymarket.
Her Majesty's, Haymarket.
Palladium, 8 Argyll Street.
Piccadilly, Denman Street.
The Queen's Theatre, Shaftesbury Avenue.
Odeon, Leicester Square (formerly the Alhambra).

MAYFAIR/OXFORD STREET WALK

Curzon, Curzon Street.

MARYLEBONE/REGENT'S PARK WALK

Open Air Theatre, Queen Mary's Gardens, Regent's Park.

Brompton/Hyde Park Walk

Royal Albert Hall, Kensington Gore.

SHOPS MENTIONED IN WALKS BY CATEGORY

Art, Antiques, and Jewelry

Agnew's, 43 Bond Street. (MAYFAIR/OXFORD STREET WALK)

Asprey's, 166 New Bond Street. (MAYFAIR/OXFORD STREET WALK)

Bonham and Sons, Montpelier Street. (BROMPTON/HYDE PARK WALK)

Christie's Auction House, 8 King Street. (ST. JAMES WALK)

Marlborough Fine Art Ltd., 39 Bond Street. (MAYFAIR/ OXFORD STREET WALK)

Sotheby's, 34-35 Bond Street. (MAYFAIR/OXFORD STREET WALK)

Books

Foyles, 119 Charing Cross Road. (SOHO WALK)

Hatchard's, 187 Piccadilly. (ST. JAMES WALK)

Virago, 34 Southampton Street. (COVENT GARDEN/THE STRAND WALK)

Victor Gollancz, 14 Henrietta Street (COVENT GARDEN/THE STRAND WALK)

W.H. Smith, In every railway station.

Wiley's Legal Bookstore (INNS OF COURT/FLEET STREET WALK)

Department Stores

Army & Navy, 105 Victoria Street. (WESTMINSTER WALK)

Austin Reed, Regent Street. (MAYFAIR/OXFORD STREET WALK)

Fortnum & Mason, Piccadilly. (ST. JAMES WALK)

Harrods, 87-135 Brompton Road. (BROMPTON/HYDE PARK WALK)

Selfridges, 398-429 Oxford Street. (MARYLEBONE/ REGENT'S PARK WALK)

Dickens & Jones, 224-44 Regent Street. (MAYFAIR/OXFORD STREET WALK)

John Lewis, 242-306 Oxford Street. (MAYFAIR/OXFORD STREET WALK)

Liberty's, 210-20 Regent Street. (SOHO WALK)

Marks & Spencer's, Oxford Street. (MAYFAIR/OXFORD STREET WALK)

AUTHORS, BOOKS, AND SLEUTHS BY WALK

CITY WALK: AUTHORS

Aird, Catherine	**In Harm's Way**
Bentley, E.C.	**Trent's Last Case**
Berkeley, Anthony	**The Poisoned Chocolates Case**
Brontë, Anne	—
Brontë, Charlotte	—
Carr, John Dickson	**The Mad Hatter Mystery**
Chesterton, G.K.	**The Ball and the Cross**
Christie, Agatha	**The Golden Ball**
Christie, Agatha	**The Mystery of the Blue Train**
Christie, Agatha	**The Secret Adversary**
Christie, Agatha	**The Secret of Chimneys**
Collins, Wilkie	**The Moonstone**
Dickens, Charles	—
Doyle, Sir Arthur Conan	**"A Case of Identity"**
Doyle, Sir Arthur Conan	**"The Dancing Men"**
Doyle, Sir Arthur Conan	**"The Mazarin Stone"**
Doyle, Sir Arthur Conan	**"The Three Garridebs"**

Francis, Dick	**Banker**
Francis, Dick	**Odds Against**
Grimes, Martha	**The Dirty Duck**
Heyer, Georgette	**Death in the Stocks**
Jonson, Ben	—
Keating, H.R.F.	**Inspector Ghote Hunts the Peacock**
Macaulay, Thomas Babington	—
Marsh, Ngaio	**A Surfeit of Lampreys**
Marsh, Ngaio	**A Wreath for Rivera**
Mason, A.E.W.	**The House in Lordship Lane**
Milne, A.A.	**The Red House Mystery**
Milton, John	—
Mitchell, Gladys	**Watson's Choice**
More, Sir Thomas	—
Orczy, Baroness	**Lady Molly of Scotland Yard**
Poe, Edgar Allan	—
Raleigh, Sir Walter	**The History of the World**
Rohmer, Sax	**The Trail of Fu Manchu**
Sayers, Dorothy L.	**Murder Must Advertise**
Sayers, Dorothy L.	**Whose Body?**
Shakespeare, William	**Richard III**
Symons, Julian	**The Blackheath Poisonings**
Tey, Josephine	**The Daughter of Time**
Wallace, Edgar	**The Crimson Circle**
Williams, Charles	**All Hallows Eve**
Williams, Charles	**War in Heaven**
Yorke, Margaret	**Cast for Death**

CITY WALK: BOOKS

"A Case of Identity"	Doyle, Sir Arthur Conan
All Hallows Eve	Williams, Charles
A Surfeit of Lampreys	Marsh, Ngaio
A Wreath for Rivera	Marsh, Ngaio
Banker	Francis, Dick
Cast for Death	Yorke, Margaret
Death in the Stocks	Heyer, Georgette

In Harm's Way	Aird, Catherine
Inspector Ghote Hunts the Peacock	Keating, H.R.F.
Lady Molly of Scotland Yard	Orczy, Baroness
Murder Must Advertise	Sayers, Dorothy L.
Odds Against	Francis, Dick
Richard III	Shakespeare, William
The Ball and the Cross	Chesterton, G.K.
The Blackheath Poisonings	Symons, Julian
The Crimson Circle	Wallace, Edgar
"The Dancing Men"	Doyle, Sir Arthur Conan
The Daughter of Time	Tey, Josephine
The Dirty Duck	Grimes, Martha
The Golden Ball	Christie, Agatha
The History of the World	Raleigh, Sir Walter
The House in Lordship Lane	Mason, A.E.W.
The Mad Hatter Mystery	Carr, John Dickson
"The Mazarin Stone"	Doyle, Sir Arthur Conan
The Moonstone	Collins, Wilkie
The Mystery of the Blue Train	Christie, Agatha
The Poisoned Chocolates Case	Berkeley, Anthony
The Red House Mystery	Milne, A.A.
The Secret Adversary	Christie, Agatha
The Secret of Chimneys	Christie, Agatha
"The Three Garridebs"	Doyle, Sir Arthur Conan
The Trail of Fu Manchu	Rohmer, Sax
Trent's Last Case	Bentley, E.C.
War in Heaven	Williams, Charles
Watson's Choice	Mitchell, Gladys
Whose Body?	Sayers, Dorothy L.

CITY WALK: SLEUTHS

SUPERINTENDENT BATTLE	Christie
INSPECTOR ALAN GRANT	Tey
DETECTIVE INSPECTOR C.D. SLOAN	Aird

Inspector Ghote	Keating
Lord Peter Wimsey	Sayers
Tommy Beresford	Christie
Tuppence Cowley	Christie
M. Hanaud	Mason
Sergeant Cuff	Collins
Roger Sheringham	Berkeley
Hercule Poirot	Christie
Inspector Hannasyde	Heyer
Philip Trent	Bentley
Tim Ekaterin	Francis
Roderick Alleyn	Marsh
Sir Denis Nayland Smith	Rohmer
Lady Molly	Orczy
Sid Halley	Francis
Inspector Parr	Wallace
Patrick Grant	Yorke
Dr. Gideon Fell	Carr
Superintendent Jury	Grimes
Dame Beatrice Bradley	Mitchell
Sherlock Holmes	Doyle

Inns of Court/Fleet Street Walk: Authors

Allingham, Margery	**Flowers for the Judge**
Allingham, Margery	**Tiger in the Smoke**
Babson, Marian	**The Lord Mayor of Death**
Belloc, Hilaire	—
Belloc-Lowndes, Marie	**The Lodger**
Bentley, E.C.	**Trent's Last Case**
Brand, Christianna	**Fog of Doubt**
Byrne, Muriel St. Clare, ed.	**The Lisle Letters**
Carr, John Dickson	**The Bride of Newgate**
Chesterton, G.K.	**The Man Who Was Thursday**
Chesterton, G.K.	**"The Purple Wig"**
Christie, Agatha	**"Jane in Search of a Job"**
Collins, Wilkie	**The Moonstone**

Collins, Wilkie	The Woman in White
Creasey, John	Leave It to the Toff
Dickens, Charles	Bleak House
Dickens, Charles	David Copperfield
Dickens, Charles	The Pickwick Papers
Donne, John	—
Doyle, Sir Arthur Conan	A Study in Scarlet
Doyle, Sir Arthur Conan	"The Speckled Band"
Francis, Dick	Forfeit
Freeman, R. Austin	—
Gilbert, Michael	Death Has Deep Roots
Gilbert, Michael	Smallbone Deceased
Greene, Graham	—
Grimes, Martha	The Anodyne Necklace
Hare, Cyril	Tragedy at Law
Heyer, Georgette	Death in the Stocks
Heyer, Georgette	Duplicate Death
James, P.D.	An Unsuitable Job for a Woman
James, P.D.	The Skull Beneath the Skin
James, P.D.	Unnatural Causes
Johnson, Dr. Samuel	Rasselas
Keating, H.R.F.	—
Le Carré, John	—
Marsh, Ngaio	A Surfeit of Lampreys
Marsh, Ngaio	Black as He's Painted
Marsh, Ngaio	Black Beech and Honeydew
Marsh, Ngaio	Killer Dolphin
Marsh, Ngaio	Light Thickens
Mortimer, John	"Rumpole and the Man of God"
Mortimer, John	Rumpole of the Bailey
Moyes, Patricia	Who Is Simon Warwick?
Peters, Ellis	City of Gold and Shadows
Rendell, Ruth	—
Sayers, Dorothy L.	Busman's Honeymoon
Sayers, Dorothy L.	Clouds of Witness
Sayers, Dorothy L.	Murder Must Advertise

Sayers, Dorothy L.	**Strong Poison**
Sayers, Dorothy L.	**"The Piscatorial Farce of the Stolen Stomach"**
Sayers, Dorothy L.	**The Unpleasantness at the Bellona Club**
Sayers, Dorothy L.	**Unnatural Death**
Sayers, Dorothy L.	**Whose Body?**
Shakespeare, William	**Comedy of Errors**
Shakespeare, William	**Macbeth**
Shakespeare, William	**Twelfth Night**
Stuart, Ian	**A Growing Concern**
Symons, Julian	**A Three Pipe Problem**
Symons, Julian	**The Blackheath Poisonings**
Tey, Josephine	**The Man in the Queue**
Wallace, Edgar	—
Wallace, Edgar	**The Crimson Circle**
Yorke, Margaret	—

INNS OF COURT/FLEET STREET WALK: BOOKS

A Growing Concern	Stuart, Ian
An Unsuitable Job for a Woman	James, P.D.
A Study in Scarlet	Doyle, Sir Arthur Conan
A Surfeit of Lampreys	Marsh, Ngaio
A Three Pipe Problem	Symons, Julian
Black as He's Painted	Marsh, Ngaio
Black Beech and Honeydew	Marsh, Ngaio
Bleak House	Dickens, Charles
Busman's Honeymoon (play)	Sayers, Dorothy L., with Muriel St. Clare Byrne
City of Gold and Shadows	Peters, Ellis
Clouds of Witness	Sayers, Dorothy L.
Comedy of Errors	Shakespeare, William
David Copperfield	Dickens, Charles
Death Has Deep Roots	Gilbert, Michael
Death in the Stocks	Heyer, Georgette
Duplicate Death	Heyer, Georgette

Flowers for the Judge	Allingham, Margery
Fog of Doubt	Brand, Christianna
Forfeit	Francis, Dick
"Jane in Search of a Job"	Christie, Agatha
Killer Dolphin	Marsh, Ngaio
Leave It to the Toff	Creasey, John
Light Thickens	Marsh, Ngaio
Macbeth	Shakespeare, William
Murder Musc Advertise	Sayers, Dorothy L.
Rasselas	Johnson, Dr. Samuel
"Rumpole and the Man of God"	Mortimer, John
Rumpole of the Bailey	Mortimer, John
Smallbone Deceased	Gilbert, Michael
Strong Poison	Sayers, Dorothy L.
The Anodyne Necklace	Grimes, Martha
The Blackheath Poisonings	Symons, Julian
The Bride of Newgate	Carr, John Dickson
The Crimson Circle	Wallace, Edgar
The Lisle Letters	Byrne, Muriel St. Clare, ed.
The Lodger	Belloc-Lowndes, Marie
The Lord Mayor of Death	Babson, Marian
The Moonstone	Collins, Wilkie
The Man in the Queue	Tey, Josephine
The Man Who Was Thursday	Chesterton, G.K.
The Pickwick Papers	Dickens, Charles
"The Piscatorial Farce of the Stolen Stomach"	Sayers, Dorothy L.
"The Purple Wig"	Chesterton, G.K.
The Skull Beneath the Skin	James, P.D.
"The Speckled Band"	Doyle, Sir Arthur Conan
The Unpleasantness at the Bellona Club	Sayers, Dorothy L.
The Woman in White	Collins, Wilkie
Tiger in the Smoke	Allingham, Margery
Tragedy at Law	Hare, Cyril
Trent's Last Case	Bentley, E.C.
Twelfth Night	Shakespeare, William

Unnatural Causes	James, P.D.
Unnatural Death	Sayers, Dorothy L.
Who Is Simon Warwick?	Moyes, Patricia
Whose Body?	Sayers, Dorothy L.

INNS OF COURT/FLEET STREET WALK: SLEUTHS

INSPECTOR CHARLES PARKER	Sayers
CORDELIA GRAY	James
DR. THORNDYKE	Freeman
DR. WATSON	Doyle
HENRY TIBBETT	Moyes
LORD PETER WIMSEY	Sayers
PHILIP TRENT	Bentley
SUPERINTENDENT RODERICK ALLEYN	Marsh
RUMPOLE	Mortimer
SHERLOCK HOLMES	Doyle
SUPERINTENDENT ADAM DALGLEISH	James
DAVID GRIERSON	Stuart
ALBERT CAMPION	Allingham
INSPECTOR HAZELRIGG	Gilbert
SERGEANT CUFF	Collins
GEORGE FELSE	Peters
THE TOFF	Creasy
SUPERINTENDENT JURY	Grimes
INSPECTOR PARR	Wallace
FATHER BROWN	Chesterton
INSPECTOR COCKRILL	Brand

COVENT GARDEN/THE STRAND WALK: AUTHORS

Allingham, Margery	**Tether's End**
Anthony, Evelyn	**The Defector**
Austen, Jane	**Northanger Abbey**
Bentley, E.C.	**Trent's Last Case**
Berkeley, Anthony	**The Poisoned Chocolates Case**

Blake, Nicholas	**End of Chapter**
Brett, Simon	**Murder in the Title**
Brett, Simon	**Murder Unprompted**
Brett, Simon	**Not Dead, Only Resting**
Buchan, John	**The Thirty-Nine Steps**
Carr, John Dickson	**The Bride of Newgate**
Carr, John Dickson	**The Skeleton in the Clock**
Chesterton, G.K.	**"In Defence of Detective Stories"**
Chesterton, G.K.	**"The Man in the Passage"**
Chesterton, G.K.	**The Man Who Was Thursday**
Christie, Agatha	**The Big Four**
Christie, Agatha	**The Mousetrap**
Christie, Agatha	**The Mystery of the Blue Train**
Christie, Agatha	**The Secret Adversary**
Christie, Agatha	**Witness for the Prosecution**
Creasey, John	**The Masters of Bow Street**
Crispin, Edmund	**Frequent Hearses**
Crispin, Edmund	**Swan Song**
Daviot, Gordon (Josephine Tey)	**Richard of Bordeaux**
Dickens, Charles	**Bleak House**
Dickens, Charles	**David Copperfield**
Dickens, Charles	**Oliver Twist**
Dickens, Charles	**Sketches by Boz**
Doyle, Sir Arthur Conan	**"A Scandal in Bohemia"**
Doyle, Sir Arthur Conan	**The Sign of Four**
Doyle, Sir Arthur Conan	**"The Man with the Twisted Lip"**
Eliot, T.S.	**"The Waste Land"**
Fielding, Henry	—
Fraser, Antonia	**A Splash of Red**
Heyer, Georgette	**Behold, Here's Poison**
Heyer, Georgette	**Death in the Stocks**
Heyer, Georgette	**Regency Buck**
James, P.D.	**An Unsuitable Job for a Woman**

James, P.D.	The Skull Beneath the Skin
Keating, H.R.F.	—
Lewis, C. Day (Nicholas Blake)	—
Marric, J.J. (John Creasey)	Gideon's Wrath
Marsh, Ngaio	A Surfeit of Lampreys
Marsh, Ngaio	Black Beech and Honeydew
Marsh, Ngaio	Death in Ecstasy
Marsh, Ngaio	Light Thickens
Moyes, Patricia	Who Is Simon Warwick?
Oppenheim, E. Phillips	—
Orczy, Baroness	—
Parker, Robert B.	The Judas Goat
Perry, Anne	Resurrection Row
Poe, Edgar Allan	—
Sayers, Dorothy L.	Busman's Honeymoon (play; with Muriel St. Clare Byrne)
Sayers, Dorothy L.	Strong Poison
Sayers, Dorothy L.	Love All
Sayers, Dorothy L.	"The Image in the Mirror"
Sayers, Dorothy L.	"The Man with No Face"
Sayers, Dorothy L., trans.	The Divine Comedy
Sayers, Dorothy L., trans.	Tristan of Britany
Sayers, Dorothy L.	"Introduction" to The Omnibus of Crime
Sayers, Dorothy L.	Murder Must Advertise
Sayers, Dorothy L.	The Unpleasantness at the Bellona Club
Sayers, Dorothy L.	Whose Body?
Shakespeare, William	Macbeth
Shaw, G.B.	Pygmalion
Symons, Julian	The Blackheath Poisonings
Tey, Josephine	The Daughter of Time
Tey, Josephine	The Man in the Queue
Voltaire, F.A.	—
Williams, Charles	All Hallows Eve
Winn, Dilys, ed.	Murderess Ink
Yorke, Margaret	Cast for Death

COVENT GARDEN/THE STRAND WALK: BOOKS

All Hallows Eve	Williams, Charles
An Unsuitable Job for a Woman	James, P.D.
"A Scandal in Bohemia"	Doyle, Sir Arthur Conan
A Splash of Red	Fraser, Antonia
A Surfeit of Lampreys	Marsh, Ngaio
Behold, Here's Poison	Heyer, Georgette
Black Beech and Honeydew	Marsh, Ngaio
Bleak House	Dickens, Charles
Busman's Honeymoon (play)	Sayers, Dorothy L., with Muriel St. Clare Byrne
Busman's Honeymoon	Sayers, Dorothy L.
Cast for Death	Yorke, Margaret
David Copperfield	Dickens, Charles
Death in Ecstasy	Marsh, Ngaio
Death in the Stocks	Heyer, Georgette
End of Chapter	Blake, Nicholas
Frequent Hearses	Crispin, Edmund
Gideon's Wrath	Marric, J.J. (John Creasey)
"In Defence of Detective Stories"	Chesterton, G.K.
"Introduction" to The Omnibus of Crime	Sayers, Dorothy L.
Light Thickens	Marsh, Ngaio
Love All	Sayers, Dorothy L.
Macbeth	Shakespeare, William
Murder in the Title	Brett, Simon
Murder Must Advertise	Sayers, Dorothy L.
Murder Unprompted	Brett, Simon
Murderess Ink	Winn, Dilys, ed.
Northanger Abbey	Austen, Jane
Not Dead, Only Resting	Brett, Simon
Oliver Twist	Dickens, Charles
Pygmalion	Shaw, G.B.
Regency Buck	Heyer, Georgette
Resurrection Row	Perry, Anne
Sketches by Boz	Dickens, Charles

Strong Poison	Sayers, Dorothy L.
Swan Song	Crispin, Edmund
Tether's End	Allingham, Margery
"The Adventure of the Bruce-Partington Plans"	Doyle, Sir Arthur Conan
The Big Four	Christie, Agatha
The Blackheath Poisonings	Symons, Julian
The Bride of Newgate	Carr, John Dickson
The Daughter of Time	Tey, Josephine
The Defector	Anthony, Evelyn
The Divine Comedy	Sayers, Dorothy L., trans.
"The Image in the Mirror"	Sayers, Dorothy L.
The Judas Goat	Parker, Robert B.
"The Man in the Passage"	Chesterton, G.K.
The Man in the Queue	Tey, Josephine
The Man Who Was Thursday	Chesterton, G.K.
"The Man with No Face"	Sayers, Dorothy L.
"The Man with the Twisted Lip"	Doyle, Sir Arthur Conan
The Masters of Bow Street	Creasey, John
The Mousetrap	Christie, Agatha
The Mystery of the Blue Train	Christie, Agatha
The Poisoned Chocolates Case	Berkeley, Anthony
"The Red Circle"	Doyle, Sir Arthur Conan
The Secret Adversary	Christie, Agatha
The Sign of Four	Doyle, Sir Arthur Conan
The Skeleton in the Clock	Carr, John Dickson
The Skull Beneath the Skin	James, P.D.
The Thirty-Nine Steps	Buchan, John
The Unpleasantness at the Bellona Club	Sayers, Dorothy L.
"The Waste Land"	Eliot, T.S.
Tristan of Britany	Sayers, Dorothy L., trans.
Who Is Simon Warwick?	Moyes, Patricia
Whose Body?	Sayers, Dorothy L.
Witness for the Prosecution	Christie, Agatha

COVENT GARDEN/THE STRAND WALK: SLEUTHS

INSPECTOR ALAN GRANT	Tey
CHARLES PARIS	Brett
DR. WATSON	Doyle
GIDEON	Marric
JEMIMA SHORE	Fraser
LORD PETER WIMSEY	Sayers
NIGEL STRANGEWAYS	Blake
PATRICK GRANT	Yorke
PHILIP TRENT	Bentley
RODERICK ALLEYN	Marsh
SHERLOCK HOLMES	Doyle
SIR HENRY MERRIVALE	Carr
SPENSER	Parker
TUPPENCE COWLEY	Christie
TOMMY BERESFORD	Christie
INSPECTOR HANNASYDE	Heyer
ROGER SHERINGHAM	Berkeley
DAVINA GRAHAM	Anthony
INSPECTOR PITT	Perry
ALBERT CAMPION	Allingham
CORDELIA GRAY	James
GERVASE FEN	Crispin
HENRY TIBBETT	Moyes
RICHARD HANNAY	Buchan
HERCULE POIROT	Christie
DR. GIDEON FELL	Carr
FATHER BROWN	Chesterton

BLOOMSBURY WALK: AUTHORS

Allingham, Margery	—
Babson, Marian	—
Bentley, E.C.	**Trent's Last Case**
Blake, Nicholas	**End of Chapter**
Byrne, Muriel St. Clare	—
Carr, John Dickson	**The Mad Hatter Mystery**

Chesterton, G.K.	**"The Diabolist"**
Chesterton, G.K.	**The Man Who Was Thursday**
Christie, Agatha	—
Crispin, Edmund	**Frequent Hearses**
Dante, Alighieri	**The Divine Comedy**
Dickens, Charles	**Oliver Twist**
Dickens, Charles	**The Pickwick Papers**
Doyle, Sir Arthur Conan	—
du Maurier, Daphne	—
du Maurier, George	**Trilby**
Emerson, Ralph Waldo	—
Evelyn, John	—
Forster, E.M.	—
Francis, Dick	**Forfeit**
Fraser, Antonia	**A Splash of Red**
Fraser, Antonia	**Quiet as a Nun**
Freeling, Nicholas	—
Hope, Sir Anthony	**The Prisoner of Zenda**
Household, Geoffrey	**Hostage: London**
Innes, Michael	**From London Far**
James, P.D.	**Innocent Blood**
MacInnes, Helen	—
Mann, Jessica	**Funeral Sites**
Marx, Karl	**The Communist Manifesto**
Marsh, Ngaio	**A Surfeit of Lampreys**
Morgan, Janet	**Agatha Christie**
Moyes, Patricia	**Who Is Simon Warwick?**
Parker, Robert B.	**The Judas Goat**
Perry, Anne	**Callander Square**
Rendell, Ruth	**From Doom with Death**
Sayers, Dorothy L.	**Busman's Honeymoon, stage directions**
Sayers, Dorothy L., trans.	**Divine Comedy**
Sayers, Dorothy L.	**Gaudy Night**
Sayers, Dorothy L.	**Love All**
Sayers, Dorothy L.	**Murder Must Advertise**
Sayers, Dorothy L.	**Strong Poison**

Sayers, Dorothy L.	**The Documents in the Case**
Sayers, Dorothy L.	**"The Vindictive Story of Footsteps That Ran"**
Sayers, Dorothy L., trans.	**Tristan of Britany**
Sayers, Dorothy L.	**Unnatural Death**
Sayers, Dorothy L.	**Whose Body?**
Scott, Sir Walter	—
Shaw, George Bernard	—
Strachey, Lytton	—
Symons, Julian	**The Blackheath Poisonings**
Tey, Josephine	**The Daughter of Time**
Wentworth, Patricia	**The Case Is Closed**
Woolf, Virginia	—
Yorke, Margaret	**Cast for Death**

Bloomsbury Walk: Books

Agatha Christie	Morgan, Janet
A Splash of Red	Fraser, Antonia
A Surfeit of Lampreys	Marsh, Ngaio
Busman's Honeymoon (play)	Sayers, Dorothy L., with Muriel St. Clare Byrne
Callander Square	Perry, Anne
Cast for Death	Yorke, Margaret
Divine Comedy	Sayers, Dorothy L., trans.
End of Chapter	Blake, Nicholas
Forfeit	Francis, Dick
Frequent Hearses	Crispin, Edmund
From Doom with Death	Rendell, Ruth
From London Far	Innes, Michael
Funeral Sites	Mann, Jessica
Gaudy Night	Sayers, Dorothy L.
Hostage: London	Household, Geoffrey
Innocent Blood	James, P.D.
Love All	Sayers, Dorothy L.
Murder Must Advertise	Sayers, Dorothy L.
Oliver Twist	Dickens, Charles
Quiet as a Nun	Fraser, Antonia

Strong Poison	Sayers, Dorothy L.
The Blackheath Poisonings	Symons, Julian
The Case Is Closed	Wentworth, Patricia
The Communist Manifesto	Marx, Karl
The Daughter of Time	Tey, Josephine
"The Diabolist"	Chesterton, G.K.
The Divine Comedy	Dante Alighieri
The Documents in the Case	Sayers, Dorothy L.
The Judas Goat	Parker, Robert B.
The Mad Hatter Mystery	Carr, John Dickson
The Man Who Was Thursday	Chesterton, G.K.
The Pickwick Papers	Dickens, Charles
The Prisoner of Zenda	Hope, Anthony
"The Vindictive Story of the Footsteps That Ran"	Sayers, Dorothy L.
Trent's Last Case	Bentley, E.C.
Trilby	du Maurier, George
Tristan of Britany	Sayers, Dorothy L., trans.
Unnatural Death	Sayers, Dorothy L.
Who Is Simon Warwick?	Moyes, Patricia
Whose Body?	Sayers, Dorothy L.

BLOOMSBURY WALK: SLEUTHS

ALAN GRANT	Tey
INSPECTOR PITT	Perry
GERVASE FEN	Crispin
HARRIET VANE	Sayers
JEMIMA SHORE	Fraser
LORD PETER WIMSEY	Sayers
MEREDITH	Innes
MISS MAUD SILVER	Wentworth
NIGEL STRANGEWAYS	Blake
PATRICK GRANT	Yorke
PHILIP TRENT	Bentley
SHERLOCK HOLMES	Doyle
TAMARA HOYLAND	Mann

Spenser	Parker
Dr. Gideon Fell	Carr
Henry Tibbett	Moyes
Roderick Alleyn	Marsh

Soho Walk: Authors

Aird, Catherine	—
Allingham, Margery	**Black Plumes**
Allingham, Margery	**Tether's End**
Allingham, Margery	**Tiger in the Smoke**
Bentley, E.C.	—
Berkeley, Anthony	**The Piccadilly Murder**
Berkeley, Anthony	**The Poisoned Chocolates Case**
Brand, Christianna	—
Brett, Simon	**Not Dead, Only Resting**
Buchan, John	**The Three Hostages**
Byrne, Muriel St. Clare	**Busman's Honeymoon (play)**
Carr, John Dickson	**The Bride of Newgate**
Chesterton, G.K.	**The Man Who Was Thursday**
Christie, Agatha	**The Big Four**
Christie, Agatha	**The Secret Adversary**
Christie, Agatha	**The Seven Dials Mystery**
Creasey, John	**The Masters of Bow Street**
Creasey, John	**The Toff and the Deadly Parson**
Crispin, Edmund	**Frequent Hearses**
Crispin, Edmund	**Swan Song**
Detection Club	**"Behind the Screen"**
Detection Club	**Crime on the Coast**
Detection Club	**The Floating Admiral**
Detection Club	**"The Scoop"**
Detection Club	**Verdict of 13**
Dickens, Charles	**A Tale of Two Cities**
Dickens, Charles	**Great Expectations**
Dickens, Charles	**Sketches by Boz**

Doyle, Sir Arthur Conan	**A Study in Scarlet**
Greene, Graham	—
Grimes, Martha	**The Dirty Duck**
Hanff, Helene	**Eighty-Four Charing Cross Road**
Hervey, Evelyn (H.R.F. Keating)	—
Heyer, Georgette	**Death in the Stocks**
Innes, Michael	**From London Far**
James, P.D.	**An Unsuitable Job for a Woman**
James, P.D.	**The Skull Beneath the Skin**
James, P.D.	**Unnatural Causes**
Keating, H.R.F.	—
Le Carré, John	**Tinker, Tailor, Soldier, Spy**
MacInnes, Helen	**Cloak of Darkness**
Marric, J.J. (John Creasey)	**Gideon's Wrath**
Marsh, Ngaio	**A Man Lay Dead**
Marsh, Ngaio	**Artists in Crime**
Marsh, Ngaio	**A Surfeit of Lampreys**
Marsh, Ngaio	**Death in Ecstasy**
Marsh, Ngaio	**Killer Dolphin**
Mitchell, Gladys	**Watson's Choice**
More, Sir Thomas	**Historie of Richard III**
Münster	**Cosmographia universalis**
Parker, Robert B.	**The Judas Goat**
Perry, Anne	**Bluegate Fields**
Perry, Anne	**Resurrection Row**
Perry, Anne	**The Devil's Acre**
Peters, Ellis	**The Funeral of Figaro**
Rohmer, Sax	**The Trail of Fu Manchu**
Sayers, Dorothy L.	**Busman's Honeymoon (play; with Muriel St. Clare Byrne)**
Sayers, Dorothy L.	**"The Haunted Policeman"**
Sayers, Dorothy L.	**"The Learned Adventure of the Dragon's Head"**
Sayers, Dorothy L.	**Busman's Honeymoon**
Sayers, Dorothy L.	**Clouds of Witness**

Sayers, Dorothy L.	**Murder Must Advertise**
Sayers, Dorothy L.	**The Unpleasantness at the Bellona Club**
Sayers, Dorothy L.	**Unnatural Death**
Sayers, Dorothy L.	**Whose Body?**
Shakespeare, William	—
Simpson, Helen	**Enter Sir John**
Stevenson, Robert Louis	**The New Arabian Nights**
Stewart, Mary	**The Gabriel Hounds**
Symons, Julian	**A Three Pipe Problem**
Symons, Julian	**Mortal Consequences**
Symons, Julian	**The Blackheath Poisonings**
Tey, Josephine	**The Daughter of Time**
Tey, Josephine	**The Man in the Queue**
Truman, Margaret	—
Wallace, Edgar	**The Crimson Circle**
Winn, Dilys, ed.	**Murderess Ink**
Yorke, Margaret	**Cast for Death**

SOHO WALK: BOOKS

A Man Lay Dead	Marsh, Ngaio
An Unsuitable Job for a Woman	James, P.D.
Artists in Crime	Marsh, Ngaio
A Study in Scarlet	Doyle, Sir Arthur Conan
A Surfeit of Lampreys	Marsh, Ngaio
A Tale of Two Cities	Dickens, Charles
A Three Pipe Problem	Symons, Julian
"Behind the Screen"	Detection Club
Black Plumes	Allingham, Margery
Bluegate Fields	Perry, Anne
Busman's Honeymoon (play)	Sayers, Dorothy L., with Muriel St. Clare Byrne
Busman's Honeymoon	Sayers, Dorothy L.
Cast for Death	Yorke, Margaret
Cloak of Darkness	MacInnes, Helen
Clouds of Witness	Sayers, Dorothy L.

Cosmographia universalis	Münster
Crime on the Coast	Detection Club
Death in Ecstasy	Marsh, Ngaio
Death in the Stocks	Heyer, Georgette
Eighty-Four Charing Cross Road	Hanff, Helene
Enter Sir John	Simpson, Helen
Frequent Hearses	Crispin, Edmund
From London Far	Innes, Michael
Gideon's Wrath	Marric, J.J. (John Creasey)
Great Expectations	Dickens, Charles
Historie of Richard III	More, Sir Thomas
Killer Dolphin	Marsh, Ngaio
Mortal Consequences	Symons, Julian
Murderess Ink	Winn, Dilys, ed.
Murder Must Advertise	Sayers, Dorothy L.
Not Dead, Only Resting	Brett, Simon
Resurrection Row	Perry, Anne
Sketches by Boz	Dickens, Charles
Swan Song	Crispin, Edmund
Tether's End	Allingham, Margery
The Big Four	Christie, Agatha
The Blackheath Poisonings	Symons, Julian
The Book of Common Prayer	—
The Bride of Newgate	Carr, John Dickson
The Crimson Circle	Wallace, Edgar
The Daughter of Time	Tey, Josephine
The Devil's Acre	Perry, Anne
The Dirty Duck	Grimes, Martha
The Floating Admiral	Detection Club
The Funeral of Figaro	Peters, Ellis
The Gabriel Hounds	Stewart, Mary
"The Haunted Policeman"	Sayers, Dorothy L.
The Judas Goat	Parker, Robert B.
"The Learned Adventure of the Dragon's Head"	Sayers, Dorothy L.
The Man in the Queue	Tey, Josephine

The Man Who Was Thursday	Chesterton, G.K.
The Masters of Bow Street	Creasey, John
The New Arabian Nights	Stevenson, Robert Louis
The Piccadilly Murder	Berkeley, Anthony
The Poisoned Chocolates Case	Berkeley, Anthony
"The Scoop"	Detection Club
The Secret Adversary	Christie, Agatha
The Seven Dials Mystery	Christie, Agatha
The Skull Beneath the Skin	James, P.D.
The Three Hostages	Buchan, John
The Toff and the Deadly Parson	Creasey, John
The Trail of Fu Manchu	Rohmer, Sax
The Unpleasantness at the Bellona Club	Sayers, Dorothy L.
Tiger in the Smoke	Allingham, Margery
Tinker, Tailor, Soldier, Spy	Le Carré, John
Unnatural Causes	James, P.D.
Unnatural Death	Sayers, Dorothy L.
Verdict of 13	Detection Club
Watson's Choice	Mitchell, Gladys
Whose Body?	Sayers, Dorothy L.

SOHO WALK: SLEUTHS

INSPECTOR ALAN GRANT	Tey
CHARLES PARIS	Brett
CORDELIA GRAY	James
DR. WATSON	Doyle
GERVASE FEN	Crispin
INSPECTOR GIDEON	Creasey
LORD PETER WIMSEY	Sayers
RODERICK ALLEYN	Marsh
SPENSER	Parker
SUPERINTENDENT JURY	Grimes
TOMMY BERESFORD	Christie
TUPPENCE COWLEY	Christie

Inspector Hannasyde	Heyer
Sheridan Haynes	Symons
Richard Hannay	Buchan
The Toff	Creasey
Inspector Pitt	Perry
Patrick Grant	Yorke
Robert Renwick	MacInnes
Sir John	Simpson
Albert Campion	Allingham
Hercule Poirot	Christie
Inspector Parr	Wallace
Roger Sheringham	Berkeley
Superintendent Battle	Christie
Dame Beatrice Bradley	Mitchell

Mayfair/Oxford Street Walk: Authors

Allingham, Margery	**Black Plumes**
Allingham, Margery	**The Fashion in Shrouds**
Bentley, E.C.	**Trent's Last Case**
Berkeley, Anthony	**The Piccadilly Murder**
Berkeley, Anthony	**The Poisoned Chocolates Case**
Blake, Nicholas	**End of Chapter**
Blake, Nicholas	**Minute for Murder**
Buchan, John	**The Three Hostages**
Carr, John Dickson	**The Skeleton in the Clock**
Chesterton, G.K.	—
Christie, Agatha	**At Bertram's Hotel**
Christie, Agatha	**Mr. Parker Pyne, Detective**
Christie, Agatha	**"The Case of the Middle-Aged Wife"**
Christie, Agatha	**The Golden Ball**
Christie, Agatha	**The Mystery of the Blue Train**
Christie, Agatha	**The Secret Adversary**
Christie, Agatha	**The Secret of Chimneys**
Creasey, John	**The Baron and the Missing Old Masters**

Creasey, John	**The Toff and the Deadly Parson**
Crispin, Edmund	**Frequent Hearses**
Disraeli, Benjamin	—
Doyle, Sir Arthur Conan	**"The Adventure of the Bruce-Partington Plans"**
Doyle, Sir Arthur Conan	**"The Adventure of the Illustrious Client"**
du Maurier, George	**Trilby**
Eliot, George	—
Francis, Dick	**Forfeit**
Fraser, Antonia	**Cool Repentance**
Fraser, Antonia	**Quiet as a Nun**
Gilbert, Michael	**Death Has Deep Roots**
Grimes, Martha	**The Dirty Duck**
Heyer, Georgette	**Duplicate Death**
Heyer, Georgette	**Regency Buck**
James, P.D.	**An Unsuitable Job for a Woman**
Keating, H.R.F.	**Inspector Ghote Hunts the Peacock**
Mann, Jessica	**Funeral Sites**
Mann, Jessica	**Grave Goods**
Mann, Jessica	**No Man's Island**
Marsh, Ngaio	**A Surfeit of Lampreys**
Marsh, Ngaio	**A Wreath for Rivera**
Marsh, Ngaio	**Death in a White Tie**
Marsh, Ngaio	**Death in Ecstasy**
Marsh, Ngaio	**Killer Dolphin**
Mason, A.E.W.	—
Maugham, Somerset	—
Mortimer, John	**Rumpole of the Bailey**
Moyes, Patricia	**Who Is Simon Warwick?**
Orczy, Baroness	**Lady Molly of Scotland Yard**
Parker, Robert B.	**The Judas Goat**
Rohmer, Sax	**The Trail of Fu Manchu**
Sayers, Dorothy L.	**Busman's Honeymoon**
Sayers, Dorothy L.	**Clouds of Witness**
Sayers, Dorothy L.	**Murder Must Advertise**

Sayers, Dorothy L.	"The Article in Question"
Sayers, Dorothy L.	The Documents in the Case
Sayers, Dorothy L.	"The Haunted Policeman"
Sayers, Dorothy L.	The Unpleasantness at the Bellona Club
Sayers, Dorothy L.	Unnatural Death
Sayers, Dorothy L.	Whose Body?
Shelley, Percy B.	—
Symons, Julian	A Three Pipe Problem
Symons, Julian	The Blackheath Poisonings
Tey, Josephine	The Daughter of Time
Theroux, Paul	Half Moon Street
Wallace, Edgar	The Crimson Circle
Walpole, Horace	The Castle of Otranto
Wentworth, Patricia	Spotlight
Wilde, Oscar	—
Williams, Charles	War in Heaven
Winn, Dilys, ed.	Murder Ink
Wodehouse, P.G.	—
Yorke, Margaret	Find Me a Villain

MAYFAIR/OXFORD STREET WALK: BOOKS

An Unsuitable Job for a Woman	James, P.D.
A Surfeit of Lampreys	Marsh, Ngaio
A Three Pipe Problem	Symons, Julian
A Wreath for Rivera	Marsh, Ngaio
At Bertram's Hotel	Christie, Agatha
Black Plumes	Allingham, Margery
Busman's Honeymoon	Sayers, Dorothy L.
Clouds of Witness	Sayers, Dorothy L.
Cool Repentance	Fraser, Antonia
Death Has Deep Roots	Gilbert, Michael
Death in a White Tie	Marsh, Ngaio
Death in Ecstasy	Marsh, Ngaio
Duplicate Death	Heyer, Georgette
End of Chapter	Blake, Nicholas

Find Me a Villain	Yorke, Margaret
Forfeit	Francis, Dick
Frequent Hearses	Crispin, Edmund
Funeral Sites	Mann, Jessica
Grave Goods	Mann, Jessica
Half Moon Street	Theroux, Paul
Inspector Ghote Hunts the Peacock	Keating, H.R.F.
Killer Dolphin	Marsh, Ngaio
Lady Molly of Scotland Yard	Orczy, Baroness
Minute for Murder	Blake, Nicholas
Mr. Parker Pyne, Detective	Christie, Agatha
Murder Ink	Winn, Dilys, ed.
Murder Must Advertise	Sayers, Dorothy L.
No Man's Island	Mann, Jessica
Quiet as a Nun	Fraser, Antonia
Regency Buck	Heyer, Georgette
Rumpole of the Bailey	Mortimer, John
Spotlight	Wentworth, Patricia
"The Adventure of the Bruce-Partington Plans"	Doyle, Sir Arthur Conan
"The Adventure of the Illustrious Client"	Doyle, Sir Arthur Conan
"The Article in Question"	Sayers, Dorothy L.
The Baron and the Missing Old Masters	Creasey, John
The Blackheath Poisonings	Symons, Julian
"The Case of the Middle-Aged Wife"	Christie, Agatha
The Castle of Otranto	Walpole, Horace
The Crimson Circle	Wallace, Edgar
The Daughter of Time	Tey, Josephine
The Dirty Duck	Grimes, Martha
The Documents in the Case	Sayers, Dorothy L.
The Fashion in Shrouds	Allingham, Margery
The Golden Ball	Christie, Agatha
"The Haunted Policeman"	Sayers, Dorothy L.
The Judas Goat	Parker, Robert B.
The Mystery of the Blue Train	Christie, Agatha

The Piccadilly Murder	Berkeley, Anthony
The Poisoned Chocolates Case	Berkeley, Anthony
The Secret Adversary	Christie, Agatha
The Secret of Chimneys	Christie, Agatha
The Skeleton in the Clock	Carr, John Dickson
The Three Hostages	Buchan, John
The Toff and the Deadly Parson	Creasey, John
The Trail of Fu Manchu	Rohmer, Sax
The Unpleasantness at the Bellona Club	Sayers, Dorothy L.
Trent's Last Case	Bentley, E.C.
Trilby	du Maurier, George
Unnatural Death	Sayers, Dorothy L.
War in Heaven	Williams, Charles
Who Is Simon Warwick?	Moyes, Patricia
Whose Body?	Sayers, Dorothy L.

Mayfair/Oxford Street Walk: Sleuths

Alan Grant	Tey
Jemima Shore	Fraser
Lord Peter Wimsey	Sayers
Miss Jane Marple	Christie
Miss Maud Silver	Wentworth
Richard Hannay	Buchan
Sherlock Holmes	Doyle
Spenser	Parker
Tamara Hoyland	Mann
The Baron	Creasey
The Toff	Creasey
Albert Campion	Allingham
Rumpole	Mortimer
M. Hannaud	Mason
Inspector Hazelrigg	Gilbert
Philip Trent	Bentley
Ashenden	Maugham
Sheridan Haynes	Symons

ROGER SHERINGHAM	Berkeley
NIGEL STRANGEWAYS	Blake
SIR HENRY MERRIVALE	Carr
PARKER PYNE	Christie
INSPECTOR HANNASYDE	Heyer
RODERICK ALLEYN	Marsh
LADY MOLLY	Orczy

ST. JAMES WALK: AUTHORS

Allingham, Margery	**Black Plumes**
Brand, Christianna	**Fog of Doubt**
Buchan, John	**The Thirty-Nine Steps**
Buchan, John	**The Three Hostages**
Carr, John Dickson	**The Bride of Newgate**
Carr, John Dickson	**The Skeleton in the Clock**
Chesterton, G.K.	**"The Queer Feet"**
Christie, Agatha	**At Bertram's Hotel**
Christie, Agatha	**The Golden Ball**
Christie, Agatha	**The Mousetrap**
Christie, Agatha	**The Mystery of the Blue Train**
Christie, Agatha	**The Secret Adversary**
Christie, Agatha	**The Secret of Chimneys**
Christie, Agatha	**The Seven Dials Mystery**
Fraser, Antonia	**A Splash of Red**
Greene, Graham	**The Human Factor**
Heyer, Georgette	**Behold, Here's Poison**
Heyer, Georgette	**Death in the Stocks**
Heyer, Georgette	**Duplicate Death**
Heyer, Georgette	**Regency Buck**
Innes, Michael	**From London Far**
Mann, Jessica	**Funeral Sites**
Marsh, Ngaio	**A Wreath for Rivera**
Marsh, Ngaio	**Black as He's Painted**
Milne, A.A.	**"Buckingham Palace"**
Milne, A.A.	**The Red House Mystery**
Morgan, Janet	**Agatha Christie**

Parker, Robert B.	**The Judas Goat**
Sayers, Dorothy L.	**Busman's Honeymoon**
Sayers, Dorothy L.	**Clouds of Witness**
Sayers, Dorothy L.	**Gaudy Night**
Sayers, Dorothy L.	**Have His Carcase**
Sayers, Dorothy L.	**Love All**
Sayers, Dorothy L.	**Murder Must Advertise**
Sayers, Dorothy L.	**The Unpleasantness at the Bellona Club**
Sayers, Dorothy L.	**Unnatural Death**
Sayers, Dorothy L.	**Whose Body?**
Scott, Sir Walter	**The Waverley Novels**
Symons, Julian	**Mortal Consequences**
Symons, Julian	**The Blackheath Poisonings**
Truman, Margaret	**Murder on Embassy Row**
Wallace, Edgar	**The Crimson Circle**
Waugh, Evelyn	**Brideshead Revisited**
Wilde, Oscar	**Lady Windermere's Fan**
Yorke, Margaret	**Find Me a Villain**
Yorke, Margaret	**Cast for Death**

ST. JAMES WALK: BOOKS

Agatha Christie	Morgan, Janet
A Splash of Red	Fraser, Antonia
At Bertram's Hotel	Christie, Agatha
A Wreath for Rivera	Marsh, Ngaio
Behold, Here's Poison	Heyer, Georgette
Black as He's Painted	Marsh, Ngaio
Black Plumes	Allingham, Margery
Brideshead Revisited	Waugh, Evelyn
"Buckingham Palace"	Milne, A.A.
Busman's Honeymoon	Sayers, Dorothy L.
Cast for Death	Yorke, Margaret
Clouds of Witness	Sayers, Dorothy L.
Death in the Stocks	Heyer, Georgette
Duplicate Death	Heyer, Georgette
Find Me a Villain	Yorke, Margaret

Fog of Doubt	Brand, Christianna
From London Far	Innes, Michael
Funeral Sites	Mann, Jessica
Gaudy Night	Sayers, Dorothy L.
Have His Carcase	Sayers, Dorothy L.
Lady Windermere's Fan	Wilde, Oscar
Love All	Sayers, Dorothy L.
Mortal Consequences	Symons, Julian
Murder Must Advertise	Sayers, Dorothy L.
Murder on Embassy Row	Truman, Margaret
Regency Buck	Heyer, Georgette
The Blackheath Poisonings	Symons, Julian
The Bride of Newgate	Carr, John Dickson
The Crimson Circle	Wallace, Edgar
The Golden Ball	Christie, Agatha
The Human Factor	Greene, Graham
The Judas Goat	Parker, Robert B.
The Mousetrap	Christie, Agatha
The Mystery of the Blue Train	Christie, Agatha
"The Queer Feet"	Chesterton, G.K.
The Red House Mystery	Milne, A.A.
The Secret Adversary	Christie, Agatha
The Secret of Chimneys	Christie, Agatha
The Seven Dials Mystery	Christie, Agatha
The Skeleton in the Clock	Carr, John Dickson
The Thirty-Nine Steps	Buchan, John
The Three Hostages	Buchan, John
The Unpleasantness at the Bellona Club	Sayers, Dorothy L.
The Waverley Novels	Scott, Sir Walter
Unnatural Death	Sayers, Dorothy L.
Whose Body?	Sayers, Dorothy L.

ST. JAMES WALK: SLEUTHS

FATHER BROWN	Chesterton
LORD PETER WIMSEY	Sayers
RICHARD HANNAY	Buchan

RODERICK ALLEYN	Marsh
SHERLOCK HOLMES	Doyle
SPENSER	Parker
RAFFLES	Hornung
INSPECTOR PARR	Wallace
TUPPENCE AND TOMMY	Christie
DETECTIVE-INSPECTOR FARRELL	Christie
INSPECTOR COCKRILL	Brand
INSPECTOR HANNASYDE	Heyer
INSPECTOR BUTLER	Greene
SIR HENRY MERRIVALE	Carr
SUPERINTENDENT BATTLE	Christie
HERCULE POIROT	Christie
TAMARA HOYLAND	Mann
MISS MARPLE	Christie
PATRICK GRANT	Yorke
JEMIMA SHORE	Fraser

MARYLEBONE/REGENT'S PARK WALK: AUTHORS

Allingham, Margery	**Death of a Ghost**
Allingham, Margery	**Tether's End**
Anthony, Evelyn	**The Defector**
Babson, Marian	**The Twelve Deaths of Christmas**
Barrett, Elizabeth	—
Belloc, Hilaire	—
Belloc-Lowndes, Marie	**The Lodger**
Bentley, E.C.	**Trent's Last Case**
Berkeley, Anthony	—
Blake, Nicholas	**Minute for Murder**
Boswell, James	**Life of Samuel Johnson**
Brand, Christianna	**Fog of Doubt**
Brett, Simon	**Not Dead, Only Resting**
Browning, Robert	—
Buchan, John	**The Three Hostages**
Buchan, John	**The Thirty-Nine Steps**

Byrne, Muriel St. Clare	**Busman's Honeymoon** (play with Dorothy Sayers)
Byron, Lord	—
Chesterton, G.K.	**Robert Browning**
Chesterton, G.K.	**The Man Who Was Thursday**
Chesterton, G.K.	**The Napoleon of Notting Hill**
Collins, Wilkie	**The Moonstone**
Christie, Agatha	**At Bertram's Hotel**
Christie, Agatha	**The Secret of Chimneys**
Crofts, Freeman Wills	—
Dane, Clemence	—
Detection Club	**"Behind the Screen"**
Detection Club	**Crime on the Coast**
Detection Club	**The Floating Admiral**
Detection Club	**"The Scoop"**
Dickens, Charles	**A Christmas Carol**
Dickens, Charles	**David Copperfield**
Dickens, Charles	**Dombey and Son**
Dickens, Charles	**Martin Chuzzlewit**
Dickens, Charles	**The Old Curiosity Shop**
Doyle, Sir Arthur Conan	**"A Scandal in Bohemia"**
Doyle, Sir Arthur Conan	**"The Adventure of the Illustrious Client"**
Doyle, Sir Arthur Conan	**"The Final Problem"**
Doyle, Sir Arthur Conan	**"The Mazarin Stone"**
Doyle, Sir Arthur Conan	**"The Valley of Fear"**
Ferrars, E.X.	**The Root of All Evil**
Francis, Dick	**Forfeit**
Fraser, Antonia	**A Splash of Red**
Fraser, Antonia	**Jemima Shore Investigates**
Fraser, Antonia	**Quiet as a Nun**
Gibbon, Edward	**Decline and Fall of the Roman Empire**
Gilbert, Michael	**The Killing of Katie Steelstock**

Hervey, Evelyn (H.R.F. Keating)	**The Man of Gold**
Heyer, Georgette	**Regency Buck**
James, Henry	**The Turn of the Screw**
James, P.D.	**Innocent Blood**
James, P.D.	**The Skull Beneath the Skin**
Keating, H.R.F.	**Inspector Ghote Hunts the Peacock**
Knox, Ronald	—
Marsh, Ngaio	**Death in a White Tie**
Mason, A.E.W.	**The House in Lordship Lane**
Moyes, Patricia	**Who Is Simon Warwick?**
Orczy, Baroness	**Lady Molly of Scotland Yard**
Orczy, Baroness	**"The Woman in the Big Hat"**
Orwell, George	**1984**
Parker, Robert B.	**The Judas Goat**
Sayers, Dorothy L.	**Busman's Honeymoon**
Sayers, Dorothy L.	**Busman's Honeymoon (play; with Muriel St. Clare Byrne)**
Sayers, Dorothy L.	**Gaudy Night**
Sayers, Dorothy L.	**Love All**
Sayers, Dorothy L.	**The Emperor Constantine**
Sayers, Dorothy L.	**The Unpleasantness at the Bellona Club**
Sayers, Dorothy L.	**Whose Body?**
Shaw, G.B.	—
Symons, Julian	**A Three Pipe Problem**
Tey, Josephine	**The Daughter of Time**
Tey, Josephine	**The Man in the Queue**
Thackeray, W.M.	**Vanity Fair**
Trollope, Anthony	—
Wallace, Edgar	**The Crimson Circle**
Walpole, Hugh	—
Wentworth, Patricia	—

MARYLEBONE/REGENT'S PARK WALK: BOOKS

A Christmas Carol	Dickens, Charles
"A Scandal in Bohemia"	Doyle, Sir Arthur Conan
A Splash of Red	Fraser, Antonia
At Bertram's Hotel	Christie, Agatha
A Three Pipe Problem	Symons, Julian
"Behind the Screen"	Detection Club
Busman's Honeymoon	Sayers, Dorothy L.
Busman's Honeymoon (play)	Sayers, Dorothy L., and Byrne, Muriel St. Clare
Crime on the Coast	Detection Club
David Copperfield	Dickens, Charles
Death in a White Tie	Marsh, Ngaio
Death of a Ghost	Allingham, Margery
Decline and Fall of the Roman Empire	Gibbon, Edward
Dombey and Son	Dickens, Charles
Fog of Doubt	Brand, Christianna
Forfeit	Francis, Dick
Gaudy Night	Sayers, Dorothy L.
Innocent Blood	James, P.D.
Inspector Ghote Hunts the Peacock	Keating, H.R.F.
Jemima Shore Investigates	Fraser, Antonia
Lady Molly of Scotland Yard	Orczy, Baroness
Life of Samuel Johnson	Boswell, James
Love All	Sayers, Dorothy L.
Martin Chuzzlewit	Dickens, Charles
Minute for Murder	Blake, Nicholas
1984	Orwell, George
Not Dead, Only Resting	Brett, Simon
Quiet as a Nun	Fraser, Antonia
Regency Buck	Heyer, Georgette
Robert Browning	Chesterton, G.K.
Tether's End	Allingham, Margery
"The Adventure of the Illustrious Client"	Doyle, Sir Arthur Conan
The Crimson Circle	Wallace, Edgar

The Daughter of Time	Tey, Josephine
The Defector	Anthony, Evelyn
The Emperor Constantine	Sayers, Dorothy L.
"The Final Problem"	Doyle, Sir Arthur Conan
The Floating Admiral	Detection Club
The House in Lordship Lane	Mason, A.E.W.
The Judas Goat	Parker, Robert B.
The Killing of Katie Steelstock	Gilbert, Michael
The Lodger	Belloc-Lowndes, Marie
The Man in the Queue	Tey, Josephine
The Man of Gold	Hervey, Evelyn (H.R.F. Keating)
The Man Who Was Thursday	Chesterton, G.K.
"The Mazarin Stone"	Doyle, Sir Arthur Conan
The Moonstone	Collins, Wilkie
The Napoleon of Notting Hill	Chesterton, G.K.
The Old Curiosity Shop	Dickens, Charles
The Root of All Evil	Ferrars, E.X.
"The Scoop"	Detection Club
The Secret of Chimneys	Christie, Agatha
The Skull Beneath the Skin	James, P.D.
The Thirty-Nine Steps	Buchan, John
The Three Hostages	Buchan, John
The Turn of the Screw	James, Henry
The Twelve Deaths of Christmas	Babson, Marian
The Unpleasantness at the Bellona Club	Sayers, Dorothy L.
"The Valley of Fear"	Doyle, Sir Arthur Conan
"The Woman in the Big Hat"	Orczy, Baroness
Trent's Last Case	Bentley, E.C.
Vanity Fair	Thackeray, W.M.
Who Is Simon Warwick?	Moyes, Patricia
Whose Body?	Sayers, Dorothy L.

MARYLEBONE/REGENT'S PARK WALK: SLEUTHS

SUPERINTENDENT CHARLES KNOTT	Gilbert
CHARLES PARIS	Brett
DR. WATSON	Doyle
INSPECTOR GHOTE	Keating
JEMIMA SHORE	Fraser
LADY MOLLY	Orczy
LORD PETER WIMSEY	Sayers
RICHARD HANNAY	Buchan
RODERICK ALLEYN	Marsh
SHERLOCK HOLMES	Doyle
SPENSER	Parker
ANDREW BASNETT	Ferrars
INSPECTOR COCKRILL	Brand
CORDELIA GRAY	James
ALBERT CAMPION	Allingham
NIGEL STRANGEWAYS	Blake
MISS UNWIN	Hervey
DET. SUPERINTENDENT KNOWLES	Babson
SHERIDAN HAYNES	Symons
SERGEANT CUFF	Collins
SUPERINTENDENT BATTLE	Christie
REGGIE FORTUNE	Bailey
ALAN GRANT	Tey
INSPECTOR PARR	Wallace
HENRY TIBBETT	Moyes
MISS MARPLE	Christie
SEXTON BLAKE	—

WESTMINSTER WALK: AUTHORS

Aird, Catherine	—
Allingham, Margery	**Black Plumes**
Allingham, Margery	**Tether's End**
Anthony, Evelyn	**The Defector**

Bentley, E.C.	**Trent's Last Case**
Berkeley, Anthony	**The Piccadilly Murder**
Berkeley, Anthony	**The Poisoned Chocolates Case**
Blake, Nicholas	**Minute for Murder**
Buchan, John	**The Thirty-Nine Steps**
Carr, John Dickson	**Fire Burn!**
Carr, John Dickson	**The Mad Hatter Mystery**
Carr, John Dickson	**The Skeleton in the Clock**
Chaucer, Geoffrey	—
Chesterton, G.K.	**"The Eye of Apollo"**
Chesterton, G.K.	**The Man Who Was Thursday**
Crispin, Edmund	**Frequent Hearses**
Christie, Agatha	**At Bertram's Hotel**
Christie, Agatha	**The Big Four**
Christie, Agatha	**The Secret Adversary**
Christie, Agatha	**The Secret of Chimneys**
Christie, Agatha	**The Seven Dials Mystery**
Creasey, John	**The Masters of Bow Street**
Dickens, Charles	—
Dickson, Carter (John Dickson Carr)	—
Doyle, Sir Arthur Conan	**"His Last Bow"**
Doyle, Sir Arthur Conan	**"The Adventure of the Bruce-Partington Plans"**
Doyle, Sir Arthur Conan	**The Hound of the Baskervilles**
Doyle, Sir Arthur Conan	**"The Noble Bachelor"**
Doyle, Sir Arthur Conan	**"The Priory School"**
Doyle, Sir Arthur Conan	**"The Red-Headed League"**
Doyle, Sir Arthur Conan	**"The Second Stain"**
Fraser, Antonia	**A Splash of Red**
Fraser, Antonia	**Quiet as a Nun**
Gilbert, Michael	**Death Has Deep Roots**
Hare, Cyril	—
Honeycombe, Gordon	**The Murders of the Black Museum**
James, Henry	**The Turn of the Screw**

James, P.D.	An Unsuitable Job for a Woman
James, P.D.	Innocent Blood
Keating, H.R.F.	—
Lewis, C.S.	—
Mann, Jessica	Funeral Sites
Marsh, Ngaio	A Surfeit of Lampreys
Marsh, Ngaio	A Wreath for Rivera
Marsh, Ngaio	Black as He's Painted
Milton, John	—
Mitchell, Gladys	Watson's Choice
Orczy, Baroness	Lady Molly of Scotland Yard
Parker, Robert B.	The Judas Goat
Perry, Anne	Resurrection Row
Pope, Alexander	—
Rohmer, Sax	The Trail of Fu Manchu
Sayers, Dorothy L.	Busman's Honeymoon
Sayers, Dorothy L.	Clouds of Witness
Sayers, Dorothy L.	Gaudy Night
Sayers, Dorothy L.	Murder Must Advertise
Sayers, Dorothy L.	The Documents in the Case
Sayers, Dorothy L.	The Unpleasantness at the Bellona Club
Sayers, Dorothy L.	Thrones, Dominations
Sayers, Dorothy L.	Whose Body?
Shakespeare, William	Macbeth
Snow, C.P.	Corridors of Power
Symons, Julian	A Three Pipe Problem
Symons, Julian	Mortal Consequences
Tey, Josephine	The Daughter of Time
Tey, Josephine	The Man in the Queue
Wallace, Edgar	The Crimson Circle
Williams, Charles	All Hallows Eve
Winn, Dilys, ed.	Murderess Ink
Winn, Dilys, ed.	Murder Ink
Wordsworth, William	—
Yorke, Margaret	Cast for Death

WESTMINSTER WALK: BOOKS

All Hallows Eve	Williams, Charles
An Unsuitable Job for a Woman	James, P.D.
A Splash of Red	Fraser, Antonia
A Surfeit of Lampreys	Marsh, Ngaio
At Bertram's Hotel	Christie, Agatha
A Three Pipe Problem	Symons, Julian
A Wreath for Rivera	Marsh, Ngaio
Black as He's Painted	Marsh, Ngaio
Black Plumes	Allingham, Margery
Busman's Honeymoon	Sayers, Dorothy L.
Cast for Death	Yorke, Margaret
Clouds of Witness	Sayers, Dorothy L.
Corridors of Power	Snow, C.P.
Death Has Deep Roots	Gilbert, Michael
Fire Burn!	Carr, John Dickson
Frequent Hearses	Crispin, Edmund
Funeral Sites	Mann, Jessica
Gaudy Night	Sayers, Dorothy L.
"His Last Bow"	Doyle, Sir Arthur Conan
Innocent Blood	James, P.D.
Lady Molly of Scotland Yard	Orczy, Baroness
Minute for Murder	Blake, Nicholas
Mortal Consequences	Symons, Julian
Murderess Ink	Winn, Dilys, ed.
Murder Ink	Winn, Dilys, ed.
Murder Must Advertise	Sayers, Dorothy L.
Quiet as a Nun	Fraser, Antonia
Resurrection Row	Perry, Anne
Tether's End	Allingham, Margery
"The Adventure of the Bruce-Partington Plans"	Doyle, Sir Arthur Conan
The Big Four	Christie, Agatha
The Crimson Circle	Wallace, Edgar
The Daughter of Time	Tey, Josephine
The Defector	Anthony, Evelyn

The Documents in the Case	Sayers, Dorothy L.
"The Eye of Apollo"	Chesterton, G.K.
The Hound of the Baskervilles	Doyle, Sir Arthur Conan
The Judas Goat	Parker, Robert B.
The Mad Hatter Mystery	Carr, John Dickson
The Man in the Queue	Tey, Josephine
The Man Who Was Thursday	Chesterton, G.K.
The Masters of Bow Street	Creasey, John
The Murders of the Black Museum	Honeycombe, Gordon
"The Noble Bachelor"	Doyle, Sir Arthur Conan
The Piccadilly Murder	Berkeley, Anthony
The Poisoned Chocolates Case	Berkeley, Anthony
"The Priory School"	Doyle, Sir Arthur Conan
"The Red-Headed League"	Doyle, Sir Arthur Conan
"The Second Stain"	Doyle, Sir Arthur Conan
The Secret Adversary	Christie, Agatha
The Secret of Chimneys	Christie, Agatha
The Seven Dials Mystery	Christie, Agatha
The Skeleton in the Clock	Carr, John Dickson
The Thirty-Nine Steps	Buchan, John
The Toff and the Deadly Parson	Creasey, John
The Trail of Fu Manchu	Rohmer, Sax
The Turn of the Screw	James, Henry
The Unpleasantness at the Bellona Club	Sayers, Dorothy L.
Thrones, Dominations	Sayers, Dorothy L.
Trent's Last Case	Bentley, E.C.
Watson's Choice	Mitchell, Gladys
Whose Body?	Sayers, Dorothy L.

WESTMINSTER WALK: SLEUTHS

ALAN GRANT	Tey
ALBERT CAMPION	Allingham

CHIEF INSPECTOR HEMMINGWAY	Heyer
CORDELIA GRAY	James
DAME BEATRICE BRADLEY	Mitchell
DR. WATSON	Doyle
FATHER BROWN	Chesterton
GERVASE FEN	Crispin
HERCULE POIROT	Christie
JEMIMA SHORE	Fraser
LORD PETER WIMSEY	Sayers
NIGEL STRANGEWAYS	Blake
PATRICK GRANT	Yorke
RICHARD HANNAY	Buchan
RODERICK ALLEYN	Marsh
SHERLOCK HOLMES	Doyle
SIR HENRY MERRIVALE	Dickson (Carr)
SPENSER	Parker
SUPERINTENDENT BATTLE	Christie
THE TOFF	Creasey
TOMMY BERESFORD	Christie
TUPPENCE COWLEY	Christie
ADAM DALGLEISH	James
DR. GIDEON FELL	Carr
SHERIDAN HAYNES	Symons
INSPECTOR PARR	Wallace
SIR DENIS NAYLAND SMITH	Rohmer
PHILIP TRENT	Bentley
ROGER SHERINGHAM	Berkeley
CHIEF INSPECTOR HAZELRIGG	Gilbert
DAVINA GRAHAM	Anthony
INSPECTOR PITT	Perry

BROMPTON/HYDE PARK WALK: AUTHORS

Anthony, Evelyn	**Avenue of the Dead**
Brand, Christianna	**Fog of Doubt**
Chesterton, G.K.	**The Man Who Was Thursday**

Christie, Agatha	The Big Four
Christie, Agatha	The Secret Adversary
Creasey, John	The Masters of Bow Street
Francis, Dick	Odd Man Out
Fraser, Antonia	A Splash of Red
Heyer, Georgette	An Infamous Army
Heyer, Georgette	Behold, Here's Poison
Heyer, Georgette	Death in the Stocks
Heyer, Georgette	Duplicate Death
Heyer, Georgette	Regency Buck
Household, Geoffrey	Hostage: London
James, P.D.	Innocent Blood
Mann, Jessica	Funeral Sites
Marsh, Ngaio	A Surfeit of Lampreys
Marsh, Ngaio	Black as He's Painted
Marsh, Ngaio	Black Beech and Honeydew
Marsh, Ngaio	Death in Ecstasy
Mortimer, John	Rumpole of the Bailey
Orczy, Baroness	Lady Molly of Scotland Yard
Parker, Robert B.	The Judas Goat
Sayers, Dorothy L.	Murder Must Advertise
Symons, Julian	A Three Pipe Problem
Symons, Julian	The Blackheath Poisonings
Tey, Josephine	The Daughter of Time
Tey, Josephine	The Man in the Queue
Thackeray, W.M.	—
Wentworth, Patricia	The Case of William Smith
Yorke, Margaret	Cast for Death

BROMPTON/HYDE PARK WALK: BOOKS

An Infamous Army	Heyer, Georgette
A Splash of Red	Fraser, Antonia
A Surfeit of Lampreys	Marsh, Ngaio
A Three Pipe Problem	Symons, Julian
Avenue of the Dead	Anthony, Evelyn
Behold, Here's Poison	Heyer, Georgette
Black as He's Painted	Marsh, Ngaio

Black Beech and Honeydew	Marsh, Ngaio
Cast for Death	Yorke, Margaret
Death in Ecstasy	Marsh, Ngaio
Death in the Stocks	Heyer, Georgette
Duplicate Death	Heyer, Georgette
Fog of Doubt	Brand, Christianna
Funeral Sites	Mann, Jessica
Hostage: London	Household, Geoffrey
Innocent Blood	James, P.D.
Lady Molly of Scotland Yard	Orczy, Baroness
Murder Must Advertise	Sayers, Dorothy L.
Odd Man Out	Francis, Dick
Regency Buck	Heyer, Georgette
Rumpole of the Bailey	Mortimer, John
The Big Four	Christie, Agatha
The Blackheath Poisonings	Symons, Julian
The Case of William Smith	Wentworth, Patricia
The Daughter of Time	Tey, Josephine
The Judas Goat	Parker, Robert B.
The Man Who Was Thursday	Chesterton, G.K.
The Masters of Bow Street	Creasey, John
The Secret Adversary	Christie, Agatha

BROMPTON/HYDE PARK WALK: SLEUTHS

HERCULE POIROT	Christie
JEMIMA SHORE	Fraser
RODERICK ALLEYN	Marsh
RUMPOLE	Mortimer
SPENSER	Parker
TOMMY BERESFORD	Christie
TUPPENCE COWLEY	Christie
TAMARA HOYLAND	Mann
INSPECTOR HANNASYDE	Heyer
SID HALLEY	Francis
ALAN GRANT	Tey
LORD PETER WIMSEY	Sayers

DAVINA GRAHAM	Anthony
LADY MOLLY	Orczy
INSPECTOR COCKRILL	Brand
SHERIDAN HAYNES	Symons
SHERLOCK HOLMES	Doyle
PATRICK GRANT	Yorke

BELGRAVIA/PIMLICO WALK: AUTHORS

Allingham, Margery	Flowers for the Judge
Berkeley, Anthony	The Poisoned Chocolates Case
Chesterton, G.K.	"The Blue Cross"
Chesterton, G.K.	The Innocence of Father Brown
Chesterton, G.K.	"The Queer Feet"
Christie, Agatha	—
Dickens, Charles	—
Doyle, Sir Arthur Conan	The Sign of Four
Fraser, Antonia	A Splash of Red
Fraser, Antonia	Cool Repentance
Fraser, Antonia	Quiet as a Nun
Heyer, Georgette	Death in the Stocks
Heyer, Georgette	Duplicate Death
James, P.D.	Innocent Blood
James, P.D.	The Skull Beneath the Skin
Le Carré, John	—
Mackey, Aidan	Mr. Chesterton Comes to Tea
Mann, Jessica	Grave Goods
Marsh, Ngaio	A Wreath for Rivera
Marsh, Ngaio	Death in a White Tie
Marsh, Ngaio	Death in Ecstasy
Moyes, Patricia	Who Is Simon Warwick?
Perry, Anne	The Devil's Acre
Radcliffe, Ann	—
Rendell, Ruth	—
Rohmer, Sax	The Trail of Fu Manchu

Sayers, Dorothy L., trans.	**The Song of Roland**
Sayers, Dorothy L.	**Unnatural Death**
Snow, C.P.	**A Coat of Varnish**
Snow, C.P.	**Brothers and Strangers**
Tey, Josephine	**The Man in the Queue**
Wentworth, Patricia	—
Williams, Charles	**All Hallows Eve**

BELGRAVIA/PIMLICO WALK: BOOKS

A Coat of Varnish	Snow, C.P.
All Hallows Eve	Williams, Charles
A Splash of Red	Fraser, Antonia
A Wreath for Rivera	Marsh, Ngaio
Brothers and Strangers	Snow, C.P.
Cool Repentance	Fraser, Antonia
Death in a White Tie	Marsh, Ngaio
Death in Ecstasy	Marsh, Ngaio
Death in the Stocks	Heyer, Georgette
Duplicate Death	Heyer, Georgette
Flowers for the Judge	Allingham, Margery
Grave Goods	Mann, Jessica
Innocent Blood	James, P.D.
Mr. Chesterton Comes to Tea	Mackey, Aidan
Quiet as a Nun	Fraser, Antonia
"The Blue Cross"	Chesterton, G.K.
The Devil's Acre	Perry, Anne
The Innocence of Father Brown	Chesterton, G.K.
The Man in the Queue	Tey, Josephine
The Poisoned Chocolates Case	Berkeley, Anthony
"The Queer Feet"	Chesterton, G.K.
The Sign of Four	Doyle, Sir Arthur Conan
The Skull Beneath the Skin	James, P.D.
The Song of Roland	Sayers, Dorothy L., trans.
The Trail of Fu Manchu	Rohmer, Sax

Unnatural Death	Sayers, Dorothy L.
Who Is Simon Warwick?	Moyes, Patricia

BELGRAVIA/PIMLICO WALK: SLEUTHS

ALAN GRANT	Tey
DR. WATSON	Doyle
FATHER BROWN	Chesterton
GEORGE SMILEY	Le Carré
HENRY TIBBETT	Moyes
JEMIMA SHORE	Fraser
LORD PETER WIMSEY	Sayers
MISS MARPLE	Christie
RODERICK ALLEYN	Marsh
SHERLOCK HOLMES	Doyle
INSPECTOR HANNASYDE	Heyer
CORDELIA GRAY	James
ROGER SHERINGHAM	Berkeley
ALBERT CAMPION	Allingham
SIR DENIS NAYLAND SMITH	Rohmer
INSPECTOR PITT	Perry
TAMARA HOYLAND	Mann

BIBLIOGRAPHY

BIBLIOGRAPHY

These are the books that were especially helpful in preparing this guide:

Cawelti, John G. *Adventure, Mystery and Romance*. Chicago: The University of Chicago Press, n.d.

Clarke, Stephen P. *The Lord Peter Wimsey Companion*. New York: The Mysterious Press, 1985.

Crowl, Philip A. *The Intelligent Travellers Guide to Historic Britain*. New York: Congdon & Weed, Inc., 1983.

Dale, Alzina Stone. *Maker and Craftsman*. Grand Rapids, MI: William B. Eerdmans, 1978.

———. *The Outline of Sanity*. Grand Rapids, MI: William B. Eerdmans, 1982.

Francis, Dick. *The Sport of Queens*. London: Pan Books, 1974.

Han, Robert W., ed. *Sincerely, Tony/Faithfully, Vincent, The Correspondence of Anthony Boucher and Vincent Starrett*. Privately printed, 1975.

Haycraft, Howard, ed. *The Art of the Mystery Story*. New York: Grosset & Dunlap, 1946.

———. *Murder for Pleasure*. New York: Carroll & Graf Publishers, Inc., 1984.

Hodge, Jane Aiken. *The Private World of Georgette Heyer*. London: The Bodley Head, 1984.

Honeycombe, Gordon. *The Murders of the Black Museum 1870–1970*. Special rev. ed. London: Arrow Books, 1984.

Keating, H.R.F., ed. *Agatha Christie, First Lady of Crime*. New York: Holt, Rinehart, and Winston, 1977.

Lejeune, Anthony. *The Gentlemen's Clubs of London*. New York: Dorset Press, 1984.

Marsh, Ngaio. *Black Beech and Honeydew, An Autobiography.* London: Collins, 1966.

Morgan, Janet. *Agatha Christie.* London: Collins, 1984.

Morley, Frank. *Literary Britain.* New York: Dorset Press, 1983.

Penzler, Otto, ed. *The Great Detectives.* New York: Penguin Books, 1979.

Sanders, Ann. *The Art and Architecture of London.* Oxford: Phaidon Press, 1984.

Sayers, Dorothy L., and Muriel St. Clare Byrne. *Love All.* Alzina Stone Dale, ed. Kent, OH: Kent State University Press, 1984.

Symons, Julian. *Great Detectives.* New York: Harry N. Abrams, Inc., Publishers, 1981.

————. *Mortal Consequences.* New York: Schocken Books, 1973.

————. *The Tell-Tale Heart, The Life and Works of Edgar Allan Poe.* Middlesex: Penguin Books, 1978.

Winks, Robin W. *Modus Operandi, An Excursion into Detective Fiction.* Boston: David R. Godine, Publisher, n.d.

Winn, Dilys, ed. *Murder Ink.* New York: Workman Publishing, 1977.

————, ed. *Murderess Ink.* New York: Bell Publishing, 1981.

INDEX

INDEX

S

Sabine, Martin, 151
St. Agnes of Powder Hill, 11
St. Andrew's, 32
St. Anne's Soho, xix, 88, 93, 95
St. Bartholomew's Hospital, 33
St. Bartholomew the Great, 33
St. Bride's Church, 35-36
St. Clement Dane's Church, 21, 29, 40
St. Dunstan's in the West, 30
St. George's, Hanover Square, 107-8
St. George's Square, 211, 212
St. Giles-in-the-Fields, 96-97
St. James, 124-40
St. James Church, 136
St. James's Palace, 124, 125, 132, 139
St. James's Park, 138-39, 163, 176, 187
St. James Theatre, 133
St. John, Chapel of, 15
St. John's Wood, 159
St. Margaret's Church, 15, 163, 182-83
St. Martin's-in-the-Fields, 43, 44
St. Martin's Theatre, 43, 50
St. Marylebone Parish Church, 155
St.-Mary-le-Bow, 3, 9
St. Mary Mead, 118
St. Mary's le Strand, 40
St. Michael's Church, 207, 208
St. Paul's Cathedral, xviii, 2, 6, 7, 8, 56
St. Paul's Church, 43, 56
St. Peter ad Vincula, Chapel of, 15, 16
St. Peter's Eaton Sq., 206
St. Peter's Square, 32
St. Savior's, 212
St. Sepulchre, Crusaders' Church of, 32-33
St. Stephen's Porch, 183
St. Stephen's Tavern, 163, 170
St. Thomas' Tower, 14
Salisbury Pub, The, 44, 49
Sallet Square, xviii, 137
Sasanov, 51
Savile Row, 107
Savoy Chapel, 61
Savoy Grill, 61
Savoy Hotel, 42, 60-62
Sayers, Dorothy L., xviii, xix, 4, 7, 9, 10, 17, 22, 24, 25, 27, 29, 30, 31,

35, 36, 37, 47, 48, 52, 53, 55, 57, 59, 64, 67, 70, 71, 72, 73, 75, 76, 77, 84, 85, 88, 89, 90, 91, 92, 93, 95, 97, 99, 100, 104, 106, 108, 111, 112, 115, 116, 117, 121, 122, 126, 128, 129, 130, 132, 133, 135, 137, 145, 146, 147, 148, 150, 152-53, 159, 160, 165, 169, 170, 171, 174, 177, 182, 183, 184, 195, 211, 212, 213
Sayers Historical and Literary Society, 56, 88, 93
Say When!, 48
"Scandal in Bohemia, A," 44, 151
Scase, Mr., 179, 211
Schoenberg, Harry, 14
Science Museum, 188, 195
"Scoop, The," 92
Scotland Yard, 14, 20, 40, 64, 97, 128, 162, 163, 165, 167, 170-75, 178
Scott, Gloria, 116, 175
Scott, Sir Walter, 71, 135
Seaton-Carew, Mr., 134
"Second Stain, The," 169
Secret Adversary, The, 4, 46, 61, 84, 85, 87, 98, 110, 112, 129, 138, 165, 168, 176, 196
Secret of Chimneys, The, 16, 110, 111, 137, 147, 184
Seddar, Van, 17
Seeton, Maurice, 36, 95
Selfridges, 146
Serpentine, 198
Seven Dials, 96
Seven Dials Club, 96
Seven Dials Mystery, The, 93, 96, 134
Seven Dials Society, 173
Shakespeare, William, 8, 15, 24, 36, 38, 87, 88, 175
Shaw, George Bernard, 56, 73, 152
Shepherd Market, xix, 102, 113
Shepherd Market Pub, 113
Shepherd's Tavern, 104, 113
Sheringham, Roger, 120, 122, 172, 206
Sherlock Holmes Pub, 91, 163, 166
Sholto, Phoebe, 182
Sholto, Rosamund, 69, 109, 136, 139, 189
Shore, Jemima, xvi, xviii, 47, 49, 54, 67, 69, 70, 71-72, 73, 77, 109, 111, 140, 147, 152, 154-55, 160, 165, 184, 189, 210, 213

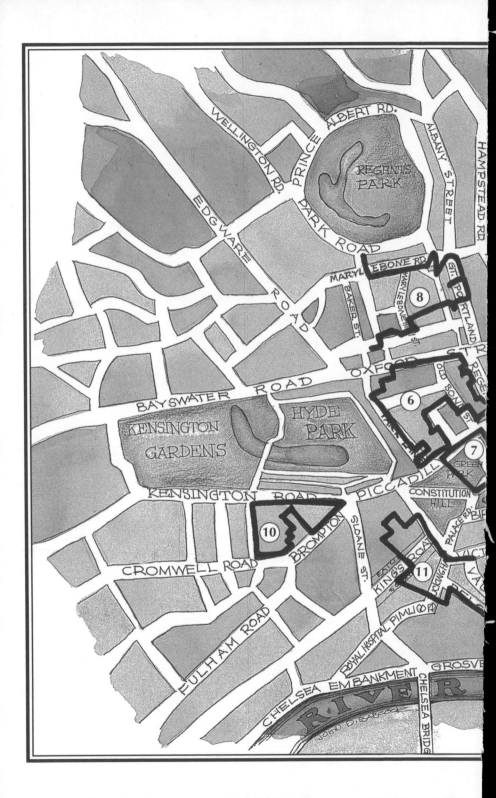